Series Editor
Jean-Charles Pomerol

Computer Memories 1

Core Concepts

Philippe Darche

iSTE

WILEY

First published 2026 in Great Britain and the United States by ISTE Ltd and John Wiley & Sons, Inc.

ISTE Ltd
27-37 St George's Road
London SW19 4EU
UK

www.iste.co.uk

John Wiley & Sons, Inc.
111 River Street
Hoboken, NJ 07030
USA

www.wiley.com

Library of Congress Control Number: 2025944878

British Library Cataloguing-in-Publication Data
A CIP record for this book is available from the British Library
ISBN 978-1-83669-024-5

The manufacturer's authorized representative according to the EU General Product Safety Regulation is Wiley-VCH GmbH, Boschstr. 12, 69469 Weinheim, Germany, e-mail: Product_Safety@wiley.com.

Contents

Quotation

To help them get rid of everything they weren't supposed to know, the Shadoks had created the Anti-memory. It was a big contraption made of subtle mechanisms such as drawer trash bins, knowledge crushers, understanding grinders, etc.

The Shadoks[1],
regarding the computer

1 Created by Jacques Rouxel, the Shadoks are the main characters from an experimental cartoon produced by the Research Department of the Office de Radiodiffusion-Télévision Française (ORTF). The two-minute-long episodes of this daily cult series were broadcast on ORTF's first channel (the only one at the time!) beginning in 1968. The birds were drawn simply and quickly using an experimental device called an animograph.

The Shadoks are ridiculous, stupid and mean. Their intellectual capacities are completely unusual. For example, they are known for bouncing up and down, but it is not clear why! Their vocabulary consists of four words: GA, BU, ZO and MEU, which are also the four digits in their number system (base 4) and the musical notes in their four-tone scale. Their philosophy is comprised of famous mottos such as the one cited in this book.

Preface

Computer systems (both hardware and software) are becoming increasingly complex, buried and transparent. It then becomes difficult to find the basic concepts to thoroughly understand how they work.

One way to do this is to look into the history of the field. A second way is to immerse ourselves in the technology by reading patents and datasheets of electronic components. Last and not least is to read research articles. We have tried to follow these three paths throughout the writing of this book series, with the goal of explaining how memory works in hardware, either as a component or a complete (sub-)system such as a mass storage device.

About this series and this book

In this second book series, we focus on an essential function of the computer: memory; the two other functions are computation, covered in Volumes 1–5 of *Microprocessor* (Darche 2021a, 2021b, 2021c, 2021d, 2021e), and communication. The order in which memory models are presented was chosen based on interface simplicity or the increasing complexity of memory concepts.

This first volume serves as a prologue to the field. After presenting the main features of a generic memory, past and present technologies, and the concept of memory hierarchy, we focus more specifically on random access solid-state memory models.

Volumes 2 and 3 cover the different categories of solid-state random access memory, or RAM, i.e. static and dynamic models in their asynchronous versions, called SRAM (static RAM) and DRAM (dynamic RAM). They detail their timing and electrical and mechanical characteristics.

Volumes 4 and 5 cover their synchronous versions, based on communication by cycle (SSRAM and SDRAM – the S stands for synchronous) and by packet (RDRAM for Rambus DRAM and SLDRAM for synchronous-link DRAM).

Volume 6 discusses solid-state read-only memory and emerging non-volatile memory (NVM for non-volatile memory). ROM, or read-only memory, is essential to a computer, whether it is general-purpose or a specialized embedded system. Its main feature is non-volatility – i.e. it does not lose data when the power is off. It stores, in particular, boot and test programs that run at startup and configuration data, without which the computer could not start at all. Current integrated circuit manufacturing technologies are reaching their limits. Experts call this the red brick wall (see section 1.5 of Darche (2021a)), which is the physical limit of how finely integrated circuits can be etched. Emerging memories aim to overcome this limitation. They are at the industrial stage, the prototype stage or even just the memory cell or concept stage. The industrial models presented are ferroelectric, magnetic and phase-change memories.

Volume 7, on specialty memory or specialized memories products, looks at memory management strategies or policies other than random access policy. Simple strategies such as “first-in, first-out” for a queue or “last-in, first-out” for a stack are studied first. Then, memory models with interfaces or internal structures that differ from classic DRAM, but still offer random access – at least through one communication port – are presented. These include pseudo-interface memories, buffer memories and application-specific memories, especially for display.

Volume 8 addresses the notion of cache. This functionally transparent mechanism plays a key role in the memory hierarchy, because it significantly improves the performance of modern microprocessors (i.e. those developed since the 1990s) and peripherals, mainly storage devices.

Volume 9 explains the concept of virtual memory. It was proposed to meet three essential needs of the computer. These are protection, memory area translation and expanding the size of the programming space. The overall solution is address mapping, separating logical and physical memory via distinct address spaces.

References in the text follow this convention: “see section V5-2.3”, for example, means refer to section 2.3 of Volume 5. If no volume number is given, the reference is from the current volume.

Italics are used for terms from foreign languages such as French or ancient ones such as Latin.

A multi-level structure

Each volume in the series gradually moves from concepts to hardware implementation. My primary focus has been on pedagogy, without neglecting formal precision. The reading is meant to work on multiple levels. Each reader will extract the knowledge needed before tackling the more difficult parts. Except for a few exceptions, the knowledge is presented linearly and as exhaustively as possible. Concrete examples from past and present technologies illustrate theoretical concepts.

When needed, exercises deepen the study of certain mechanisms. Each volume ends with bibliographic references pointing to research articles, books or patents – both foundational and recent – that reflect the state of the art. These references help the reader find further theoretical or technical information. A list of acronyms used and an index covering the entire volume are also included.

This series of books on memory in computers is the result of over 40 years of exploration in electronics, microelectronics and computing. I hope it brings you enough practical and theoretical knowledge to later specialize in one of these fields. I wish you, for this first book, a pleasant journey through these different worlds.

NOTE.– This is not a book on memory chip manufacturing technology, although the topic is discussed. There are specialized reference books on that subject such as Prince (1996, 1999), Itoh (2001), Haraszti (2002), Sharma (2002a, 2002b), Chen (2003), Redaelli and Pellizzer (2022), and Yu (2022), including some for specific memory families (Brown and Brewer 1997; Keeth and Baker 2000; Campardo et al. 2005; Brewer and Gill 2008).

Since this is an introductory book on memory, examples of commercial components from all eras are cited. Company names are listed as originally known, even if some have since merged. This will allow readers to find the datasheets of the mentioned integrated circuits online, and to study the original documentation alongside this book.

The concepts presented are based on ideas covered in previous volumes (Darche 2000, 2002, 2003, 2004, 2021a, 2021b, 2021c, 2021d, 2021e), which are recommended reading.

October 2025

Introduction

This volume is dedicated to one of the three subsystems of the so-called "von Neumann" machine model (von Neumann 1945): memory[1]. The memory function, essential to processor operation, has gradually become more complex to meet growing demands for capacity, security, speed and now energy efficiency. It is everywhere. It is found in primary memory and cache, of course, as well as in the processor and I/O interfaces. Primary memory is made up of integrated components specialized in storage, most often soldered on one or both sides of a small printed circuit board (called a "module" or "memory"). Memory can also be a block within a more complex chip, such as a microprocessor (μP or MPU for microprocessor unit) or a microcontroller (μC or MCU for microcontroller unit). In that case, it may be a register bank, also called a register file, or larger integrated memory zones, such as a cache[2] or a small primary memory. It is then called "embedded". It is also found in I/O controllers as registers, cache or as a buffer managing data flow using the "first in, first out" or FIFO policy. A peripheral device may also have a FIFO buffer or cache and a storage area. Examples include a printer or a mass storage unit with hard disk(s) or hard disk drive (HDD) or solid-state memory or a solid-state disk (SSD). In the latter case, the device is considered mass memory due to the amount of stored data. It then belongs to the category of secondary or tertiary memory.

1 The other two subsystems are input/output (I/O) and the processor, respectively discussed in Darche (2003) and Darche (2021a, 2021b, 2021c, 2021d, 2021e).

2 The origin of this term is French. It refers to a secret storage place, a synonym being "*cachette*", which is reserved for the parallel version. This is why we used the feminine gender for this word in the French edition of this book.

Memory and its environment – i.e. its controller, if any, and its communication bus, also called a "channel" – have a direct impact on computer performance (processing power, power consumption, etc.) and its cost. It is therefore essential for electronics and computer engineers to fully understand how it works and the associated technologies. The electronics engineer uses it to design this subsystem and its controller. Computer scientists, for their part, optimize programs, particularly in scientific computing.

This first volume, an introduction to the field, is organized into six chapters. The first chapter begins with a presentation of the main characteristics of a generic memory. The most important characteristic is probably its size, and the associated standardized unit of measurement is explained in detail. The goal of computer architecture researchers and industry has been to invent reliable and fast memory technologies at minimal or acceptable cost. Past and current technologies are then described. Finally, the concept of memory hierarchy is explored. Chapter 2 focuses more specifically on random access solid-state memory models. It details their internal functional organization with the main logic blocks. Chapter 3 builds on the previous one with blocks specific to some models, such as the phase-locked loop or PLL. Chapter 4 examines modular organizations such as the block (or memory subzone) and the bank, and discusses multithreaded architectures. The second-to-last chapter looks at external aspects to increase data width and capacity. It also addresses interleaving, address decoding and interfacing. This volume ends with a few additional concepts such as alignment, data ordering, memory topography, and error detection and correction. Appendix 1 is an introduction to error detection and correction codes.

1

The Memory Function

Memory is the second function of the computer, between computation and communication. Since the invention of the modern computer in the last century, memory has received the full attention of researchers, and later, of industry. It takes physical form as a component or a system, such as a memory subsystem or a mass storage device.

This chapter begins with a presentation of the characteristics of a generic memory. The most essential is likely its size, and the standardized multiples of its unit of measure are detailed in this context. The technological and historical aspects provide an opportunity to present the different memory families. These different memory families form a hierarchy in the computer, a concept that is then defined.

1.1. Main characteristics

Memory is mainly characterized by its medium, its total storage[1] capacity C and its organization, the memory access method or policy, the type of access or operation, and the permanence (or non-volatility) of the information.

1.1.1. *Memory medium*

The type of medium characterizes the technology used to store the information. Information storage can be done through the presence or absence of a material (mechanical technology), such as a hole in a punched card (see section 5.6 of Darche

1 In English, the term "storage" is generally reserved for a direct or sequential access device, such as an HDD or magnetic tape storage, while the term "memory" is used for random-access components like random access memory (RAM) or read-only memory (ROM). This distinction also applies in French, with the terms "*stockage*" and "*mémoire*".

(2003) and section 3.3 of Darche (2000)). Today, it involves a semiconductor (SC) or a magnetic, optical or magneto-optical material. In electronics, storage is done, for example, by moving or storing electric charges. In mass storage memory, it uses the change in orientation of a ferromagnetic material's magnetic field (originally iron oxide) on a flexible (floppy disk[2] or FD) or rigid (hard disk or HD) support, or, as in rewritable optical memory, a phase change.

French term	English term	Format n (bits)
Chiffre binaire	Bit (b)	1
Quartet ou demi-octet	Nibble	4
Octet	Byte[a] (B)	8
Mot	Word Dualoct	16
Double mot	Double word Quadlet quadoct	32
Quadruple mot	Quad(ruple) word Octlet (IEEE 1996) Octbyte	64

a. A contraction of the English word "bite", meaning "a mouthful", created to follow the word "bit".

Table 1.1. *Vocabulary used to describe a group of bits*

1.1.2. *Storage capacity and units of measurement*

The binary elements, 0 and 1, were named "bits" by statistician John Wilder Tukey, as a contraction of binary digit, although other terms such as bigit and binit were also suggested. The term was adopted by the community following its appearance in his famous article on information theory (Shannon 1948). The unit of measurement for memory capacity C is therefore the bit. Table 1.1 reminds us of the vocabulary used to describe a set of bits. In the era of 16-bit microprocessors (µP, microprocessor unit or MPU) in the 1980s, a word represented 16 bits. With the advent of 32-bit microprocessors, the term double word was introduced. Then came the next generation with the term quad word. But be careful – the word "word" can sometimes refer to any format depending on context, and not necessarily a multiple of the byte. We also speak of memory density, which refers to the number of bits stored per unit area (in^2 or mm^2).

2 The corresponding unit is called the floppy disk drive or FDD (FD drive).

IEC symbols and prefixes	Origin	Factors	Examples	SI symbols and prefixes (reminder)
Ki, kibi	Kilobinary	2^{10} (= 1 024)	1 Kib (formerly 1 KB)	k (kilo) = 10^3
Mi, mebi	Megabinary	2^{20} (= 1 048 576)	1 Mib (formerly 1 Mb)	M (mega) = 10^6
Gi, gibi	Gigabinary	2^{30}	1 Gib (formerly 1 Gb)	G (giga) = 10^9
Ti, tebi	Terabinary	2^{40}	1 Tib (formerly 1 Tb)	T (tera) = 10^{12}
Pi, pebi	Petabinary	2^{50}	1 Pib (formerly 1 Pb)	P (peta) = 10^{15}
Ei, exbi	Exabinary	2^{60}	–	E (exa) = 10^{18}
Zi, zebi	Zettabinary	2^{70}	–	Z (zetta) = 10^{21}
Yi, yobi	Yottabinary	2^{80}	–	Y (yotta) = 10^{24}

Table 1.2. *New standardized prefixes for capacity units*

Table 1.2 shows the symbol and prefix (or name) for the multiples of the bit. To distinguish the SI prefix kilo (10^3) from the kilo used in memory sizing, the uppercase letter K is commonly used in computing. For example, we have 1 Kb (kilobit) meaning 1,024 bits and 1 KB (kilobyte) meaning 1,024 bytes. A technical term used is computer kilo. To eliminate ambiguity, the International Electrotechnical Commission (IEC), an international standards organization, approved a new naming convention for powers of 2 with the kilobinary symbol Ki, named kibi (IEC 2000). Self (1999) explains this aspect in detail. The Institute of Electrical and Electronics Engineers (IEEE), a US-based technical professional standards body, later standardized it (IEEE 2002a, 2002b).

Figure 1.1 shows a graphic reminder of these new measurement units for semiconductor memory and the relationships between them.

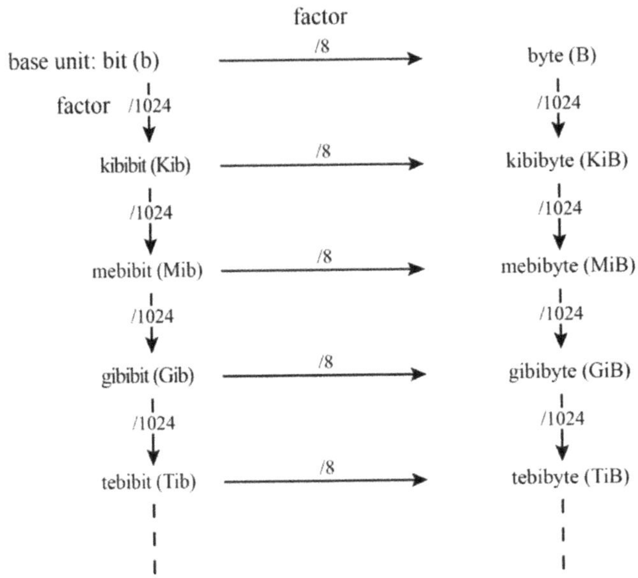

Figure 1.1. *Base unit and standardized prefixes for a semiconductor memory*

Currently, not all professionals use these two new standards, which causes some confusion. Manufacturers of semiconductor memory continue to use the old prefixes. This confusion persists with the sizes of hard disk mass memory units, where the ratio or factor between this unit and its multiples is equal to $10^{3 \times k}$ ($k \in \mathbb{N}^*$). For examples and details, see section 7.2.2 and the associated exercise 7.3 of Darche (2003).

Figure 1.2 recalls the unit of measurement for mass memory capacity and the ratios between it and its multiples, specifying its first multiples. The shaded area defines a nonexistent capacity, since the first industrial disk, the IBM 350 disk storage unit (1956) by IBM, had a capacity of 3.75 MB (5×10^6 characters or 6-bit words). Its presence is justified only to recall the kilo ratio of 10^3.

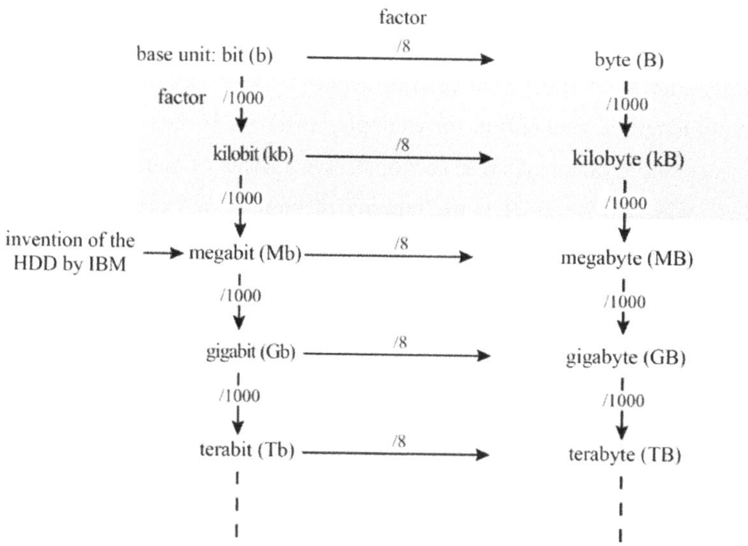

Figure 1.2. *Unit of measurement of mass memory capacity and its first multiples*

And to be complete, operating systems (OS) convert mass storage capacity into a power of 2. The Linux OS even uses the new standardized prefixes. Universal serial bus (USB) keys, which use semiconductor memories, still follow powers of 2!

1.1.3. *Organization*

The memory cell is the smallest subdivision (atomic entity) of memory in which it is possible to read or write information. A cell or memory word has a format or width[3] 1 or n or a size. We speak, for example, of the width of a register (concept detailed in section 3.1 of Darche (2021c)). This format mainly depends on the memory system format and the data bus width or mechanisms such as interleaving (see section 5.2.4). It can be a byte or a word multiple of the byte or another format (n = 9 bits, for example, in the case of error detection and correction, see section 6.4). Each bit bi of the cell of format n has a position i numbered, from right to left, from 0 to n–1 (i ∈ [0, n–1]; see Figure 1.3).

3 Some authors have used the term "length" for the format (Meinadier 1988 or Ciminiera and Valenzano 1987). This term was not retained in this book because it is reserved here for the number of words.

The organization refers to the physical arrangement of the cells in the memory. It allows us, from the total size, to specify the distribution between the format n of the memory cell and the number L of cells or depth D. We speak of input/output (I/O) organization length L × width n, for example, 16 Ki × 16 bits. In the case where there are several internal banks (see section 4.3), we speak of bank organization B × length L × width n, where B is the number of banks, for example, 8 × 2 Ki × 16 bits. The total capacity C of the memory is then equal to:

$$C = B \times L \times n \qquad [1.1]$$

1.1.4. *Access policies*

The memory cell is called by Cragon the "memory-addressable unit" (AU) (Cragon 1996). It is the atomic element (i.e. the smallest addressable word) that the MPU can address in the main memory (or primary memory, acronym MP), i.e. a byte or a word of n bits.

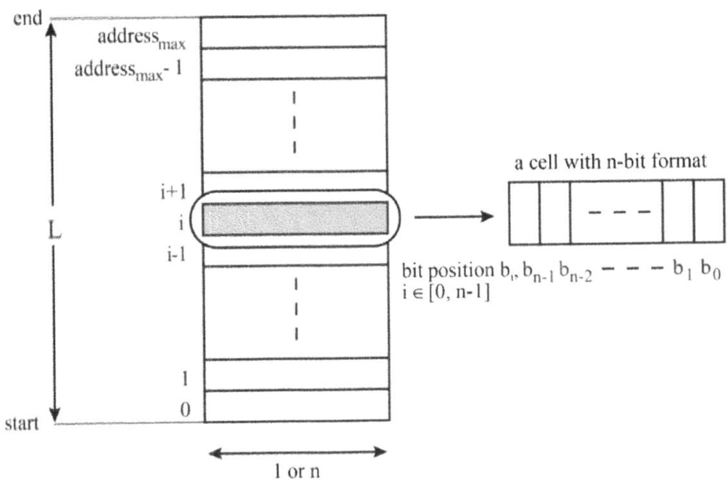

Figure 1.3. *Organization and addressing of a memory*

The memory access method or policy specifies how the memory is accessed. In the case of location-based or coordinate addressing, the memory cell is accessed using an address (address-based storage and retrieval) which is an integer. This integer generally belongs to the subset of natural numbers, a counterexample being the address used to move to increasing or decreasing addresses relative to a reference address (see section 1.2.3.2 of Darche (2021d)). If we number each memory cell starting from 0[4], then the cell's address is this number (see Figure 1.3). The interest of this figure is to facilitate the transition from this abstract model, which I call "the dresser"[5] by analogy, to the logical implementation of Figure 2.5.

If the cell is the smallest addressable element, then the format m of address A numbered from 0 is equal to:

$$m = \lfloor \log_2 address_{max} \rfloor + 1\ bits \qquad [1.2]$$

where the mathematical symbols "⌊"and"⌋" represent the "smallest integer less than or equal to" the function (floor() function) and with the $address_{max} \neq 0$.

And we have:

$$L = 2^m \qquad [1.3]$$

The access policy (management strategy or policy) specifies how to access a memory cell. Figure 1.4 classifies them. In address-based access, random access[6] means that any memory cell can be accessed directly by providing its address with a constant access time t_a (see section 1.1.7). In the case of serial or sequential access, the memory cells are accessed in a specific order that characterizes the policy. An example of a policy is "first data in is first data out" (FIFO) for a queue, or "last data in is first data out" (LIFO) for a stack. It should not be confused with serial location, an example of which is magnetic tape, which is not a semiconductor memory. Its records are read one after another by reading their header to determine which one is sought. In content-based access (by content), the information is accessed by partial match, as we would do with a phone directory where the contact name is used to retrieve the number (Belady et al. 1981). The data must therefore contain a key or an identifier. This type of policy is well suited for information retrieval. Thus, content-addressable memory (CAM), which is associative memory, is particularly used in network devices and in the cache (see Volumes 7 and 8, respectively). Associative addressing is a generalization of content-based addressing because it does not require an exact match (Chisvin and Duckworth 1989).

4 Justification of this initial value in section 2.2.6.

5 By analogy with this piece of furniture where each numbered drawer is a memory cell.

6 This adjective should especially not be confused with randomness or a probability law. Direct access could be a synonym. However, it is actually reserved to define one of the modes of addressing a memory location by a processor (microprocessor or microcontroller). For a mass memory like an HDD, we also speak of direct addressing, but it must be known that the access time then depends on the location of the information and the position of the read head, unlike a semiconductor memory where this time is constant.

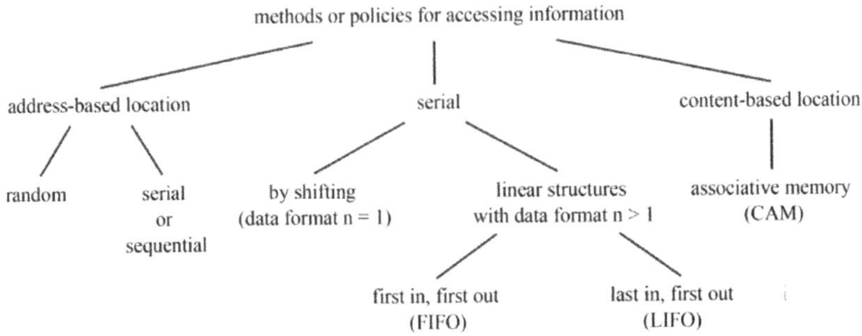

Figure 1.4. *Memory access policies*

1.1.5. *Types of access*

The type of access specifies the requested operation, which can be read, write, read–write or read–modify–write. Read–write means the stored data can be read and then another data stored at the same address during the same cycle. The last operation is a special case where the data read is modified and then stored at the same address, still in the same cycle. This last type of access is useful, for example, for error detection and correction (ED(A)C, error detection (and) correction, ECC error-correcting code; see section 6.4). The type of access may have given the memory its name, such as ROM (read-only memory), an electronic component, or WORM or WOM (write-once read-many-times memory), a mass memory device.

1.1.6. *Data permanence*

Data permanence indicates whether information is lost when power is off, or if it remains stored. This permanence is characterized by the data-retention time. A memory that loses its stored data when power is lost or due to the storage material's properties is called "volatile". It is also called RAM.

Considering data retention or usage duration, memory may be termed immediate-, very short-, short-, mid- or long-term memory. For example, a register is a very short-term memory, while a magnetic tape is a very long-term memory.

1.1.7. *Timing characteristics*

To characterize a memory in time (see section V2-1.2 for the semiconductor version), the read access and cycle times (access time and cycle time, respectively) are specified. Access time t_a is the time from presenting the address to presenting the output data. Note, it is defined only for the read operation. Cycle time t_c is the total time for a read or write operation. This cycle time can vary, depending on the operation, into a write cycle time t_{WC} and a read cycle time t_{RC}. Note that t_a is less than or equal to t_c (actually t_{RC}). An important note: in random access, both times are independent of the memory cell's position.

At the module or component level, other times are used to refine timing characterization. They depend on memory type and the organization of the subset. So, they are detailed in relevant chapters and volumes.

For successive accesses, also called block or burst mode (see Volumes 3 and 4), throughput must be considered. Throughput is divided into I/O rate and data rate (Chen and Patterson 1993). The first, measured in accesses per second, applies when few bytes are transferred per access, such as in transaction processing. This definition applies to storage systems such as hard disk drives.

In this book, we distinguish two types of throughput: raw throughput or data rate, and effective throughput. Raw throughput is the maximum rate a component can provide at the hardware level. Effective throughput is the average rate available to the requester, usually a memory controller or processor. Data rate is measured in bits (or bit multiples, typically bytes) transferred per unit of time. It depends on the data format n. So, the basic unit is bits per second (bit/s). Throughput multiples follow powers of 10. Thus, 1 KB/s or kbps (note the lowercase k from SI) equals 1,000 bits/s. For semiconductor memory, raw throughput can be expressed in b/s/pin[7] (or bpspp), i.e. n = 1 bit. If the data transfer format is larger, total throughput equals that value multiplied by n. Throughput is the inverse of t_c (see Exercise V2-E1.1). Access is usually by blocks[8] to maximize throughput. This is called burst mode access. Table 1.3 lists some typical I/O throughput values (see Exercise E1.1 for the first three values).

A more relevant parameter is the fill frequency (FF). It describes the global performance of the memory system. It is defined by the equation:

$$\text{fill frequency (Hz)} = \frac{throughput\ (b/s)}{memory\ size\ (b)} \qquad [1.4]$$

7 From the component's package.

8 As opposed to random access.

This fill frequency applies to a full memory system and to the component itself, helping to quantify market demand (market requirement FF) (Przybylski 1996). Typical values are: 10 Hz for a workstation, 30 Hz for a PC (personal computer) and 100 Hz for a GUI (graphical user interface) accelerator. This indicator indicates here that a graphics accelerator needs high bandwidth, or that a workstation's memory system bandwidth is well used. Also, if a memory component's FF is below FF market requirements, it is not suitable (see Figure 2 of Przybylski (1996)).

Application or interface	**Bandwidth**	**Raw throughput**
High-fidelity (Hi-Fi) mono sound	20 kHz	88.2 KB/s (CD (compact disc))
Fast Ethernet (100Base-T) – IEEE Std 802.3™	–	100 Mb/s
Luminance video signal	Approximately 6 MHz	135 MB/s
Uncompressed digital video image (n = 24 bits) XGA (extended graphics array)	–	118 MB/s
Gigabit Ethernet (1000Base-T) – IEEE Std 802.3™	–	1 Gb/s
Disk interface PATA (parallel advanced technology attachment)	–	133 MB/s
Disk interface SATA (serial advanced technology attachment)	–	150 MB/s (SATA 1.0a – 2003) 300 MB/s (SATA 2.0 – 2004) 600 MB/s (SATA 3.0 – 2009)
DVI (digital visual interface) single link	165 MHz	3.96 Gb/s
PCI (peripheral component interconnect) Express bus	–	4 Gb/s (× 1, unencoded) 64 Gb/s (× 16, unencoded)

Application or interface	Bandwidth	Raw throughput
USB	–	1.5 et 12 Mb/s (USB 1.0 – 1996) 480 Mb/s (USB 2.0 – 2000) 5 Gb/s (USB 3.0 – 2008) 10 Gb/s (USB 3.1 – 2013) 20 Gb/s (USB 3.2 – 2017) 40 Gb/s (USB 4.0 – 2019) 40 Gb/s (USB 4.2 – 2019)
HDMI (high-definition multimedia interface)	165 MHz 340 MHz 600 MHZ 1,200 MHZ	4.95 Gb/s (1.0 – 2002) 10.2. Gb/s (1.3 – 2006) 18 Gb/s (2.0 – 2013) 48 Gb/s (2.0 – 2013)

Table 1.3. *Bandwidth of various applications and interfaces*

It is also useful to have an external characterization of the memory subsystem at the level of a bus master such as a processor. Katayama (1997) proposes to evaluate system performance using equations [1.5] and [1.7], comparable to Gene Amdahl's empirical rules. Coefficients k_1 and k_2 adjust the performance. B is the number of banks and N is the total number of memory components. We can deduce that the term in [1.9] is actually a fill frequency when comparing it to relation [1.4]:

$$\text{MPU performance} = k_1 \times \text{memory system bandwidth} \quad [1.5]$$

$$= k_1 \times \frac{N}{K} \times \text{throughput of one memory} \quad [1.6]$$

and

$$\text{MPU performance} = k_2 \times \text{memory system capacity} \quad [1.7]$$

$$= k_2 \times N \times \text{size of one memory} \quad [1.8]$$

From [1.6] and [1.8], we can deduce:

$$\text{throughput of one memory} = B \times \text{size of one memory} \times \frac{k_1}{k_2} \quad [1.9]$$

Another important parameter is latency[9], which is the total time between presenting the address and the availability of the data (read) or its acknowledgment (write). It includes all delays in the data path (DP, see section 3.2.2.1 of Darche (2021a)). This is an upper bound. In block access, latency concerns access to the first element. So, as before, throughput must also be considered. It depends on memory-related times (read access and cycle time), subsystem-related times (organization, controller) and exchange times between the memory subsystem, bus and processor. For the bus, this includes its access protocol, especially arbitration, its clock frequency and its width. For the processor, this concerns its protocol and cycle time. Latency and throughput(s) are the two most used parameters to evaluate the performance of a memory subsystem.

More generally, in computing, latency is the time elapsed between initiating an operation and the moment its result appears. This characteristic also appears in the networking domain.

1.2. Modeling

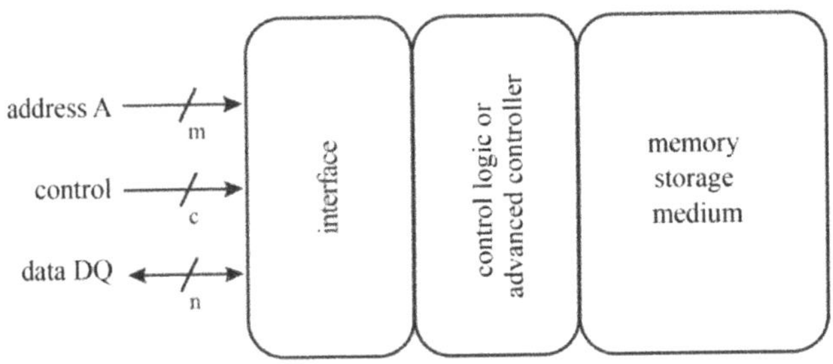

Figure 1.5. *Memory modeling*

A memory, as a component or subsystem, can be modeled with three subunits: the storage medium, the controller and the interface (see Figure 1.5; see also Figure 9.1). The latter two can perform complex operations. The storage medium

9 For an HDD memory unit, rotational latency or rotational delay is the time it takes for the head to find the beginning of a given sector once the arm is positioned on the addressed track (see section 7.2 of Darche (2003)).

may be removable, such as in a CD-ROM, or fixed. At the interface level, address information A in m-bit format can be exchanged bit by bit (serial interface) or by n-bit ($n > 1$) in a single exchange (parallel interface). The name DQ refers to the signals of a D-type flip-flop (see section 2.1). This exchange can be synchronous, meaning an external clock is needed to pace the operation (see clock notion in sections 3.1.2 and 3.1.4 of Darche (2002)). Otherwise, it is asynchronous, meaning it occurs within a bounded time frame. The control signal group includes at least one signal specifying the access type (R/#W or #WE), and generally, a memory select signal (#CE for chip enable or #CS for chip select). The latter controls the component's sleep mode. In a synchronous approach, a clock signal Clk is present. The controller generates internal control signals from the external control signals.

A computer system can be graphically described using symbolic elements, as shown in Figure 1.6 with a parallel memory architecture of the NUMA (non-uniform memory architecture) type. The compute element, such as a microprocessor or core, can be represented by a compute element or PE/PU (processing element/unit), a memory by a memory element or ME/MU (memory element/unit) and a peripheral (input-output) with its controller by an I/O element or IOE/IOU (I/O element/unit).

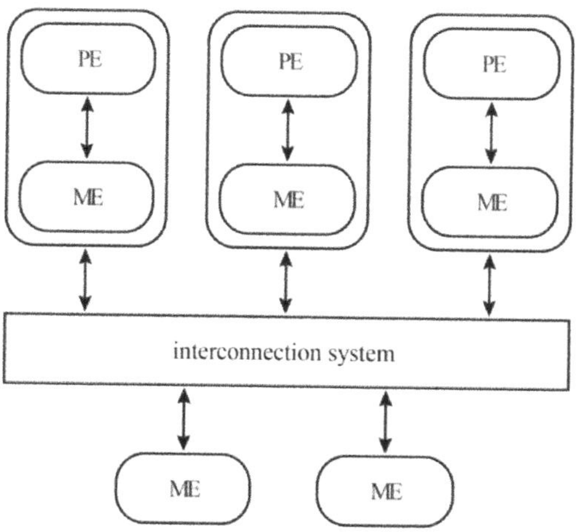

Figure 1.6. *Shared and distributed NUMA memory architecture*

1.3. Technological and historical aspects

It is impossible to discuss computing without addressing the technologies used or still used to design computer elements. This section details them, serving as a pretext to begin examining the various memory components or systems. It then becomes possible to finally define the concept of memory hierarchy.

1.3.1. *Mechanical calculator technologies*

The pursuit of researchers in computer architecture and manufacturers has been to invent memory technologies that are reliable, fast, and low-cost or economically viable. Any physical phenomenon or system with n stable states (n = 2 in the case of binary logic, the most common) is a candidate for use in a memory system. Memory can also be analog.

To find memory in a machine, we must go back about 300 years before Christ with the Chinese abacus, or to the 17th century with the mechanical accumulators in the mechanical calculators of Blaise Pascal (idea dating from 1642) and Gottfried Wilhelm Leibniz (1646–1716). The 18th and 19th centuries saw the emergence of programmable mechanical machines. These were the looms of Jacques de Vaucanson (in 1728, see Figure 1.8 of Darche (2021)) and Joseph-Marie Jacquard (in 1804), whose weaving programs were stored as punched cards. This latter format had been invented by Basile Bouchon in 1725 as a punched paper tape for the weaving industry. Jean-Baptiste Falcon improved it by transforming the tape into a series of punched cards linked by cords. These cards stored the weaving pattern. More details and illustrations are given in Marguin (1994).

Another example in this technology is the second difference engine of Charles Babbage (see Figure 1.6 of Darche (2021a)). It introduced the basic architecture of a computer and its programming (Hartree 1948). It included a mill playing the role of the modern CPU and a store serving as main memory (see Figure 1.7 of Darche (2021a)). There were also the concepts of registers (major axes) and data buses (transfer paths). To program it, Babbage also proposed the punched card. Detailed explanations of its operation are provided in Bromley (1982). This memory principle was reused with Herman Hollerith's punched card, which stored the data and instructions of tabulating machines (1890) (IEEE Spectrum 00; Kistermann 1991, 2005).

1.3.2. *Main memory technologies in modern computers*

The term "modern computer" often refers to electronic technology, but generation 1 (Darche 2021a) were electromechanical calculators (1937–1945). The basic component is the electromechanical relay or EMR (see Figure 1.7).

The vacuum tube (or thermionic tube, Figure 1.8) was then the first electronic component used. Tube-based memories do not all use the same principle. The flip-flop, also called bistable (English or French term), is the basic element for data storage and synchronization, and by extension, for the operation of automata, including microprocessor cores (see Darche (2002)).

The first flip-flop implementation was the circuit by Eccles and Jordan (1919), made of two triode vacuum tubes, also called electronic tubes, and six resistors (see an example with the electronic numerical integrator and computer (ENIAC) in Burks (1947)).

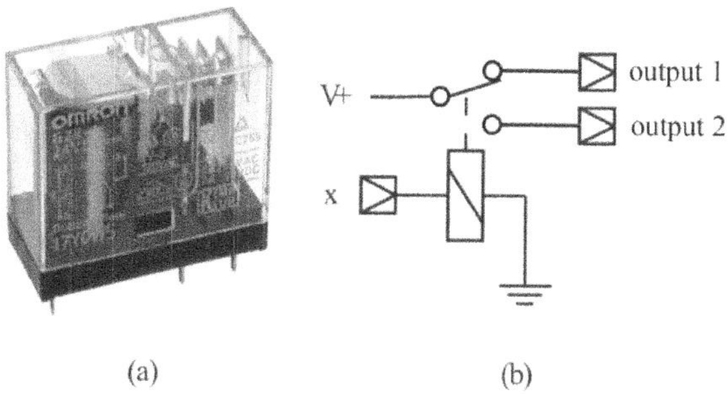

Figure 1.7. *A modern electromechanical relay and its equivalent circuit diagram (source: left part of Figure 1.11 from Darche (2020a))*

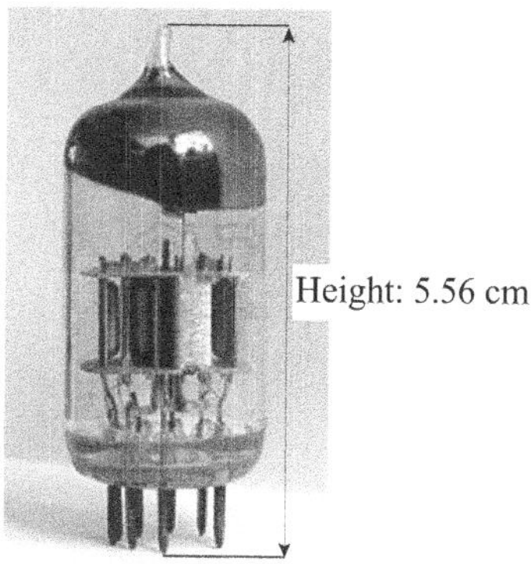

Figure 1.8. *An RCA 5965 type vacuum tube (source: left part of Figure 1.12 from Darche (2020a))*

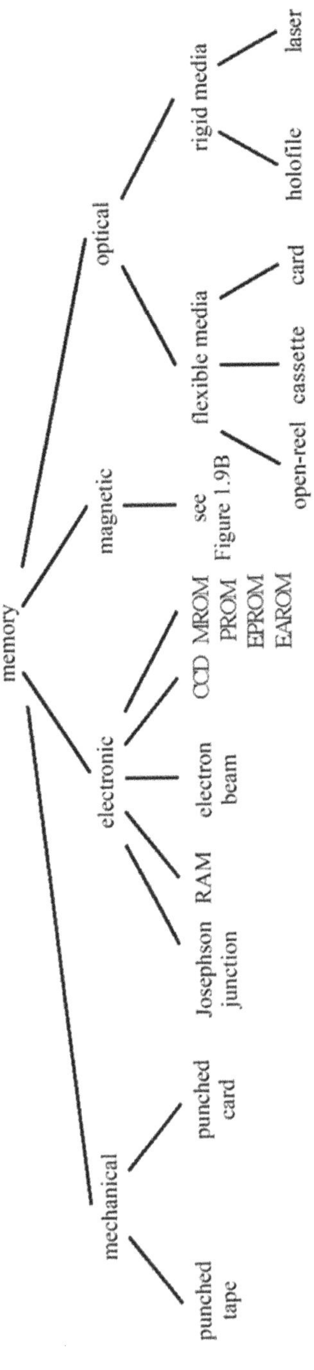

Figure 1.9(A). *Memory classification in 1978 (according to Puthuff (1978))*

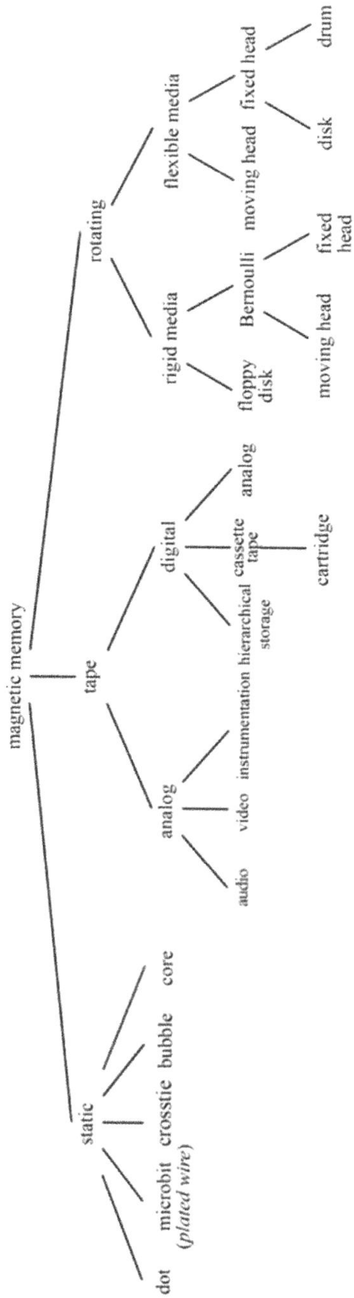

Figure 1.9(B). *Memory classification in 1978 (according to Puthuff (1978)) (continued)*

A main memory of several KiB made with tube-based flip-flops would have had significant weight and, most of all, occupied too much space. Also, researchers tested other technologies. Some of these made use of the properties of the electrostatic tube (see section 1.3.2.1). The first main memory (MM) technologies used the propagation time of a signal through a medium or component (delay line, see section 1.3.2.2) or the physical properties of materials, for example, magnetic properties with the core (see section 1.3.2.3). Large size, heavy weight and high power consumption characterized these early technologies.

Bell et al. (1978) reproduced a classification of the memory components and subassemblies of the time, taken from a study by Puthuff (1978) from Memorex (see Figure 1.9(A)). Four technological domains, both old and modern, are present: mechanical, electronic, magnetic and already optical. Computer peripherals using paper or cardboard as storage media were described in sections 5.6 and 6.5 of Darche (2003). Semiconductor technology (see section 1.3.2.4) with the transistor gradually replaced the electronic tube in the early 1960s and was later integrated. Note the presence of charge-coupled device (CCD) memory, which is also used as an optical sensor.

It was gradually replaced by the transistor (see Figure 1.17(a)).

The magnetic domain has the most branches, as shown in Figure 1.9(B). The magnetic medium in the form of a tape or disk is in motion. If it is static, it may be used as a component forming the cell of an MM. The core in particular is often used (see section 1.3.2.3).

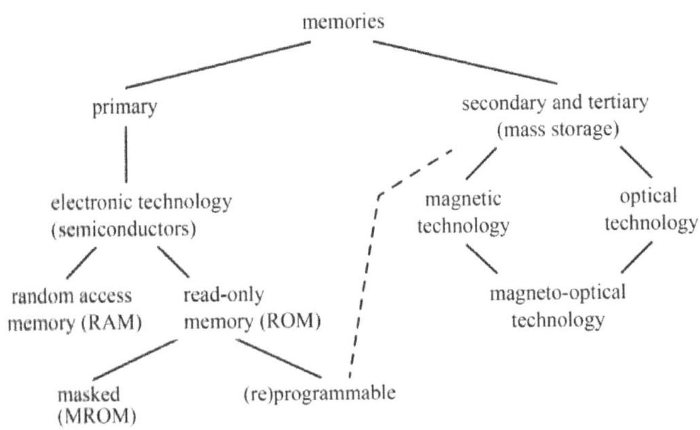

Figure 1.10. *The different memory technologies of a modern computer*

In 2025, technology is electronic, magnetic or optical. But the current trend is toward the elimination of moving components (electric motors, platters (i.e. disk) arms, etc.). Thus, the use of reprogrammable ROM such as flash memory (dotted line in Figure 1.10; see also Volume 6) as components of secondary memory is becoming dominant. Each level of the memory hierarchy corresponds to one of these three technologies, as shown in Figure 1.10.

The next three sections detail some representative legacy families.

1.3.2.1. *Electrostatic memories*

The first representative is the Williams–Kilburn tube (Chu and Klein 1952). Eckert (1949) and Julian and Samuel (1949) describe it as a classical cathode-ray tube, or CRT (see Figure 1.11), which stores binary information as a small light dot on the screen or as a dash.

Figure 1.11. *The Williams–Kilburn tube and a view of its screen (source: left image: https://en.wikipedia.org/wiki/File:Williams-tube.jpg; right image: National Institute of Standards and Technology, Public Domain, https://commons.wikimedia.org/w/index.php?curid=31539966)*

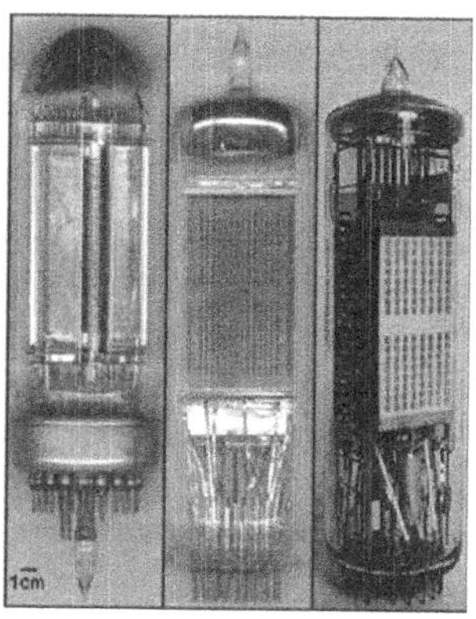

Figure 1.12. *The Selectron (source: https://rhartshorne.com/summer-2013/jamesralph/Multimedia%20Project/Evolution%20of%20RAM.html)*

The second is the Selectron (Selective Electrostatic Storage Tube), which was a special electronic tube (see Figure 1.12) able to store the value of a bit as a stable electric potential (holding beam memory tube). This type of memory could store 256 bits in a tube 3'' (= 7.62 cm) in diameter and 7'' (= 17.78 cm) tall. The highest capacity achieved was 4,096 bits. The access time was approximately 10 µs. This should be compared to the access time of early semiconductor memories, which was several hundred ns. It was first described in 1947 (Rajchman 1948) and given a detailed description by Rajchman (1949, 1951) and Knoll and Kazan (1952). This tube was manufactured by RCA (Radio Corporation of America). Due to lack of reliability, the Williams tube was preferred.

1.3.2.2. *The delay line*

A delay line slows the propagation of an electrical or mechanical signal (acoustic delay line). If the delay is long enough, it can store a train of logic pulses, provided the end of the line is looped back to its input. Thus, the delay line can serve as memory (delay-line memory). The delay can be caused by a material such as mercury (mercury sonic delay line) or quartz, or by a passive electronic component such as an inductor (i.e. a coil). The access time varies depending on the structure, and its maximum value equals the time to cross the line.

For example, the BINAC (Binary Automatic Computer) had, depending on the source, 18 memory channels of 32 words of 36 bits, giving a total capacity of 20,736 bits (20.25 KiB) (Eckert 1953), or 16 channels of 32 words of 31 bits, totaling 15,872 bits (15.5 KiB) (Schmitt 1988). The UNIVAC (Universal Automatic Computer), the first commercial computer, had 100 channels of 10 words of 91 bits, giving a total of 91,000 bits (nearly 90 KiB).

For more information on this component, Eveleth (1965) presents an overview of ultrasonic delay lines, and Zilberstein (1965) describes a variable-delay version.

1.3.2.3. *Ferrite core memory*

Ferromagnetic technology was the first used to create a non-volatile memory (ferromagnetic memory). Binary data was stored as a change in the orientation of a magnetic field in a fired toroidal ferrite core. The material properties are described by Greifer (1969). Figure 1.13 shows the curve $\Phi = f(I)$ of a ferrite core with a current-carrying wire passing through its center. Depending on the direction of the current, the core can be magnetized in one of two directions. It has two stable states when there is no supply current.

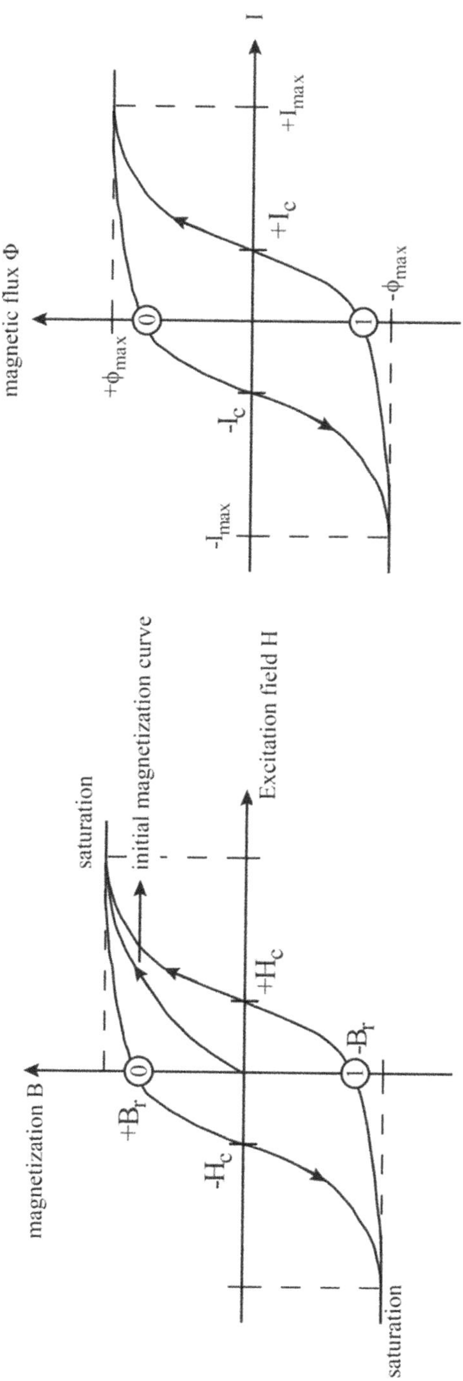

Figure 1.13. *Hysteresis curves of a ferrite core*

The sides of the loop were deliberately slanted to clearly show the key points of the cycle. Those of a real component are nearly vertical. It is thus easy to model the loop as a rectangle, as shown in Figure 1.14.

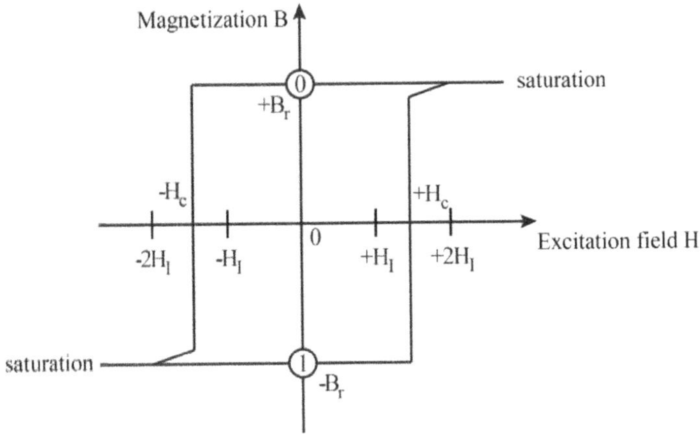

Figure 1.14. *Modeling of a ferrite core hysteresis loop*

The memory area was a wired matrix, with a core mounted at each intersection (gray oval in Figure 1.15), hence the name core memory. The typical outer diameter ranged from 0.08" (2.032 mm) to 0.4" (10.16 mm), with an inner diameter of 0.05" (1.27 mm). A specific core was addressed by coincidence. Writing was done by sending a current pulse simultaneously on one row and one column (coincident current selection). The polarity of these currents determined the magnetization direction. A single pulse was not enough to flip the magnetization of other cores on the same row or column as the selected core (half-select currents). Reading required a dedicated read wire passing through all the cores in series (three-wire core). Reading was performed by writing a known logic state, say "0". If the selected core held the opposite state, a large current spike appeared on the read line. If not, no current spike was detected. Reading was therefore destructive. A rewrite was required if the state had changed.

A trick even allowed doubling the number of cores (i.e. capacity) per address plane by using the anti-current concept. Indeed, for a given core, there are four possible current combinations: two useful (i.e. switching possible) and two that cancel out the produced magnetic field. Depending on the current direction, one of two cores could be selected, as shown in Table 1.4 and Figure 1.16.

a)

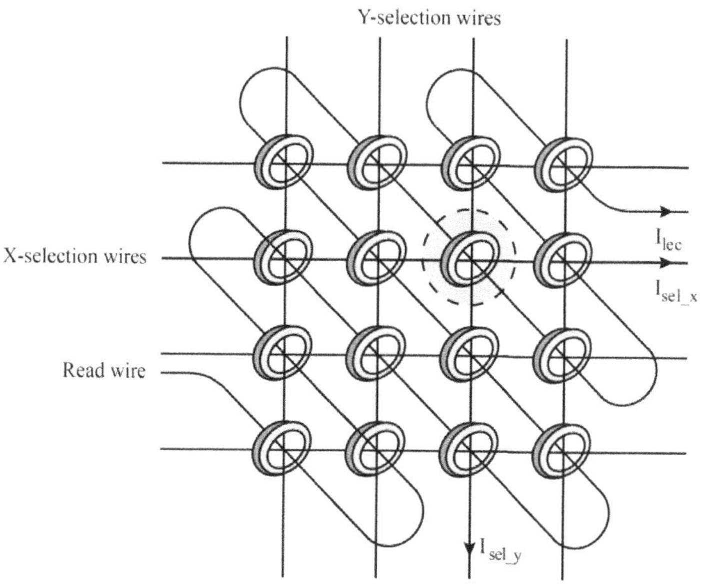

b)

Figure 1.15. *a) Matrix-organized core memory (according to Rajchman (1957)), and b) a real memory (source: The MITRE Corporation)*

Selection		State	
X	Y	C_1	C_2
–	–	0	–
–	+	–	1
+	–	–	1
+	+	1	–

Table 1.4. *Truth table: state = f (current direction)*

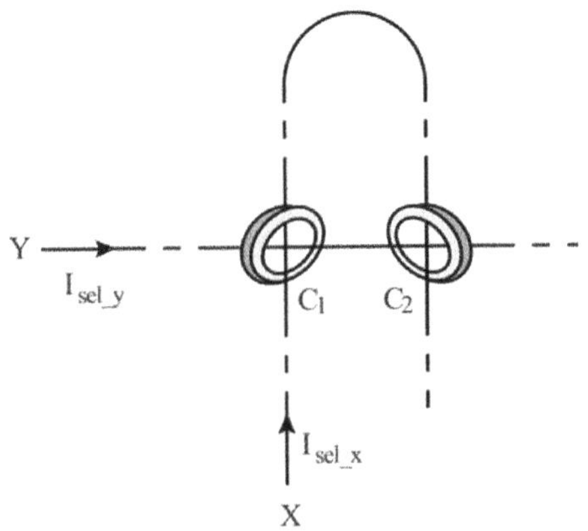

Figure 1.16. *Selection of one of two cores using anti-current technique*

The selection current ranged from 400 to 800 mA. The write time was between 3 and 5 µs. Since reading (a pulse of 50–75 mV) was destructive, the information had to be regenerated. Depending on the source, the invention is attributed to An Wang, researcher at Harvard Computing Lab in 1948 (Wang 1955), or to Jay Forrester of the Whirlwind project (Forrester 1951), who held the patent (Forrester 1956). Wang and Woo (1950) proposed a magnetic delay-line approach, while Forrester (1951) preferred the matrix-based solution. He even discussed a three-dimensional structure (3D, see section 3.7). An example of the patent is Bornhauser (1964). Rajchman (1957) reviews the early memories. In 1968, a core memory had a capacity of 4,096 bits with an access time of 120 ns. The Apollo 11 AGC (Apollo Guidance Computer) used core memory organized as 2 Ki × 15-bit RAM and 36 Ki × 15-bit RAM. Using that much ROM was not surprising, as it helped resolve the problem of overwriting of information (code or data) by a program, whether malicious or faulty (see memory protection problem in Volume 9). This memory was later developed in various formats, such as toristor, thin-film dot memory and cylindrical (magnetic rod).

Pugh et al. (1981) and Chapter 7 of Bashe et al. (1986) provide details about these memories in IBM (International Business Machines Corporation) computers. For detailed specifications, see Scrupski (2001). ANSI/IEEE standard 393 (ANSI/IEEE 1991) defines vocabulary and test procedures related to this component. With the development of discrete-transistor and then integrated memories in 1965–1966, core memories gradually disappeared since they could not compete in size, weight, power consumption, capacity and cost with their integrated counterparts. The final core models had an outer diameter as small as 0.0015" (0.0381 mm). DRAM in its modern form, first commercialized by Intel in 1971, marked the end of this technology. There remained niche markets, such as radiation-hardened memory, since radiation could cause storage errors (soft errors; see section 6.4). For instance, NASA's first shuttle used core memory of 104 Ki × 32 bits with an access time t_a de 400 ns. A presentation of this memory is given by Pugh (2000).

1.3.2.4. *Semiconductor memories*

Semiconductor memories, initially in discrete form, using diodes and then transistors (invention by Bardeen and Brattain (1948)), and from the 1970s in integrated form (see Figure 1.17(b)), have continually increased in capacity. Manufacturing technologies have evolved over 60 years, but the memory principles and internal structure have paradoxically changed very little. Memories represent one of the largest market shares of integrated circuits, but paradoxically yield little profit.

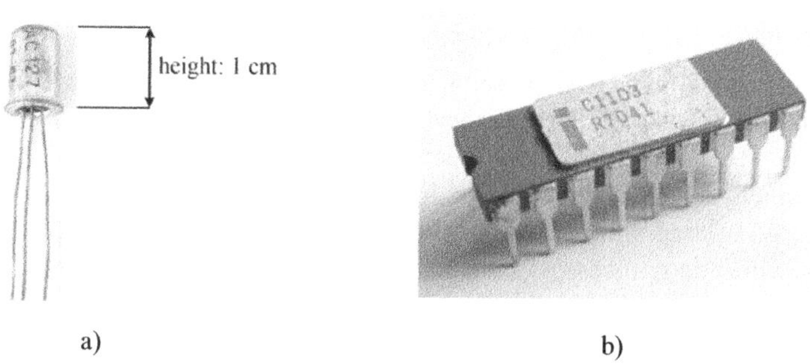

Figure 1.17. *a) Germanium transistor and b) Intel's 1103 P-channel MOS DRAM (source: Wikipedia)*

The industrial market is mainly segmented into three parts: static RAM (SRAM), dynamic RAM (DRAM) and programmable ROMs, represented by EEPROMs (electrically EPROM), flash, or FEEPROM. They are used in all subsystems and components of a computer – inside the processor, in primary memory, in intermediate memory between the processor and main memory (cache), in I/O interfaces, and in peripherals.

The static model uses a memory principle based on self-sustained electrical states. Thus, the storage is persistent without auxiliary mechanisms and is not very sensitive to external disturbances such as radiation or electrical noise (see Volume 2).

The dynamic model, however, uses the principle of storing electric charge in a capacitor (stored-charge memory). This capacitor is imperfect and has a leakage current. The stored information is not persistent and must be periodically refreshed. DRAM originally operated with a clock (synchronous model), then quickly became asynchronous in 1971 (see Volume 3). Since 1996, dynamic RAM evolved again toward synchronous operation for speed, with models such as synchronous communication per cycle (SDRAM; see Volume 4) and communication per packet (see Volume 5).

The information in ROM was implemented using a photolithographic mask (MROM or mask-programmed ROM (JEDEC)). Programmable models, or PROM (programmable ROM), then reprogrammable models, erasable by ultraviolet light (UV), such as EPROM (erasable PROM), or electrically via EAROM (electrically alterable ROM) and EEPROM (electrically EPROM) later appeared (see Volume 6).

1.3.2.5. *Historical timeline*

In summary, Figure 1.18 presents a chart inspired by Proebster (1992) that recalls, for each level of the memory hierarchy, the technologies used to store information. Technological shifts were gradual due to practical and economic reasons, which are not shown in the figure for graphical clarity. Starting in the 1970s, the LSI (large scale integration) generation enabled the emergence of early memories with microprocessors built using bipolar and unipolar technologies. The first category included the "standardized" TTL (transistor-transistor logic) and ECL (emitter-coupled logic; see section 2.3.3 of Darche (2004)) families. The second was called MOS (metal–oxide semiconductor), with PMOS (positive-channel), then NMOS (negative-channel) and later CMOS (complementary MOS) subfamilies. Gallium arsenide (GaAs) technology is mentioned anecdotally. VLSI circuits (very LSI) appeared in the 1980s. Subsequent decades saw the emergence of ULSI (ultra LSI) and GSI (gigascale integration), the latter allowing the integration of an entire digital system or SoC (system on a chip). It is noteworthy that punch cards were still (occasionally) used in the 1980s, for example, to dump memory on Bull's Mitra 625–725 machines (personal experience). A mass memory, or MSD (mass storage device), stores large quantities of data. Excluding tape and punch cards, the initial technology was magnetic, with hard disk drives and floppy disks. A mass storage system, or MSS, automatically manages a set of magnetic tapes as cartridges or cassettes (see section 1.5). For more information, Williams (1997) presents a historical overview of all the technologies discussed in this chapter. Eckert (1953), in turn, presents other technologies based on optical, magnetic or even thermal properties! Pugh (1984, 1985, 2000) details the key role played by IBM in developing memory technologies.

1.4. Memory in a microcomputer

Figure 1.19 shows memory in a modern PC-type microcomputer. The main element is the microprocessor, the sole master of data exchanges[10]. The other components, which are slaves, are the main memory and the I/O interfaces. All these subsystems communicate via buses. In electronics, a bus is a set of electrical wires or copper traces on a printed circuit board. A bus controller manages access (see section 1.6 of Darche (2021b)). It thus prevents conflicts and ensures data validity. The figure shows a dual independent bus (DIB) architecture, with a front-side bus (FSB) and a back-side bus (BSB). The BSB connects the microprocessor to the cache memory buffer (see Volume 8). Bus controllers are integrated into a component called the HUB or bridge, which acts as a true communication hub for all subsystems.

Today, most I/O interfaces are integrated into a single chip, called the ICH (I/O controller hub) or south bridge by Intel, to reflect its diagram position. Only two interfaces (network and mass storage) are shown in the figure.

However, the display interface communicates primarily with the microprocessor and main memory, except in low-end microcomputers, where it may be integrated into the north bridge, then called the GMCH (graphics and memory controller hub) by Intel. This north bridge connects to the microprocessor via the FSB. The BIOS (basic input/output system; see Chapter 4 of Darche (2003)), the software layer (software or SW) that manages I/O controllers, is stored in the ROM (firmware or fw); for a PC, this ROM is connected to the south bridge. The main memory is then partitioned, either statically or dynamically, to be shared between the microprocessor and the display controller. This is known as unified memory architecture (UMA). Without this interface, the bridge is called the MCH (memory controller hub).

10 For our level of discussion, as other components can also manage exchanges.

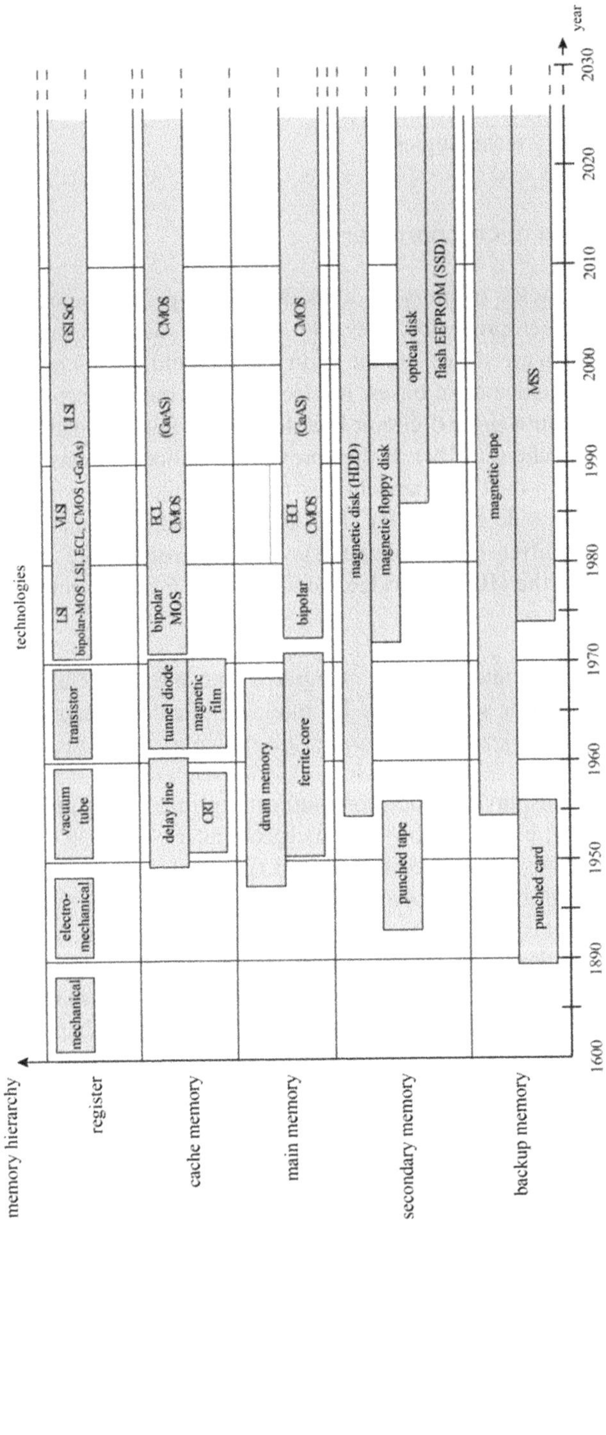

Figure 1.18. *Historical evolution of memory technologies (inspired by Proebster (1992))*

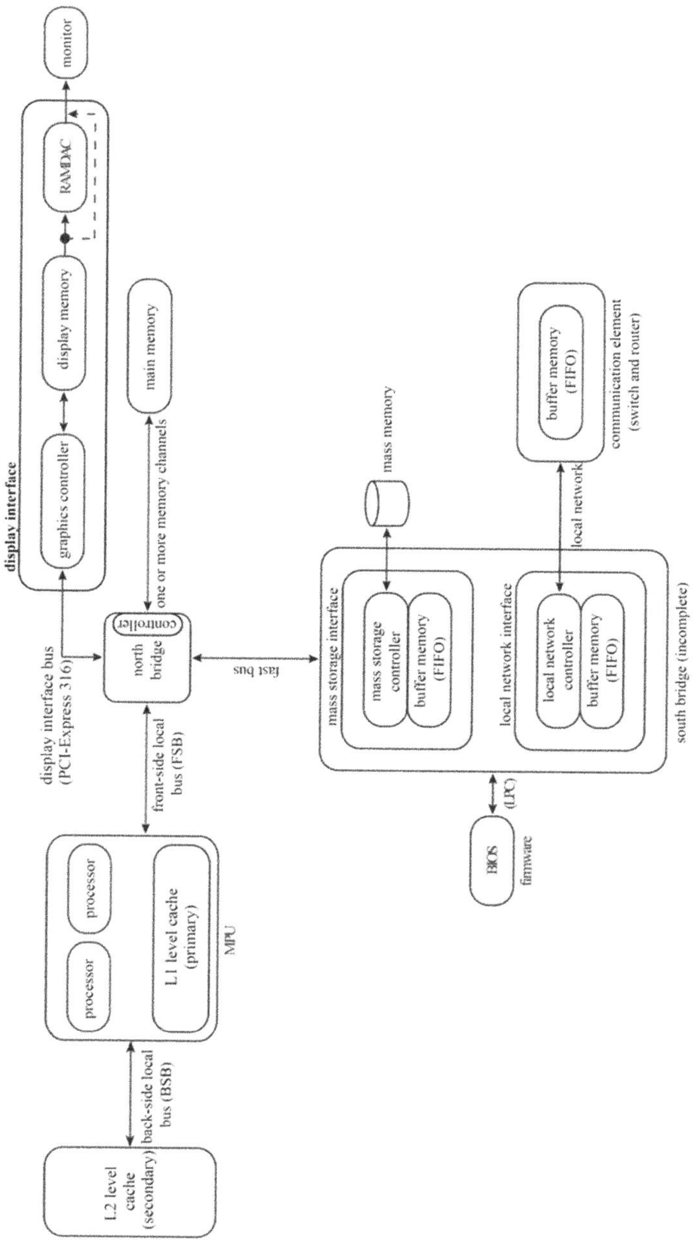

Figure 1.19. *Semiconductor memory in a modern PC-type microcomputer in 2001*

The main memory was initially a scarce resource, as the first computers had a memory of approximately a kilobyte. Mechanisms had to be created to improve its use, such as overlay (a Pascal language "overlay" module or file), virtual memory (VM) or swapping (i.e. exchanging). It must often meet contradictory criteria. For example, it must be large and fast, while taking up little space, using little power and costing less. Using buses with their associated logic introduces latencies, but integration advances have made more space on the chip for RAM and related logic. As a result, bandwidth increases while latency decreases (Patterson et al. 1997). Today, memory size is comfortable, but access time is still generally 10 times slower than that of a microprocessor register (see Table 1.5). RAM remains the second largest cost after the microprocessor when buying a personal computer. In 2004, main memory in PCs represented 50% of the DRAM market (data from Rajan (2009)).

Cache memory, inserted into the data path, improved the latency of primary memory. It is a key element in computer performance and in spatial footprint. We only have to look at a microphotograph of a multicore chip such as Core™2 Duo (Intel) to see that cache takes up nearly half its surface area (left part of Figure 1.20).

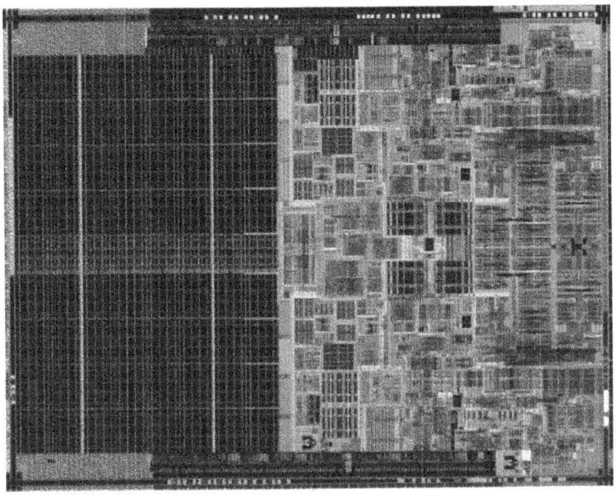

Figure 1.20. *Microphotograph of the Core™ 2 Duo microprocessor chip (source: Intel)*

As can be seen, no memory family, each of which has sometimes opposite characteristics, meets all the needs of electronic systems, whether in terms of capacity/density, volatility, access time (read) or cycle time, hence the idea of a hierarchy.

1.5. Memory hierarchization

> We are therefore forced to recognize the possibility of constructing a hierarchy of memories, each of which has greater capacity than the preceding but which is less quickly accessible (Burks et al. 1946).

It is now accepted that memory capacity and access speed needs cannot both be fully satisfied at a reasonable cost. Boland and Dollas (1994) showed that the number of processor cycles needed to access main memory doubled approximately every 6.2 years. A memory built with the same technology will, after n years, require a number of cycles equal to:

$$L(n) = L_0 \times 2^{\frac{n}{6.2}} \qquad [1.10]$$

L_0 is the base latency.

This is called the performance gap (i.e. speed) between memory and the processor (memory gap). This gap between the processor cycle time and memory time first appeared for microprocessors in the early 1980s. As a result, processors were delayed during external accesses, as shown in Figure 1.21 (f_{DRAM} = access time^{-1}). Synchronous architectures (see Volume 4) reduced this gap, though without eliminating it.

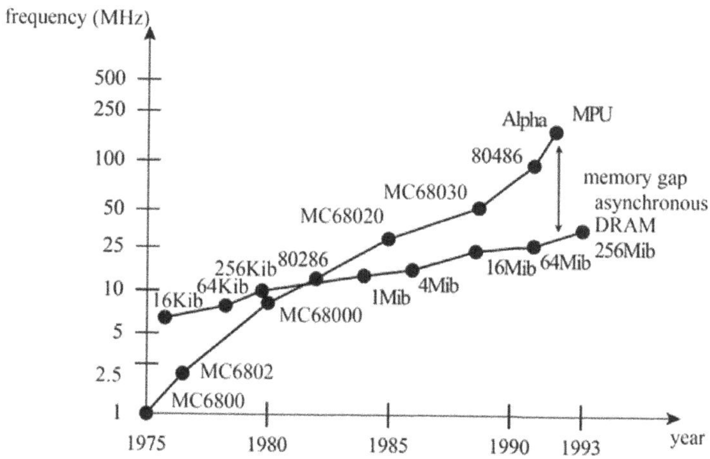

Figure 1.21. *Speed gap between MPU and asynchronous DRAM (Slater et al. 1993)*

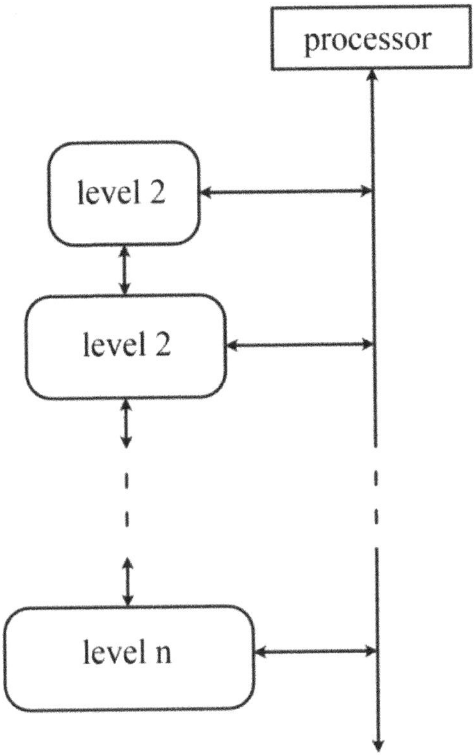

Figure 1.22. *Processor access to the memory hierarchy*

Therefore, to reduce the average access times for processor instructions and data, and for cost reasons, several memory technologies were inserted into the data path. Figure 1.22 shows the access paths available to a processor. The area of the rectangles represents access time and capacity (not to scale). Communication between levels is possible thanks to specialized controllers such as cache or DMA (direct memory access) controllers.

These different memories were modeled under the name "memory or storage hierarchy". This abstraction organizes storage components, subsets and peripherals vertically by levels (multi-level memory hierarchy) or layers, depending on their position in the data path and on a technical characteristic. The hierarchy is usually shown as a triangle or even a pyramid (Nakagomi 1993). The lower an element is, the farther it is from the PE.

Figure 1.23(b) shows a classic hierarchy. At its top is the flip-flop (in static logic implementation), a basic memory element (i.e. one bit). Next, it consists of the register, which is a set of flip-flops. The following layers include on-chip cache (internal to the MPU), or tightly coupled memory (TCM; see section 5.3), then possibly an off-chip cache, then primary, main or central memory, followed by secondary memory, and finally tertiary memory, also known as backup memory (tertiary memory system[11], offline backup storage or backing store (Handy 1998)).

Not shown here, archival memory allows for storing data over decades. These mass storage systems or MSS consist of libraries of hundreds of magnetic tape cartridges or optical disks, moved by robotic arms to insert them in reading/writing devices. Local memory is the memory integrated into the processor, i.e. registers, embedded memory and internal cache.

Since manufacturing technologies are heterogeneous, each level or layer has its own technical features, whose values rise or fall discretely, i.e. by steps (see Figure 1.23(a)). The surface or base of the trapezoid is meant to represent the magnitude of these values. In general, we focus only on four features: total storage capacity, cycle and access times, bandwidth and finally the cost per bit stored. The latter decreases as capacity increases. Thus, memory hierarchy offers the largest amount of memory at the lowest cost, while providing the fastest possible access. In general, and especially for cache levels, the frequency of access increases as you go up the hierarchy.

Figure 1.24 details types of components or devices used at each level. Tertiary memory, used for backup in case of failure, includes systems that are online, near-line (cartridge) or offline. The hierarchy is managed either by hardware or software. Cache levels are handled by dedicated controllers integrated, for example, in PCs' north bridge chipset (see section 3.3 of Darche (2021e)), now integrated into the MPU. Primary memory is managed by the dynamic memory controller. Secondary memory is managed by the virtual memory controller or MMU (memory management unit) associated with the OS.

11 Following footnote 1 of this chapter, secondary and tertiary memories are called mass storage memories: secondary and tertiary storages. The origin of these terms is found in psychophysiology, in the work of James (1890). This American psychologist called primary memory the fleeting store of thought in consciousness and secondary memory the permanent but unconscious store.

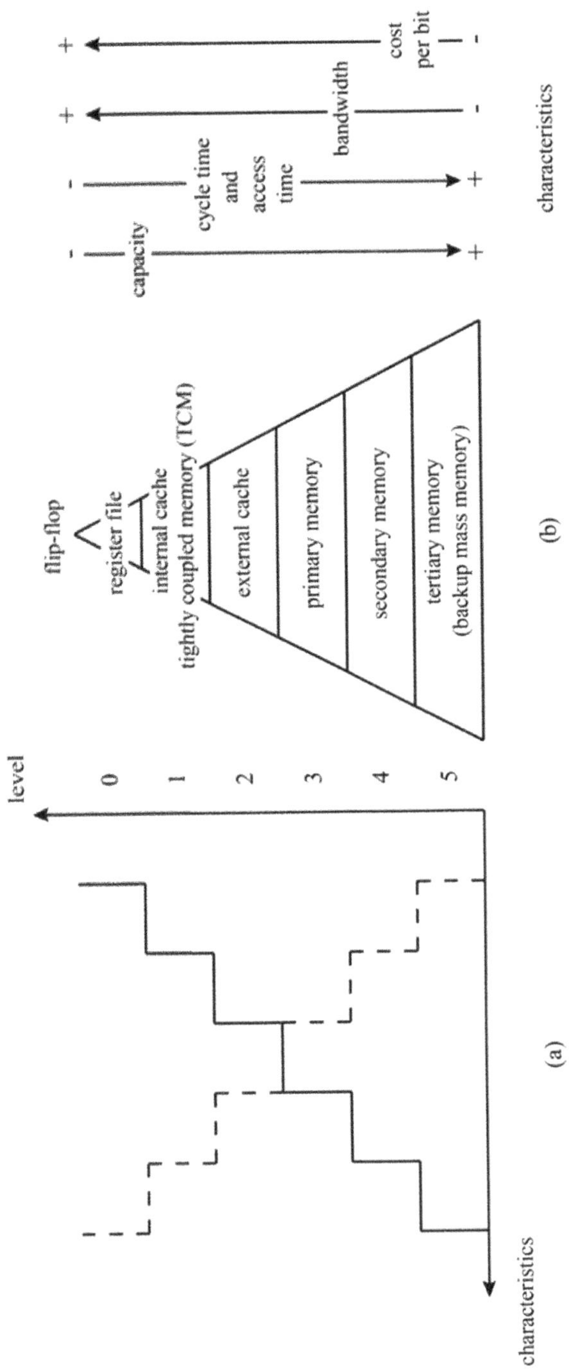

Figure 1.23. *Memory hierarchy*

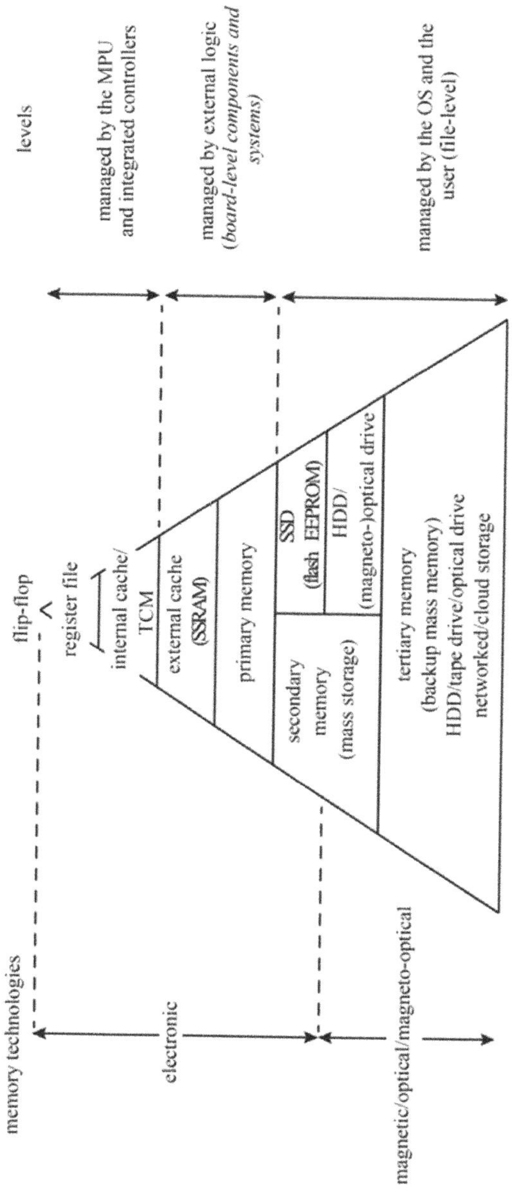

Figure 1.24. *Detailed memory hierarchy*

Cohen et al. (1989) presents an example of a memory hierarchy for a large system (mainframe) IBM 3090 (see Figure 1.25). The central unit consists of three processors, each with a cache called the HSB (high-speed buffer) (level 0). Levels 1 and 2 represent central memory (L3 and L4). Mass storage consists of hard disk units called the DASD (direct access storage device), preceded by a disk cache (Grossman 1985).

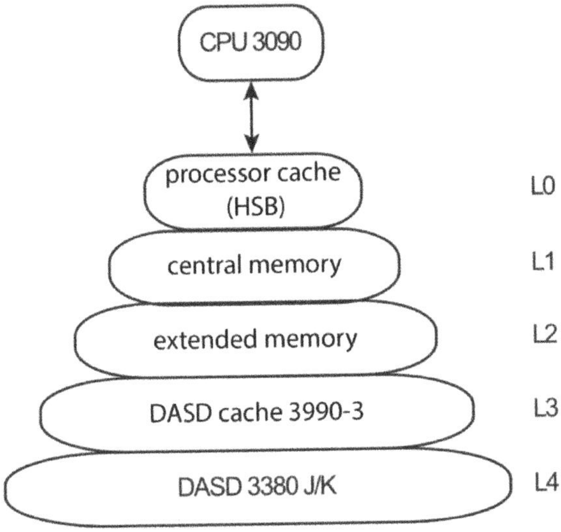

Figure 1.25. *Simplified memory hierarchy of an IBM 3090 (according to Cohen et al. (1989))*

The hierarchy is therefore not just a simple classification of memory elements by capacity, as some books have presented. It represents the various memory elements accessed successively during the execution of an instruction or when accessing data. Disregarding backup mass memory, the memory hierarchy can be viewed as a single address space available to the software architect. It is therefore a part of the hardware architecture, as defined in section 3.1.4 of Darche (2021a). To be fully complete, we must also consider the data flow exchanged between the processor and these elements, called the "storage hierarchy data flow". This diagram represents the physical structure of the hierarchy of a mainframe computer. Figure 1.26 shows the one from the previous example. It highlights a key element in operation, the system controller (system control element or SCE), which manages memory access for the processors.

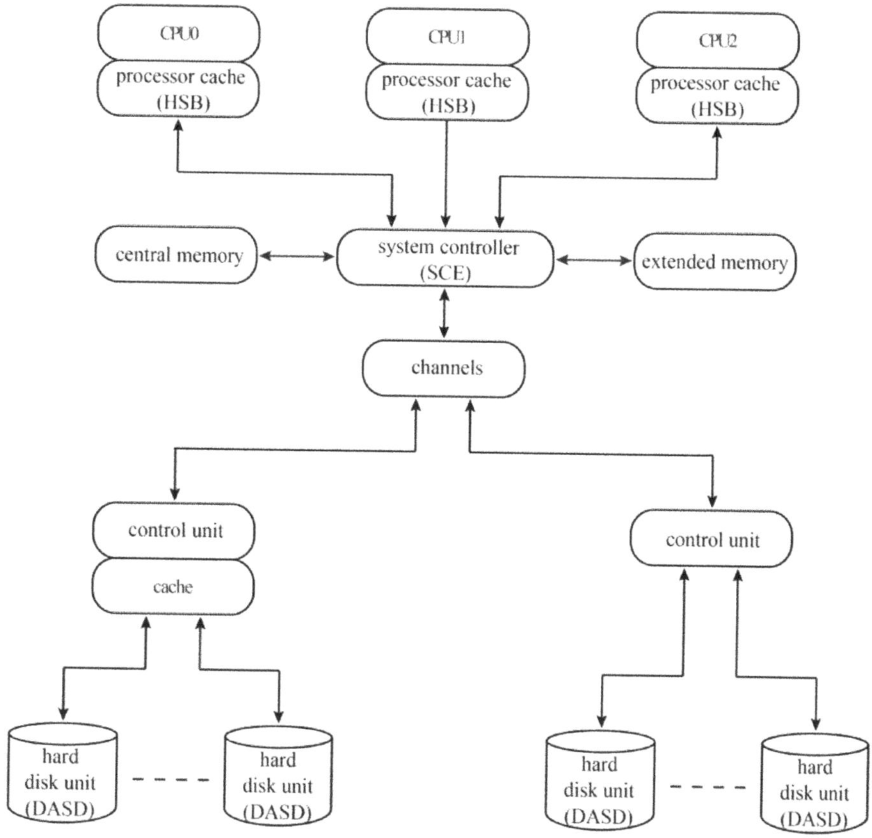

Figure 1.26. *Data flow of the memory hierarchy of an IBM 3090 (according to Cohen et al. (1989))*

Thanks to queueing theory, it is possible to model the transfer of information between the different subsystems of a computer. An example of such a study can be found in Rege (1976). From that, we can calculate theoretical throughputs. The choice of technical characteristics at each level will affect the overall computer performance and especially that of the operating system. For example, Hake and Homberg (1990) studied the impact of memory organization on matrix multiplication performance. Kaneko (1974) studied the influence of memory hierarchy on the OS task switching policy. Table 1.5 summarizes current values of the characteristics for each level. Note that the raw throughput of a memory is the intrinsic throughput of the memory. It does not involve the interface. To provide historical context, Pugh (1971) presents data from 1952 to 1972.

Level	Type	Size (bytes)	Average access time	Factor	Raw throughput (order of magnitude from access time for SC memories)	Cost/MB ($)
0	Register	Number: 8/16/32 (CISC) to 32/128/256/512 (RISC)	0.25 ns	1	32 GB/s (n = 64)	–
1	Internal L1 cache (Itanium 2 MP Intel)	32 Ki	1 ns (1 cycle)	4	8 GB/s (n = 64)	–
2	External L2 cache (Itanium 2 MP Intel)	256 Mi	5 ns (5 cycles)	20	1.6 GB/s (n = 64)	–
3	External L3 cache (Itanium 2 MP Intel)	9 Mi	12 ns (12 cycles)	48	667 MB/s (n = 64)	1.5
4	Primary memory	1 Gi	30 ns	120	267 MB/s (n = 64, random)	0.01
5	Secondary memory	1 T	10 ms (HDD)	40×10^6	250 MB/s (SATA Revision 3.0)	0.0002
6	Tertiary memory	> 10 T	30 s (average)	120×10^9	160 MB/s (LTO Ultrium 5)	0.0001

Table 1.5. *Order of magnitude of technical specs for memory levels in a microcomputer (2006)*

Level	Type	Size (bytes)	Average access time	Factor
0	Register (without pipeline)	Number: 8/16/32 (CISC) to 32/128/256/512 (RISC)	0.175 ns	1
1	Internal L1 cache/core (Zen 4 CCD AMD)	32/32 Ki (data/instructions)	0.175 ns (1 cycle)	1
2	Internal L2 cache/core (Zen 4 CCD AMD)	1 Mi	2.45 ns (14 cycles)	14
3	L3 cache/core (Zen 4 CCD AMD)	4 Mi	8,75 ns (50 cycles)	50
4	Primary memory	32 Gi (DDR5 SDRAM (DDR for Double Data Rate))	10 ns	57
5	Secondary memory	1 T	0.1 ms (SSD)	570×10^3
6	Tertiary memory	> 10 T	30 s (average)	170×10^9

Table 1.6. *Order of magnitude of technical specs for memory levels in a microcomputer (2023)*

Williams (1973) studied a memory hierarchy where the read time of mass memory (backing storage) is very small compared to that of conventional mass memories or compared to the write time, as is the case with optical mass memory units. This type of unit is called "asymmetric backing storage" and the associated hierarchy, "asymmetric memory hierarchy".

Table 1.5 should be compared with Table 1.6. Between the two dates, Moore's law remains (mostly) valid (see section 1.5 of Darche (2021a)). Integration continues across all cache levels, and multicore architecture becomes standard in MPUs. The clock frequency of processors stagnates at approximately 6 GHz. Secondary memory has changed technology. It has gradually shifted from magnetic to electronic using FEEPROM memory in SSDs. This choice improves access time by a factor of 100 compared to using an HDD.

Designing this hierarchy well is essential for computer performance. This issue is summarized as the "memory wall" by Wulf and McKee (1995), showing processor performance grows faster than memory.

1.6. Conclusion

This chapter was dedicated to the memory function. The main characteristics of a generic memory, such as capacity, organization, policies and types of access, and timing characteristics, were defined. Historical and technological aspects were then presented, leading to the presentation of the memory hierarchy.

The designer of a memory system must make a compromise between storage density, latency and throughput, power consumption and the cost of each layer in the hierarchy.

Chapter 2 presents the internal organization of a random-access semiconductor memory with its main functional subunits.

2

Internal Organization of a Random-Access Semiconductor Memory

Semiconductor memory has permeated all subunits of the computer, from the processor to the peripherals. At the microprocessor level (μP or MPU for microprocessor unit), Motorola's MC6802 (1977) integrated 128 bytes of RAM, 32 of which were battery-backed. In 1989, cache was integrated into the component with the 486DX CISC (complex instruction set computer) (8 KiB unified L1 cache) and Intel's i860 RISC (reduced instruction set computer) (4 KiB for instructions and 8 KiB for data) and the ARM3 32-bit RISC (VL86C020, 4 KiB unified L1 cache). Announced in 2020, Apple's M1 SoC (system on (a) chip) is coupled with a unified memory (memory on package or MoP) and assembled in an SiP (system-in-a-package), a concept originating in multimedia systems (Shimizu et al. 1996). By definition, a microcontroller integrates both RAM (random-access memory) and ROM (read-only memory). It gained ground in embedded systems in the 1980s, such as car onboard computers, and in the early 21st century in everyday devices such as the 1998 digital music player or music player in MP3 format (MPEG-1 audio layer 3) and Apple's iPhone in 2007.

A solid-state memory technology is attractive because it enables low-cost production of high-capacity, fast, compact and lightweight memories, which are also resistant to acceleration (i.e. shocks). It also addresses the need to limit electrical power consumption due to device mobility and energy savings. The DRAM and NAND Flash EEPROM (FEEPROM for flash electrically erasable programmable ROM, see Volume 6) market represented about 30% of the global semiconductor market in 2021 and continues to grow.

This chapter presents only the general organization of random-access semiconductor memory; other access policies are covered in dedicated volumes. Its main functional subunits are detailed.

2.1. Basic internal organization

Historically, for technological reasons, the basic memory cell stores one bit[1]. The storage principle may be based on the presence or absence of one or more electronic components. The cell was initially implemented with a diode (e.g. see Jordan (1970) or Regitz (1973)), and later with a transistor (e.g. see Jordan et al. (1972)). When the electronic component is present and electrically functional, it operates in switching mode[2], meaning it has two electrical states: off (cut-off mode) or on (saturation mode). The storage principle may also rely on the creation (antifuse) or destruction (fuse) of an electrical connection. A cell may also exploit an inherent storage mechanism, such as maintaining a logic state through feedback or storing electric charge in a capacitor or insulator. The first principle is used in the flip-flop (see sections 3.3.2 and 3.4 of Darche (2002)) and is found in static RAM or SRAM (see Volumes 2 and 4). The second principle is central to dynamic RAM or DRAM (see Volumes 3–5) and reprogrammable ROMs (see Volume 6). If a transistor is used, its technology defines the memory's technological family. We then speak of bipolar memory or MOS (metal oxide semiconductor; see technologies in sections 2.3 and 2.4 of Darche (2004)) unipolar memory.

A memory's organization centers on a memory array composed of memory cells. At first glance, memory is a one-dimensional array (see Figure 2.1). Given an address in m-bit format, a selection logic composed of a binary decoder (see section 2.4.2 of Darche (2002)), also called an address decoder, selects a row I_k from 2^m ($k \in [0, 2^m - 1]$) that enables access to a memory cell (one-hot decoder). The first address is thus 0, and the last is 2^{m-1}. The requested operation – read or write – is then performed via the bitline or bit sense, also called a column. This line can be single or double: one for reading (bit sense) and one for writing[3]. In the example, it is a read operation. The cell's physical state is interpreted by a sense amplifier (SA), also called read amplifier, dedicated to the column, which logically interprets the electrical signal (comparator). An electronic buffer (see section 3.4.1 of Darche (2004)) isolates and amplifies the electrical signal for the external interface, typically a data bus. There is also an address buffer for the same isolation and amplification reasons. This selection method is called "linear" or "Cambridge-type" (Simon 1970).

---

1 Multi-level cell (MLC) technologies, which appeared in the mid-1990s, allow storing multiple bits per cell. They will be presented in Volume 6.

2 The transistor has three main operating modes, the cut-off mode, the amplification mode (linear region of its current–voltage I–V characteristic) and the switching mode (saturated region of its I–V characteristic).

3 Later, the data line will become double to increase read sensitivity using a differential method (see section 2.2.8). However, data will flow in both directions.

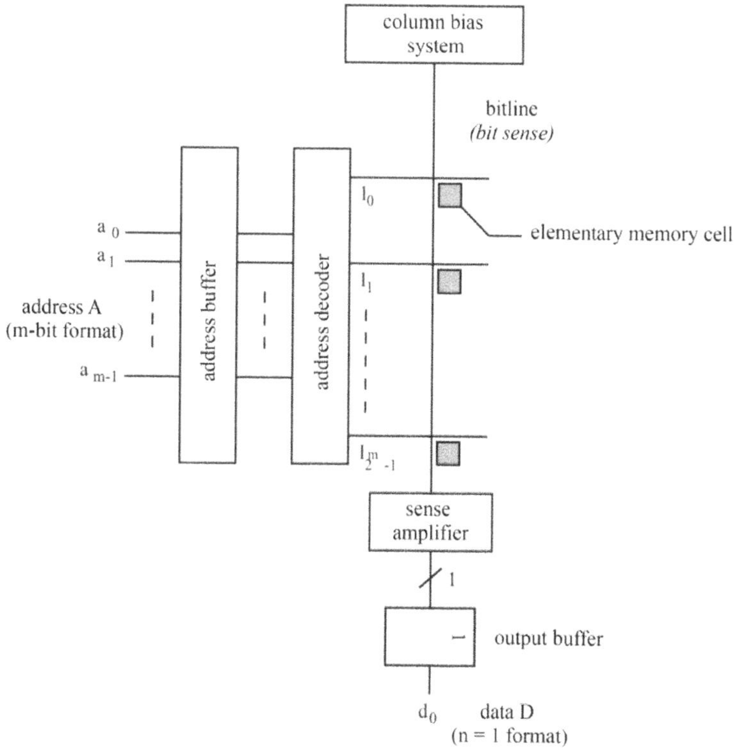

Figure 2.1. *Memory with linear selection addressing and its read system*

This selection method is called "coincident" selection or "multidimensional" (Simon 1970). To access it, the processor sends an address A in *m*-bit format which, inside the memory, is transparently split in two, the row address in *r*-bit format and the column address in *c*-bit format. Thus, we have the relationship:

$$m = r + c \qquad [2.1]$$

Static RAM operates in this way. For dynamic RAM,, it is necessary to sequentially send the row address and then the column address. This is called multiplexed addressing, implying a time-based process. It reduces the address format *m* to *m'*, which is then equal to:

$$m' = \max(r, c) \qquad [2.2]$$

A second approach, the one used, is to use a two-dimensional array (two-dimensional array or memory cell matrix). The memory cell is placed at the intersection of a wordline (WL) or row select and a bitline (BL) or bit sense, also called bit column, as shown in Figure 2.2 (space coordinates).

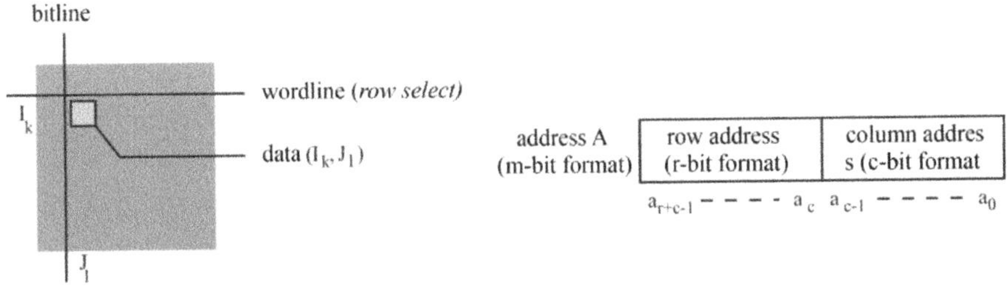

Figure 2.2. *Coincident selection and address decomposition*

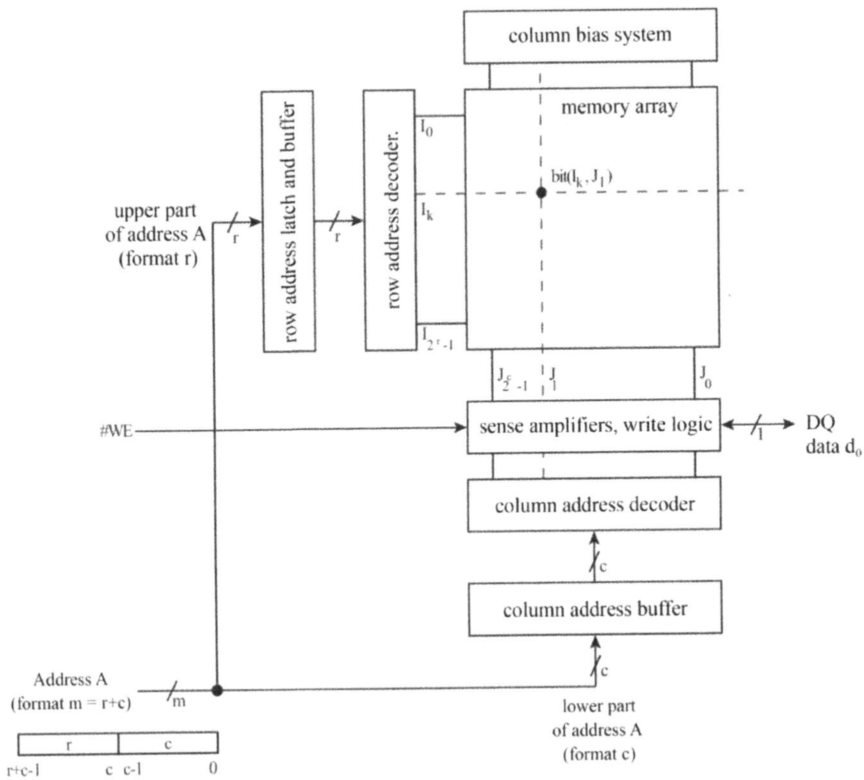

Figure 2.3. *Coincident selection addressing (modern approach)*

Figure 2.3 shows the internal organization of a memory with multiplexed addressing (address control signals not shown). The row address (X-address) is stored and decoded by the associated address decoder (row decoder or X-decoder) to select row I_k. Then, once the column address (Y-address) is entered, it is decoded (column decoder, column selector or Y-decoder) to select column J_l through logic called column selector circuitry. Column address decoders have a complemented logic output to simplify downstream logic. The column address decoder controls, depending on the type of access (read or write), the sense amplifier or the write system. The read (R) and write (W) control signals can be separated. These two signals are antagonistic during access and, to save a package pin, they can be combined, the signal then being called R/#W, with the prefix symbol # indicating that the W signal is active low. Another term, now more commonly used, is simply #WE for write enable. For more details on signal naming, see Volume 2, section 1.1.

The matrix approach offers a better spatial distribution of memory cells compared to the first approach, which is difficult to implement and route during the creation of the integrated circuit masks.

This organization is used in current memories because it allows for efficient chip area management and faster access. In addition, each row and each column require a driver amplifier, and only the columns require a bias system. For linear selection, $2^m = 2^{r+c}$ are needed, whereas for the matrix approach, $2^r + 2^c$ are required. From $m = 3$, the matrix becomes advantageous from this point of view. The numbers of rows and columns are not necessarily equal because sense amplifiers are bulky, hence an asymmetric architecture where the number of columns is limited[4].

If we introduce the height/width ratio, when the r/c ratio becomes large ($r >> c$), it is necessary to rebalance by dividing the memory area into blocks (see section 4.2). The ideal memory will also use the third dimension (three-dimensional array). Chapter 3 of Volume 2 presents the first approaches.

The memory cell is called "active" if it includes a selection transistor, and "passive" otherwise. This is then a passive grid (passive crossbar array), also called "cross-point array", as shown in Figure 2.4. The memory cell is a bistable junction. The passive grid can be described as "the ultimate memory cell" since it consists of only one component.

4 The argument is now false because there is a type of memory with a high number of columns, for example 1,024, for access known as "page mode" (see Chapter 4, Volume 3), a page being all the memory cells of a row.

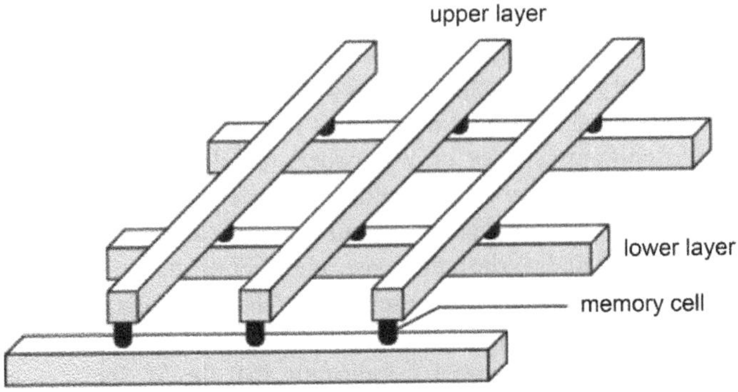

Figure 2.4. *The passive grid concept*

To increase the data width *n* of the data D in the case of linear address selection, it would suffice to increase the number of columns to get the desired width (see Figure 2.5). This solution is electrically poor because it presents strong capacitive coupling. The value of this figure is to transition from the abstract model of Figure 1.3 I call "the dresser"[5] to the logical implementation.

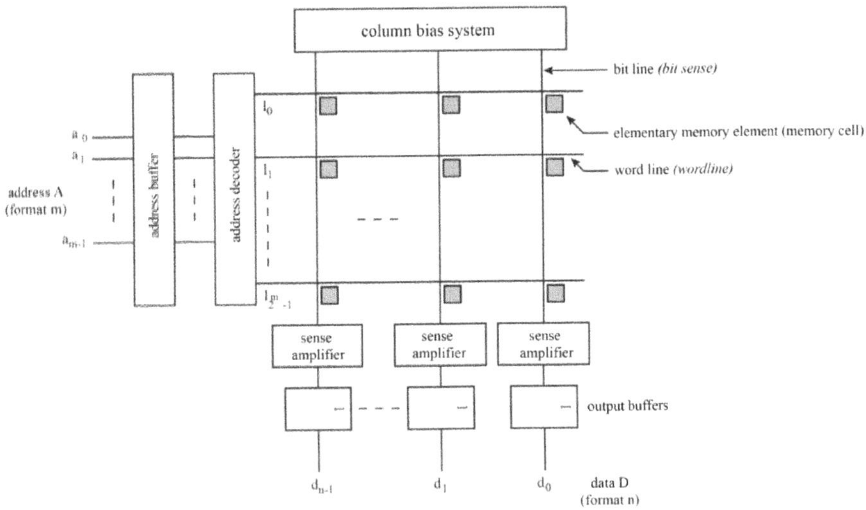

Figure 2.5. *Data width increase n for a linear-selection memory*

5 By analogy with this piece of furniture where each numbered drawer is a memory cell (see section 1.1.4).

In the matrix approach, the memory area, the address decoders and the read/write logic form an atomic logic block. This electrically and temporally validated building block will be replicated as many times (× n) as needed to obtain the data width n. This solution has generally been adopted for DRAM. For other families such as flash EEPROM (FEEPROM), since the word line has a very large width, n columns are selected for a given column address. These columns are not adjacent to limit electrical noise but are separated by other columns. Increasing the data width n of a memory comes at a connection cost because the chip package (see Chapter 3 of Volume 2) is larger. But the main advantage is the reduced inductance of the connections compared to a solution using n 1-bit packages.

To insert a memory into a microprocessor system where communication occurs via buses, access must be controlled.

The two main signals used for this are #CE and #OE (output enable). The chip enable signal #CE (chip enable), also called #CS (chip select), blocks the internal address decoders so they do not respond to any address presentation. Besides avoiding bus data collisions that, in electronics, could cause short circuits and damage the memory output stage, the benefit is also reduced power consumption. The memory component is then in standby mode when not selected. For read-only memory (ROM), only output isolation and amplification (data out buffer) are needed, performed by an electronic buffer inserted before the data exits the package. The component output selection signal #OE validates the output (see Figure 2.6). It may also be called #G. This type of stage was found in PROM (programmable ROM) where bus mounting was not required.

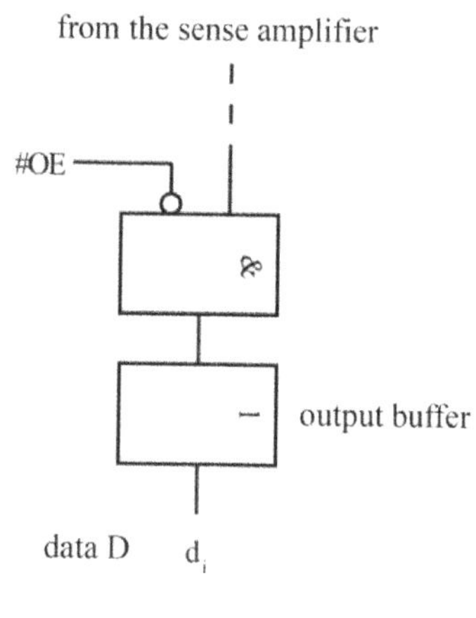

Figure 2.6. *Output stage*

But for a bus connection[6], i.e. parallel connection of data outputs from several memories, a three-state output is necessary, as open collector or open drain outputs are rarely used (see Figure 2.7(a); see sections 2.3.2 and 2.4.1 of Darche (2004) for an explanation of circuit output types). To separate chip selection from output validation (#OE), a logic function is needed (see Figure 2.7(b) and Exercise E2.1). This allows for address-based cell access and control of the read or write timing.

When the data input and output share the same chip pin, three-state electronic buffers must be used to avoid conflicts (see Figure 2.8). Previously external to the package, they are now integrated.

The name of the data input–output is "DQ", a contraction of the data input (Data) D and the output Q of a D-type flip-flop (see section 3.4 of Darche (2002)). Some manufacturers may call it I/O for input/output. With this type of I/O, when the memory switches from a read cycle to a write cycle or vice versa, bus turnaround may occur. This requires inserting a "dead" cycle, which is unproductive because it reduces the address or data bus utilization rate (see Volume 4).

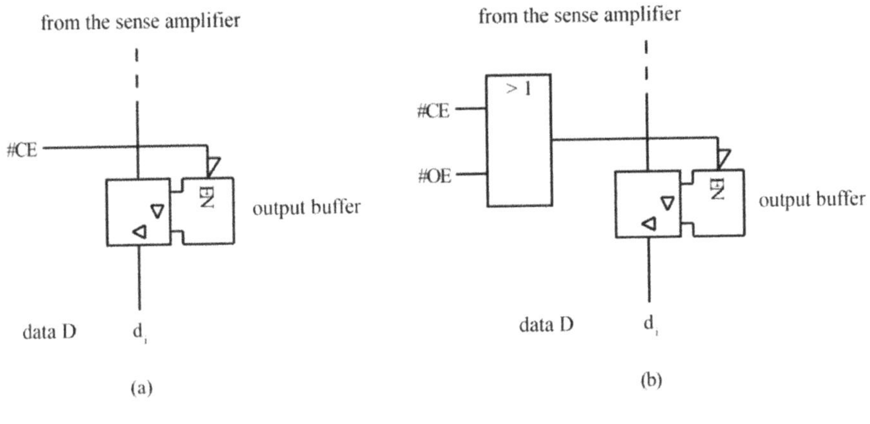

Figure 2.7. *Three-state electronic output buffer control for read-only memory*

6 A bus is a communication system with at least two elements that can communicate, but with the possibility of connecting other elements, which excludes a point-to-point link (see Chapter 1 of Darche (2021b)).

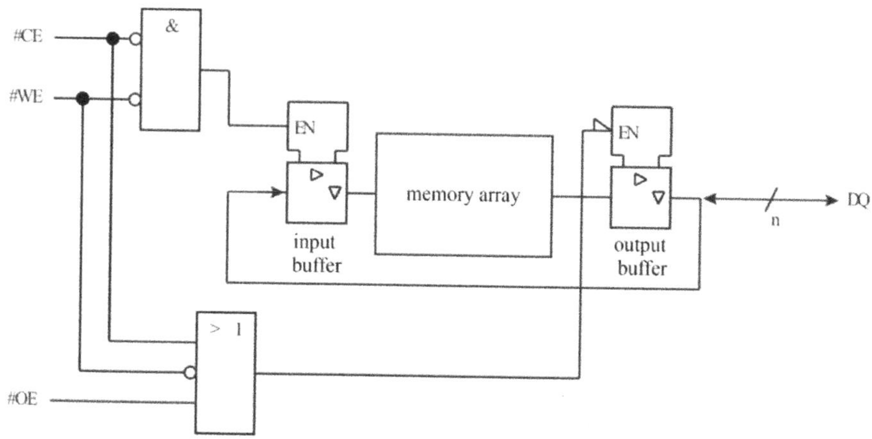

Figure 2.8. *Internal data path of a memory with shared I/O*

The figure shows the internal organization of a dynamic random-access memory. Since the output buffer can be in high impedance, the data input D and output Q can be connected without a short-circuit hazard. Note that columns are complemented for better sensitivity and noise immunity. Reading is therefore differential. The input buffer also has a differential output. The logic system composed of column transistors, the sense amplifier and the two three-state electronic data input/output buffers forms a block we call "sense amplifiers and write circuitry".

Now, it is possible to specify the timing of signal application during access. The duration of a read or write operation is called a "cycle" (read or write cycle). The other unaccessed cells are in standby cycle or may, in the case of DRAM, be in refresh cycle (see Volume 3).

In the case of non-multiplexed addressing (see Figure 2.10(a)), as for SRAM, presenting a new address generally marks the start of a cycle if the control signals #CE and #OE are not active (see fundamental timings in Volume 2). Next comes the activation of these access signals and possibly the presentation of the data if it is a write. In the case of a read, the data is provided by the memory after an access time t_a. The cycle ends either with writing into memory or with the master reading the data, i.e. the processor.

In the case of multiplexed addressing (see Figure 2.10(b)) as for DRAM, the row address is given first, followed by the column address. The cycle ends the same way as previously. This requirement to apply the address throughout the memory cycle (see section 1.5 of Volume 2) was one of the bottlenecks for increasing this component's throughput. This problem was resolved by inserting a register in the address path (see Volume 4).

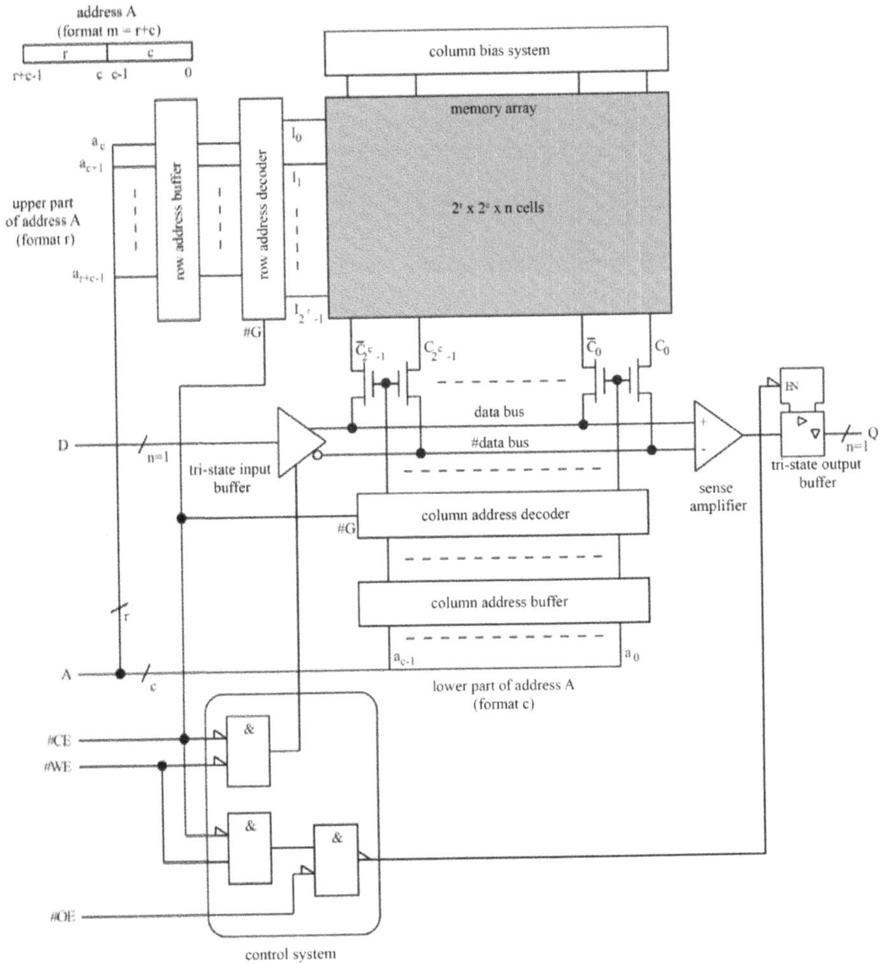

Figure 2.9. *Internal block diagram of an asynchronous static random-access memory (format n = 1)*

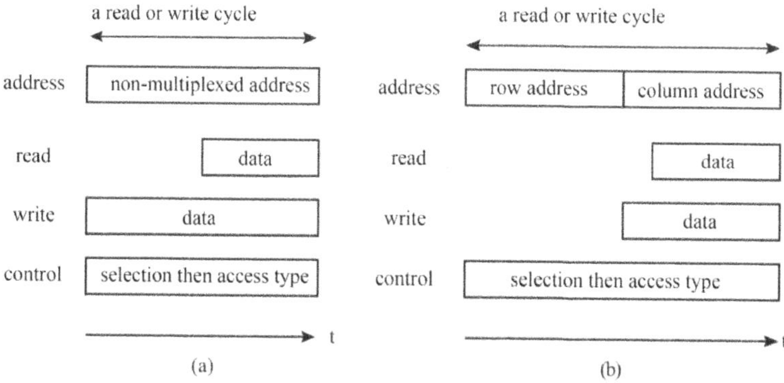

Figure 2.10. *Timing sequence of external operations*

Now, let us specify the timing order of the different steps, dividing them between the participants in the exchange – the master, i.e. the processor or memory controller, and the slave, i.e. the memory. Figure 2.11 details the steps of a read.

Figure 2.12 details the steps of a write. The presentation of the data occurs later, after activation of the write signal.

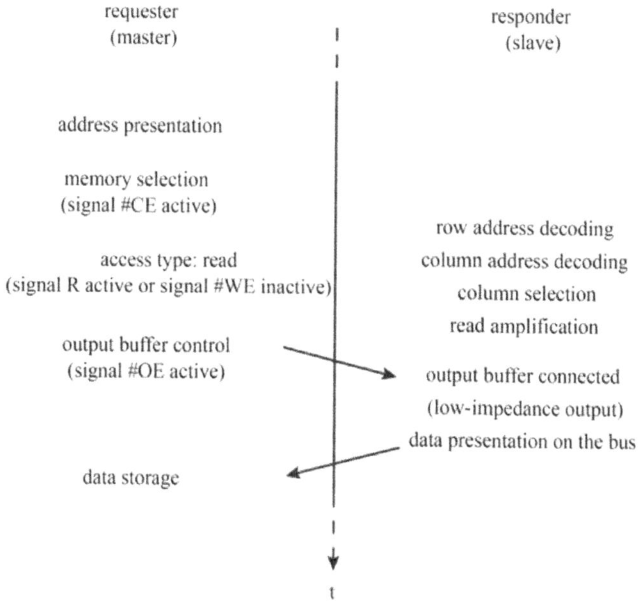

Figure 2.11. *External and internal steps of a read*

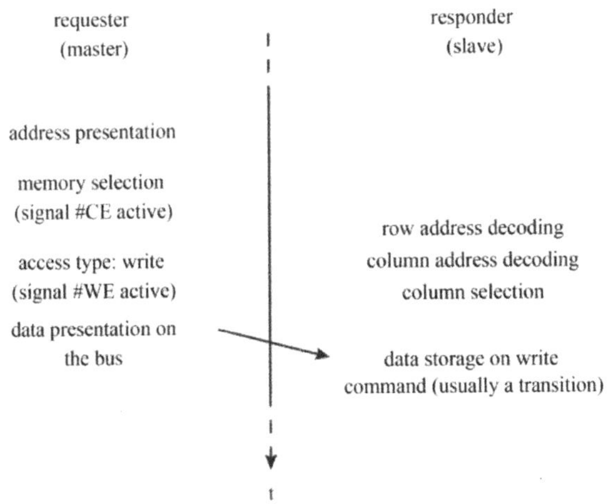

Figure 2.12. *External and internal steps of a write*

It is also possible to specify the timing sequence of internal steps and the relationships between them. Figure 2.13 shows a read. Innovations will target these different steps, attempting to parallelize them or adjust their timing. During phase 1, after address amplification/isolation, both decodings can occur in parallel if addressing is not multiplexed. The address is amplified, and possibly stored for internal operation reasons. Then comes the row and column address decodings. The selected cell delivers its electrical information, which is interpreted by the sense amplifier (phase 2). The logical information is then amplified for the outside (phase 3).

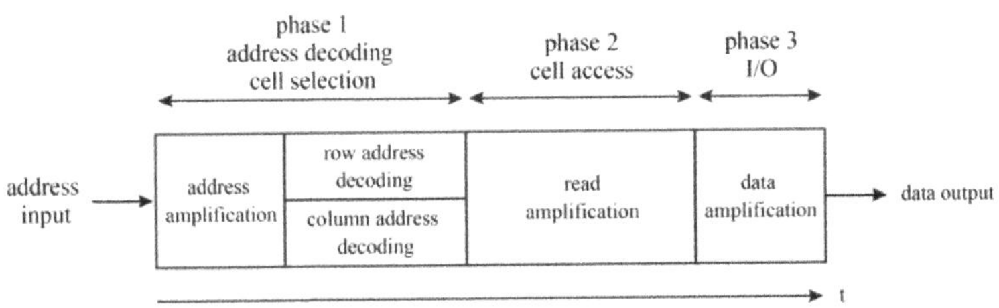

Figure 2.13. *Basic internal steps for a read access (not to scale)*

Figure 2.14 shows a write. During a write, the data can be presented during decoding (dotted in the figure), with the final deadline being actual access to the cell. The beginning of the operations is the same as the previous case. Once the cell is selected, the data is written during phase 2. These two diagrams will be refined in Volumes 3 and 4.

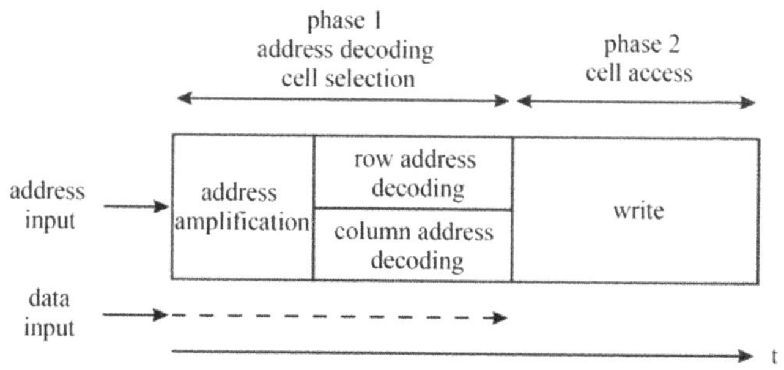

Figure 2.14. *Basic internal steps for a write access (not to scale)*

The internal operation of this memory is intrinsically asynchronous. This introduces internal timing delays, resulting in non-deterministic but bounded latency. With the current synchronous approach, which organizes internal operation based on the well-known pipeline principle, using a clock allows intermediate internal storage using one or both edges of this signal. To do this, one or more data registers at input or output are inserted in the address and data paths. These registers, by isolating the different sub-blocks, allow temporal decomposition of the operation into sub-tasks. This resembles the pipeline principle of current processors, with all associated advantages. However, this structure has high latency during bus turnaround, a phenomenon similar to a processor branch execution sequence disconnection. This synchronous operation and the notion of pipeline are detailed in Volume 4.

2.2. Detailed internal organization

This section includes examples of typical memory logic sub-blocks. The main ones are the (pre)charge system for columns, delay line, address and data transition detectors, row and column address decoders, column selector, sense amplifier, write circuit and the phase-locked and delay-locked loops discussed in Chapter 3. These logic blocks can have static or dynamic structures. Their operation may be synchronous or asynchronous.

2.2.1. *Static logic versus dynamic logic*

CMOS logic (complementary MOS; see section 2.4 of Darche (2004)) uses two types of MOS transistors: N-channel (NMOS) and P-channel (PMOS). A logic stage is made of a P-channel logic part that connects V_{DD} to the output, and an N-channel logic part that connects ground to the output (see Figure 2.15). The first is a pull-up network (PUN), and the second is a pull-down network (PDN). More details are provided in section 2.1.1 of Darche (2004). These two sub-blocks function oppositely (i.e. complementarily) to avoid a V_{DD} – Gnd short circuit.

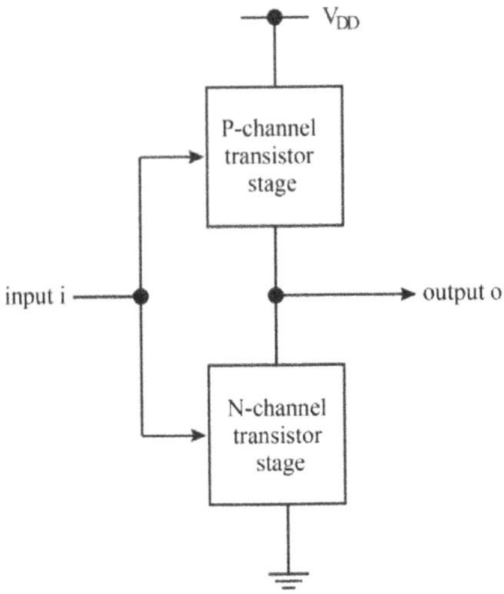

Figure 2.15. *A standard CMOS stage*

Due to the physical structure of the MOS transistor, parasitic capacitors exist. The more transistors are connected to a line and the longer that line, the higher the total capacitance. The idea of dynamic logic or precharged logic is to use these parasitic capacitors as energy reservoirs, thus as temporary memory. There are two types of precharged logic: precharged to 1 (i.e. to V_{DD}) and precharged to 0 (i.e. to Gnd). Each uses one of the CMOS logic stages, as shown in Figure 2.16. Two transistors with antagonistic operation (i.e. complementary transistors) connect the parasitic capacitor C_p or the logic stage to one of the power supply terminals. There are three very short phases: precharge, evaluation and rest. When the precharge signal Ø is active (= 1), the parasitic capacitor is charged (precharge to 1; Figure 2.16(a)) or discharged (precharge to 0; Figure 2.16(b)). During evaluation, depending on the case, the logic will discharge (a) or charge (b) the capacitor based on the logic equation. The result must be stored by the next stage, for example, such as a latch. This technique is opposed to static logic, where a logic system's output is permanently at a given state.

Figure 2.17 shows an example of use in a memory, specifically in the row address decoder. It is a classic decoder using CMOS technology, i.e. the static version with the P-channel transistor stage (top block) and the N-channel transistor stage (bottom block).

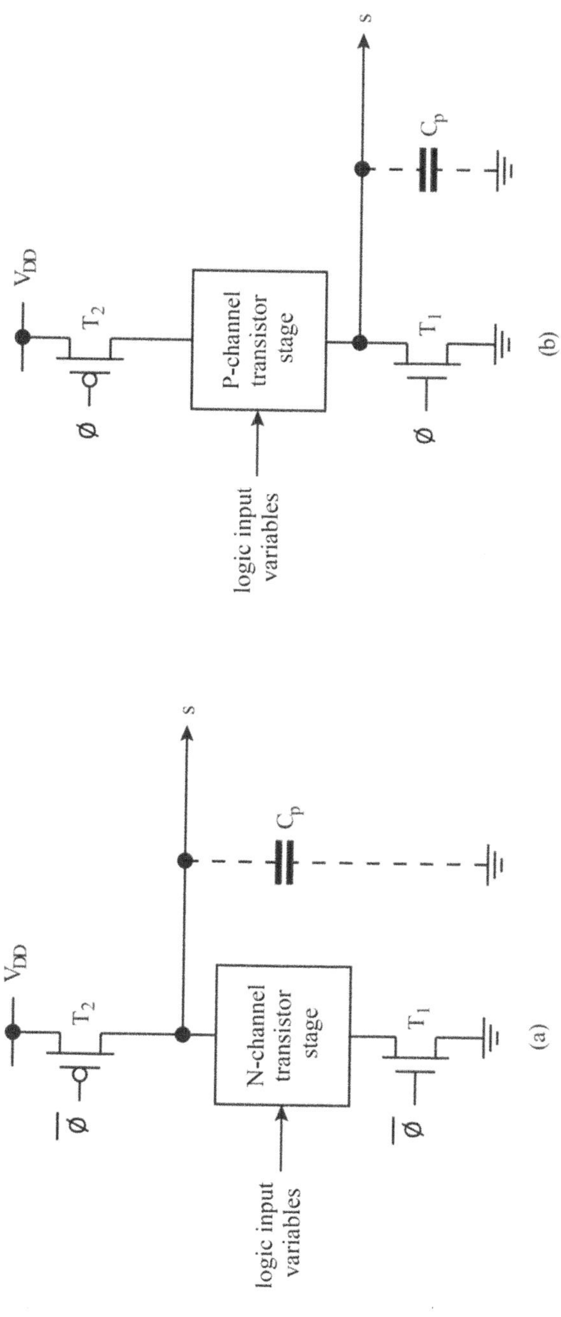

Figure 2.16. *Precharged logics to 1 (a) and to 0 (b)*

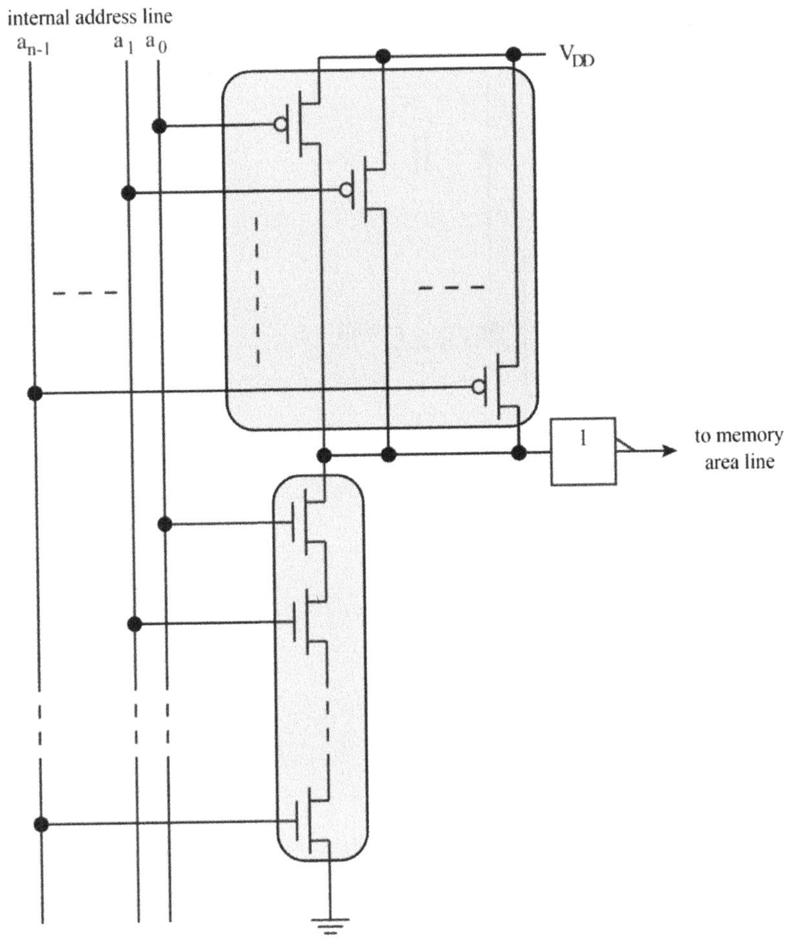

Figure 2.17. *Static logic system*

Its version with precharge (see Figure 2.18) shows that the P-channel transistors responsible for decoding have disappeared and have been replaced by two precharge transistors, T_1 and T_2. Transistor T_1 controlled by the ØATD signal (see section 2.2.4) functions to connect the column to V_{DD}. The P-channel transistor to its right forms a positive feedback loop. The N-channel transistor T_2 connects the logic system to ground. Other more complex functions use this approach, such as the latch, an example of which is described by Proebsting and Green (1975). The dynamic approach is particularly used at the column level, thus increasing memory density and speed (Stewart 1977a, 1977b). It also consumes less current since power consumption only occurs during precharge. Its disadvantage is that it requires a clock signal. Its generation must be done internally so that the technique is transparent to the designer and therefore acceptable. Moreover, it is sensitive to transient electrical phenomena.

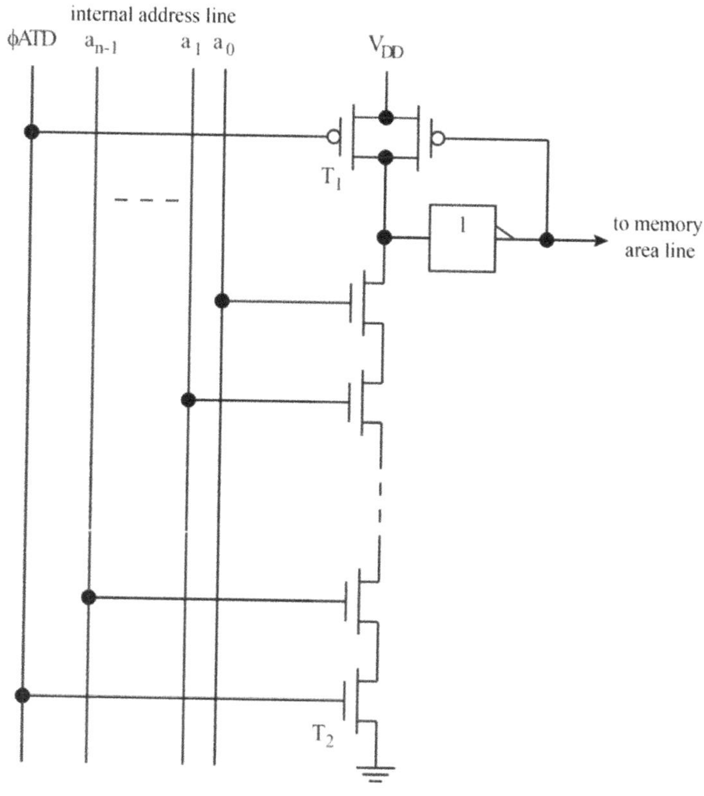

Figure 2.18. *Dynamic logic system*

The two approaches can also be combined to benefit from the strong noise immunity of the static approach and the low power consumption of the dynamic approach. Chan et al. (2006) proposed a decoder version where the input stage is static (T_1 to T_6, T_{11}, and T_{12}), while the rest of the structure is dynamic, as shown in Figure 2.19.

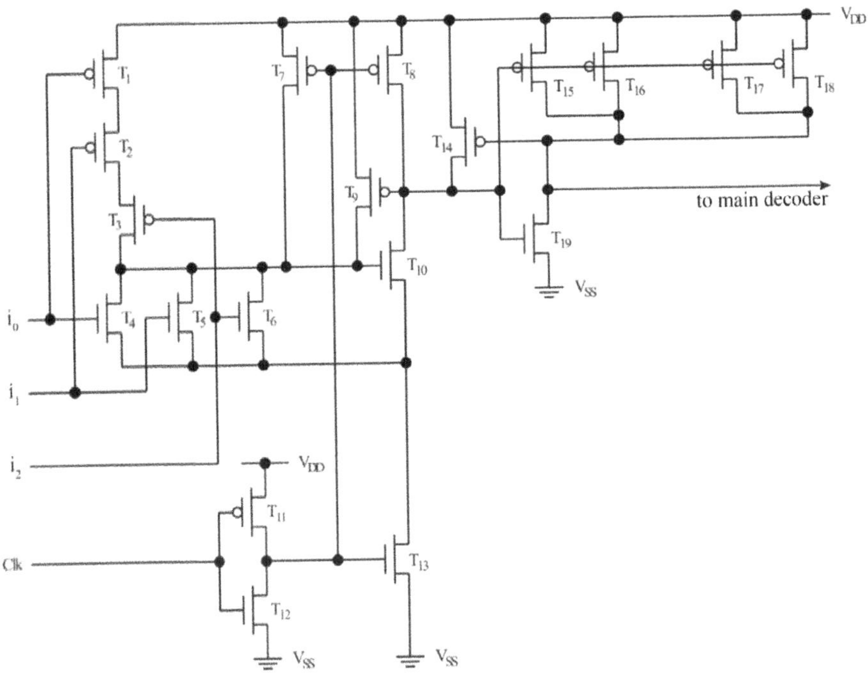

Figure 2.19. *NOR predecoder in CMOS version (based on Chan et al. (2006))*

2.2.2. Column charge and precharge systems

The memory area must be biased at the column level to set the potential. Each column is terminated at one end by a load device (sense line termination) and at the other end by a read/write system (see Figure 2.20). This is called bitline conditioning.

Several biasing approaches are possible depending on whether the load is static or a precharge technique is used. This also depends on the technology used. NMOS will use precharge to V_{DD}, PMOS to V_{SS}. CMOS will allow precharging to mid-V_{DD}. The device in Figure 2.21(a), made of an enhancement-mode NMOS transistor whose drain is connected to the gate, behaves like a voltage generator. The voltage V_{node} is equal to $V_{DD} - V_{GS(th)}$. The voltage drop is therefore constant. Furthermore, when a column is brought to a low potential, the device being at a potential near to V_{DD}, a high current flows, leading to high power dissipation. Limiting the current would result in an increase in switching speed. It is preferable to use a current generator because charging by current is faster than exponential charging due to the RC (resistor–capacitor) constant. The device acts as a nonlinear resistor. To make a current generator in MOS technology, a depletion-mode transistor must be used, connected as shown in Figure 2.21(b) so that V_{GS} is zero. When the voltage swing is high, for example, 5 V, charging or discharging a column takes time (RC constant), which increases the cell access time.

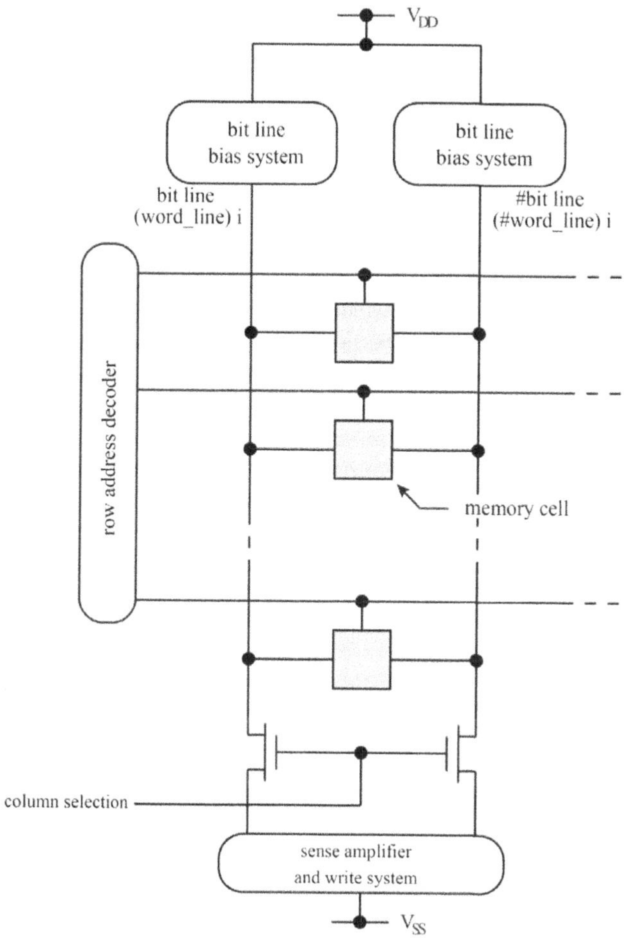

Figure 2.20. *A memory column with complementary outputs*

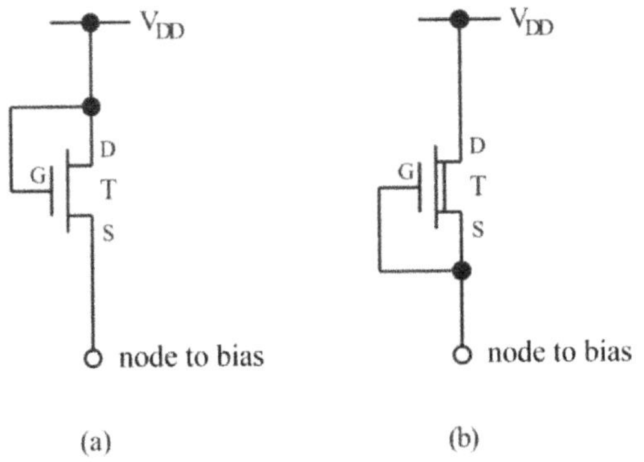

Figure 2.21. *MOS biasing devices*

The two previous approaches can be combined (see Figure 2.22(a)) to set the node potential (depletion-mode transistor T_2) while having a current generator (O'Connell and Leach 1980). This became possible once both transistor models (i.e. depletion and enhancement) could be created on the same substrate. Figure 2.22(c) shows the current versus voltage evolution of such a device, to be compared with the straight line representing that of a simple resistor. But constant-current charging takes time due to the high column capacitance. Frederick (1985) presents an improvement (see Figure 2.22(b)) by reversing the order of the transistors.

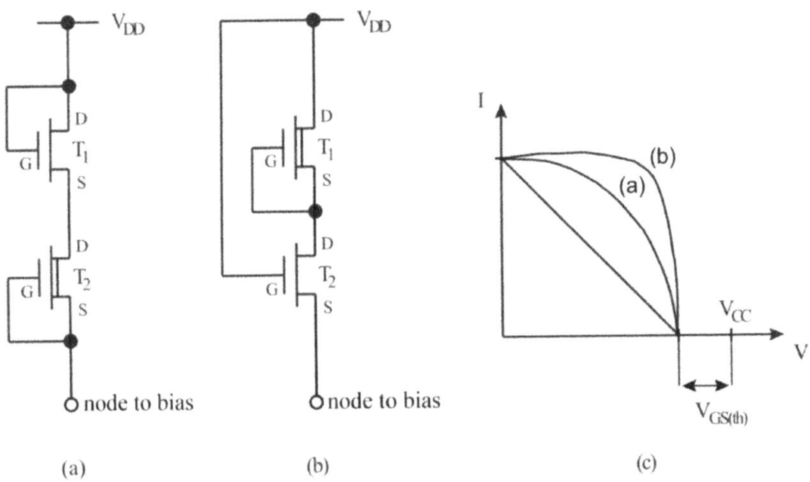

Figure 2.22. *Bias circuits and associated I = f(V) curves*

Another version is shown in Figure 2.23, which uses a P-channel transistor. Transistor T_3 equalizes the voltage between columns to minimize the differential voltage at rest and increase SA sensitivity.

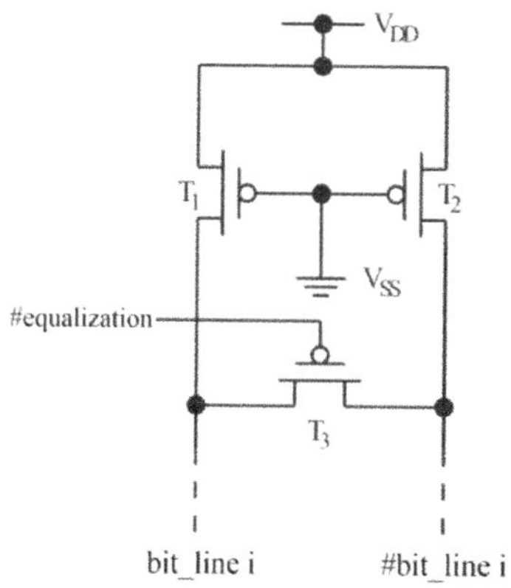

Figure 2.23. *Column charging system with precharge*

Biasing and equalization can be combined, as shown in Figure 2.24. With precharge, transistors T_1 and T_2 operating in switching mode charge the columns to V_{DD} or another voltage value. Transistor T_3 has the same function as before.

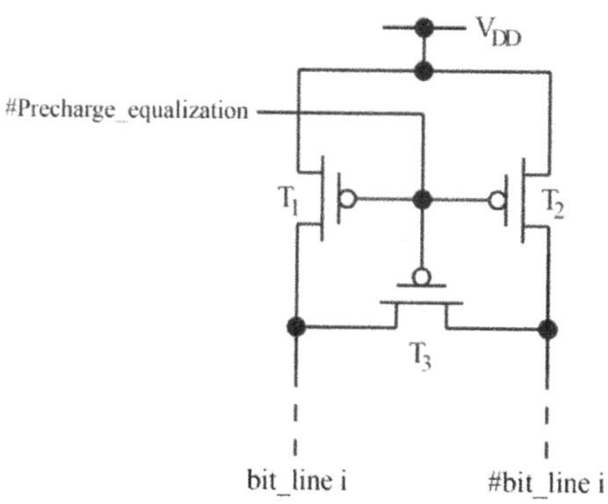

Figure 2.24. *Column precharge system*

An additional constraint to consider for large memory areas is power consumption. The column bias system must not supply too much current, as this would limit the memory area size due to power dissipation. On the other hand, too low a current would increase access time. The designer must therefore find a compromise.

2.2.3. *The delay line*

To generate a delayed clock signal, the reference circuit is the one in Figure E2.1 in Appendix 2. A delay made of a chain of inverters allows the Clk signal to be phase-shifted and to generate a time-shifted signal using the NAND gate (NOT AND). Matsui (1999) describes a use case where this circuit is used to store the output data of an SDR SDRAM (single data rate synchronous DRAM; see Volume 4). Figure 2.25 shows the standardized symbol of the delay element (IEEE 1984, 1991). The times t_1 and t_2 specify the delay relative to the rising and falling edges, respectively.

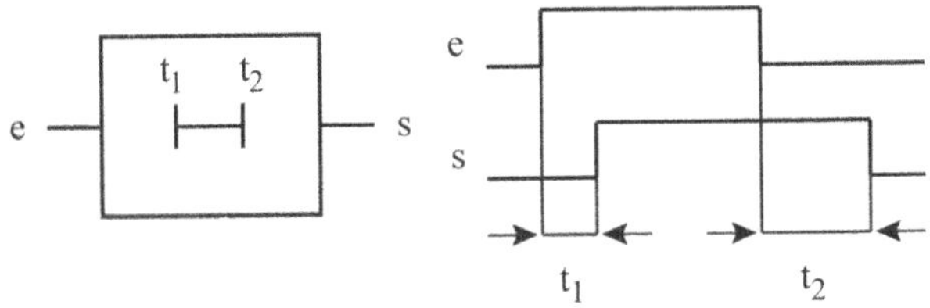

Figure 2.25. *Graphical symbol of the delay element and its associated timing diagram*

If these two times are equal, then only one time is indicated (see Figure 2.26). And the propagation delay t_{pd}, the average of the low-high t_{PLH} and high-low t_{PHL} propagation times, is then equal to:

$$t_{pd} = \frac{t_{PLH}+t_{PHL}}{2} = t_1 \qquad [2.3]$$

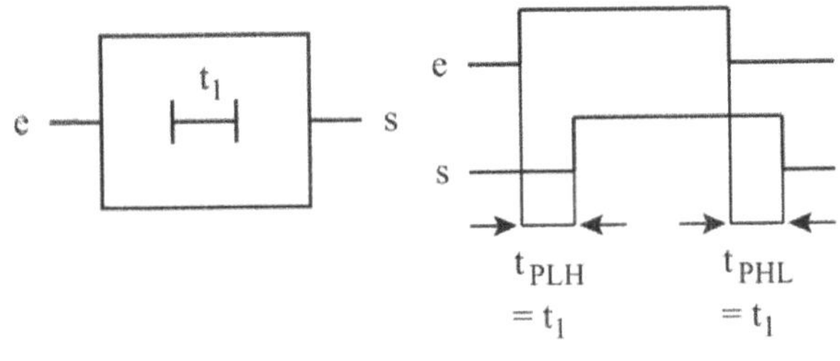

Figure 2.26. *Delay element with identical low-high and high-low propagation times*

2.2.4. *The address transition detector*

The system called ATD (address transition detection) is used to generate all internal synchronization signals for memories not using an external clock (fully asynchronous operation). The notion of address change is fundamental, as it is associated with the concept of a memory cycle. The ATD thus determines the end of one cycle and the beginning of another. For DRAM with multiplexed addressing, the address change is detected from the column address. From this address change, internal signals to generate include the wordline driver command, the column precharge and equalization signal, and the sense latch pulse. Figure 2.27 shows the basic version consisting of an edge detector (exclusive OR (XOR) gate associated with a delay line) connected to each address line and a logic operator to generate the decision. At each address change, a pulse is generated (see Figure 2.27(b)). Dubujet (1990) and Pascucci (2001) detail several examples of electronic implementation.

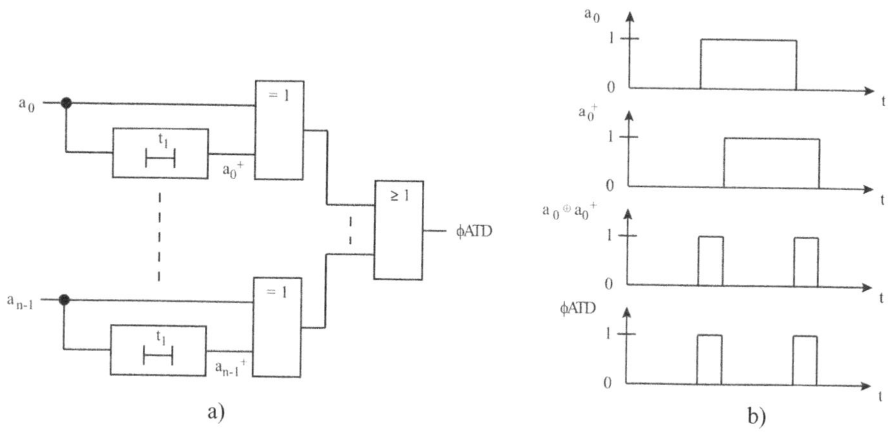

Figure 2.27. *The basic version of an address change detector with its associated timing diagrams*

Figure 2.28 shows an example of generating the column precharge pulse signal Ø. This signal is generated from the detection of an address change A or a power-up initialization (#Reset).

The address transition detector helps reduce memory access and cycle times since it allows internal memory logic (initial pulse) to be triggered before external signals request access. It can also help reduce the component's power consumption by internally controlling logical subsets, instead of using an external signal generated, for example, by the processor. Leak (1995) and exercise E2.5 detail an example.

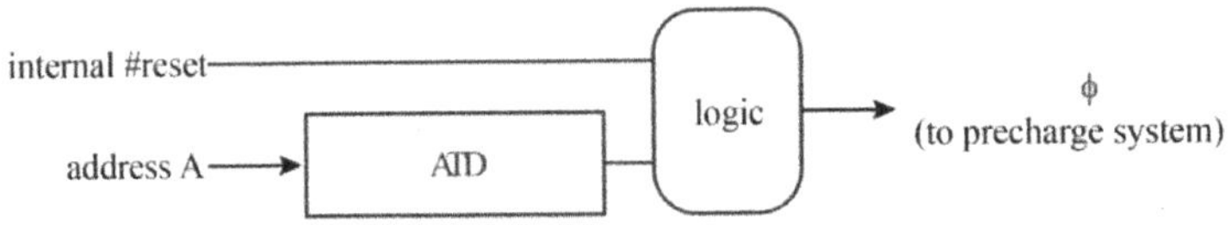

Figure 2.28. *A simplified precharge signal generator*

2.2.5. *The data-transition detector*

Called data-transition detection (DTD), this system generates a pulse at each data change for a constant address. The design of this detector is similar to that of the ATD (see section 2.2.5). It was designed to reduce power consumption during a write cycle. An example is described in Gubbels et al. (1987), which shows that this system can also be used by another signal, namely the write signal.

2.2.6. *Address decoding*

When address A in format m is applied to a memory input, an internal register or latch stores it and provides the buffered address (i.e. electrically amplified) in both its normal and complemented (logic) forms (see Figure 2.29). Next, a binary decoder (address decoder) generates the corresponding selection signals y_i ($i \in [0, 2^m - 1]$), of which only one can be active at a given time. The decoding is said to be "complete" when all address signals are involved in the decoding process. Otherwise, it is called "partial". This circuit is called an "m:2^m decoder". These signals are generally also generated in their normal and complemented forms to facilitate downstream logic. They are then amplified by electronic buffers not shown in the figure.

The internal address path is that of Figure 2.30. The address lines are distributed in their normal and complemented forms (total = 2 × m). Then, each decoding output is driven by an AND gate or by a NAND gate if operating in negative logic (see section 2.1.5. of Darche (2004)). Since the memory area is a matrix, we must distinguish between row and column address decoders.

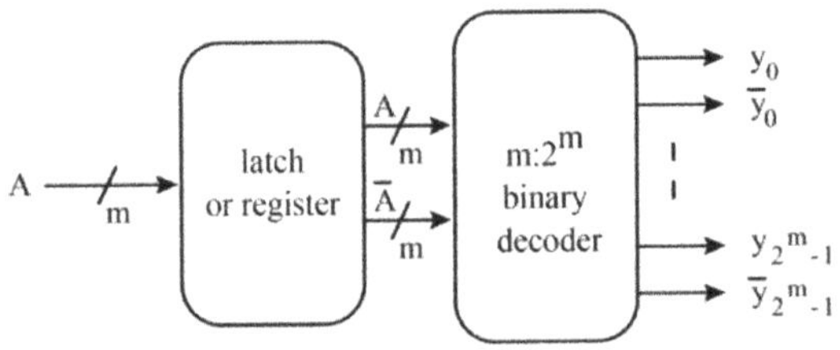

Figure 2.29. *The internal address path*

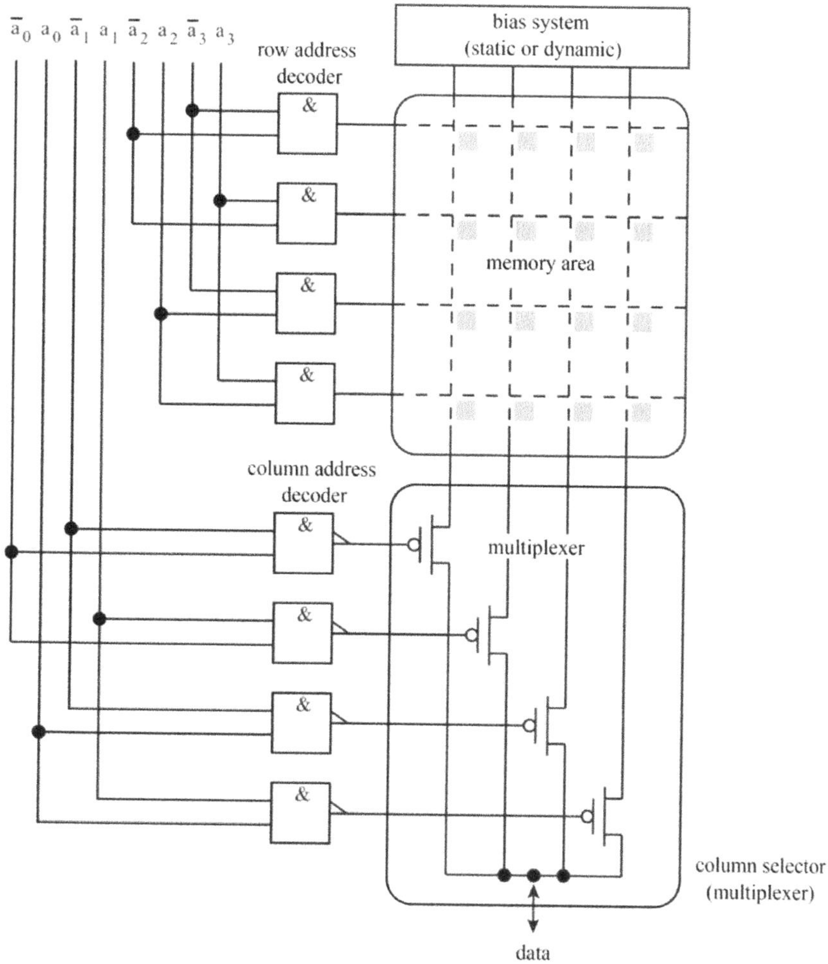

Figure 2.30. *Example of a complete address decoder in format m = 4*

An output of the decoder is a minterm, i.e. a product term (p-term) of degree m (see section 1.4.3. of Darche (2002)). The logic equation for the two extreme minterms of an AND-type decoder for an address in format m is:

$$y_0 = \overline{a_{m-1}} \cdot \cdots \cdot \overline{a_1} \cdot \overline{a_0} = \overline{a_{m-1} + \cdots + a_1 + a_0} \qquad [2.4]$$

$$y_{2^m-1} = a_{m-1} \cdot \cdots \cdot a_1 \cdot a_0 = \overline{\overline{a_{m-1}} + \cdots + \overline{a_1} + \overline{a_0}} \qquad [2.5]$$

The logic equation of an address decoder for large memory areas is thus a set of minterms of increasing degree according to the logarithm of the memory size, i.e. the address format of degree m. Each minterm is implemented using an AND, NAND, OR or NOR gate. Unfortunately, in CMOS logic, the input stage of these operators is made up of series-stacked transistors, each gate being an input (multi-input gate). This stacking is not recommended if m is very large (i.e. > 3 or 5) because it leads to degradation of switching times, which are proportional to the fan-in (see section 2.2.1 of Darche (2004)) characterizing the number of inputs of a gate. One solution would be to use a NOR gate in NMOS logic since the input stage consists of parallel transistors (see Figure 2.31). However, this technology is now rare. Exercise E2.8 presents different versions of a 3:8 address decoder.

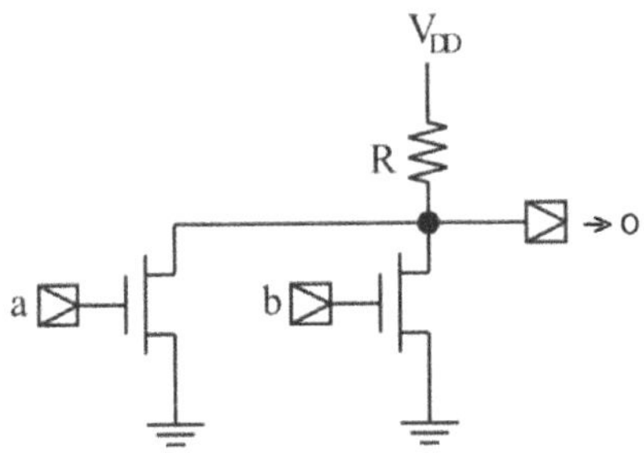

Figure 2.31. *NOR gate in NMOS logic*

It should be noted that Gerez and Woutersen (1996) proposed SRWM (sequential read-write memory), in which the address decoder is replaced by a shift register.

2.2.6.1. *Predecoding*

The commonly adopted solution to minimize the number of inputs is to perform address decoding in two steps (two-level or two-stage address decoding) called "predecoding" and "final decoding" (post or main decoding) (Hofmann and Von Basse 1978). Figure 2.32 shows an example. A predecoder (or preliminary decoder), as its name suggests, is a first level or first logic layer of address decoding. The primary goal is to reduce decoding time, knowing that a full decoding would be unnecessary. It also helps simplify the hardware by reducing the number of logic gates and their inputs, and therefore the total number of transistors. The consequence is, among other things, lower power consumption and better timing characteristics. Note that the decoding output variables are generally presented in both their normal and complemented forms to simplify downstream logic and, for the rows, amplified by electronic buffers (wordline buffer).

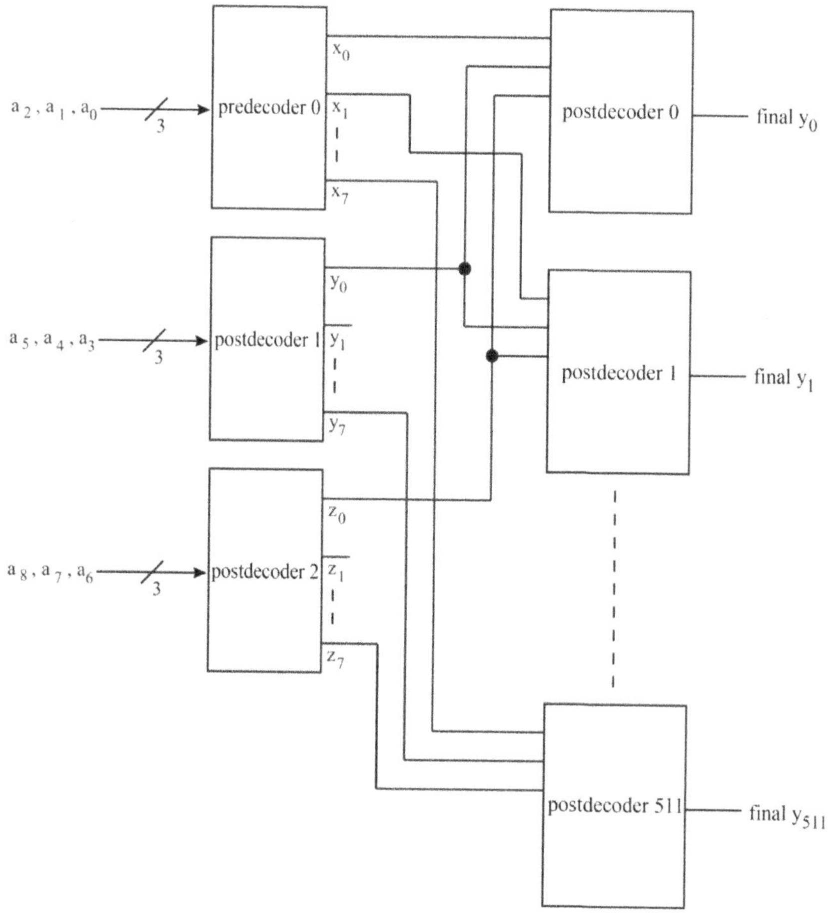

Figure 2.32. *Decomposition of address decoding into two steps*

After the classic distribution of input variables, the predecoder provides p-terms of a degree lower than m which can then be reused for final decoding. In the example in Figure 2.33, it is clear that the logic gates have a much lower fan-in than in the previous classic solution (three instead of six). In return, the propagation time increases. The gates are organized in a regular and dense manner. Another version could be a predecoding stage using NOR gates followed by a final stage using AND gates (see exercise E2.9).

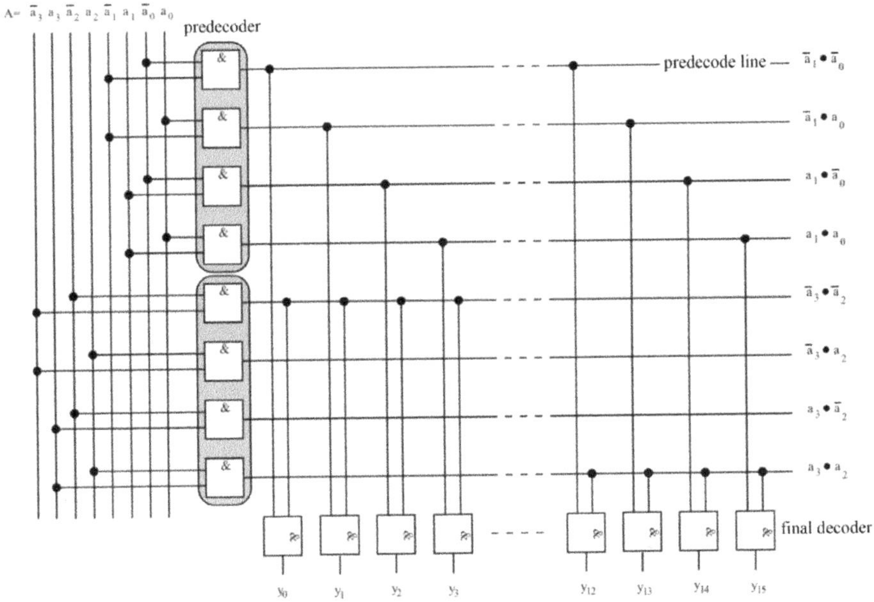

Figure 2.33. *Complete logic chain of decoding*

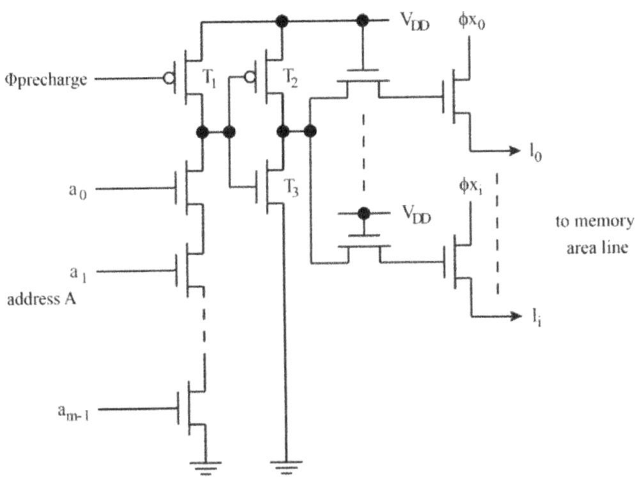

Figure 2.34. *Row address decoder in dynamic NMOS AND version (Based on Kimura et al. (1986))*

The implementation uses either static or dynamic logic. We present an example of a dynamic version of a row address decoder (see Figure 2.34) taken from Kimura et al. (1986).

Transistor T_1 is used for precharging so that the stack of transistors below performs a NAND function from the address. Transistors T_2 and T_3 then form an inverter. Then comes transistors (pass transistors) that form transmission gates that distribute the logical row selection signal based on the column decoding. Recall that the dynamic approach reduces switching times. But the drawback of the presented structure is that a transistor is inserted in the stack for each additional variable, increasing the fan-in and thus degrading the decoding response time.

In Figure 2.35, transistor T_1 still serves to precharge an output line of a NOR gate formed by the transistors below arranged in parallel. The following stages are identical to the previous case.

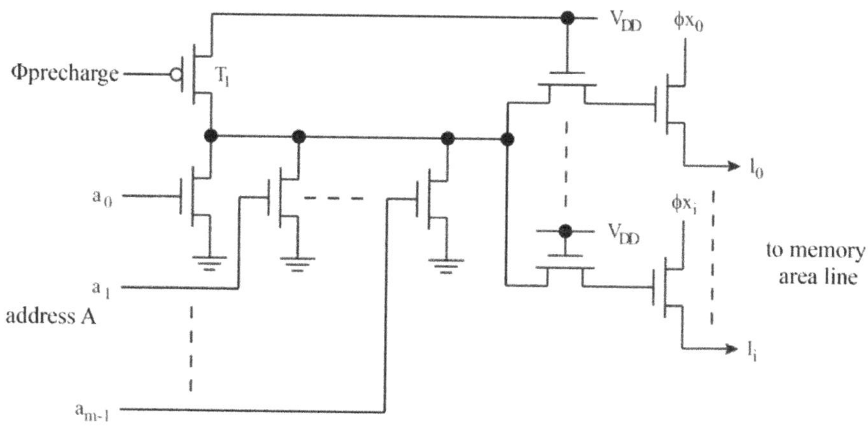

Figure 2.35. *Row address decoder in dynamic CMOS NOR version (Based on Kimura et al. (1986))*

Figure 2.36 shows the decoding and postdecoding subsystems in context[7].

---

7 The total number of columns must be multiplied by n, the data format (i.e. $2^c \times n$). To simplify decoder outputs, we assume here that n is only equal to 1. This holds true for all chapters.

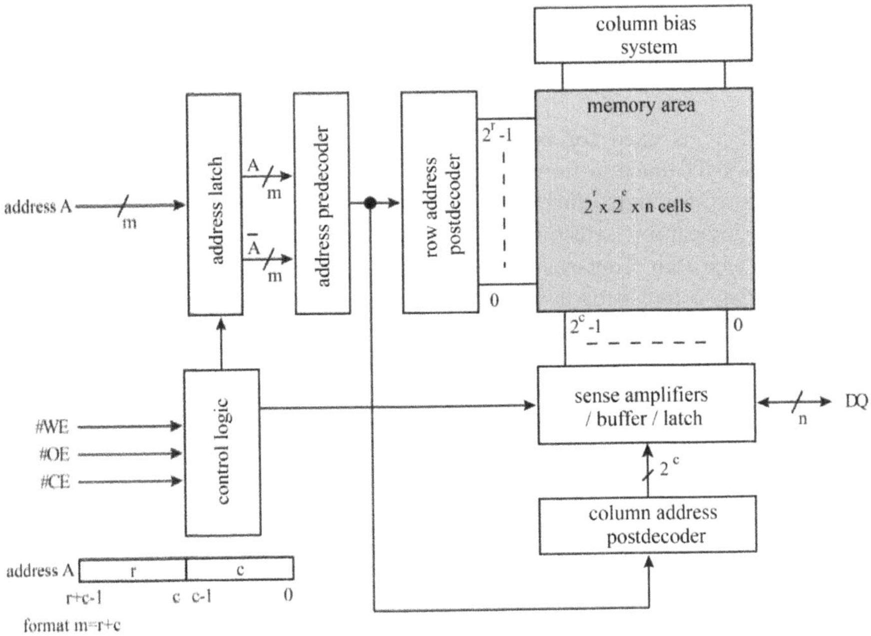

Figure 2.36. *An address predecoder in context in an SRAM*

2.2.6.2. *Other techniques*

It is possible to use other logic functions such as a comparator (see section 5.1.3) or one associated with an adder for address decoding in a cache (Heald et al. 1998a, 1998b), or SAM (sum-addressed memory). The decoder called SAD (sum-addressed decoder) is used, for example, in the Ultrasparc III MPU (Lynch et al. 1998). A programmable logic component such as a PLD (programmable logic device; see Chapter 4 of Darche (2004)) allows greater flexibility in the addressing scheme.

2.2.7. The column selector

The column selector (column selector circuitry) must allow routing the output data from one column among 2^c to the output (multiplexing function) or, conversely, the input data to one column among 2^c (demultiplexing function). If pass-transistor logic (PTL) is used, it allows implementing the multiplexing function with a minimum number of transistors (one per column). This logic subset is located downstream of the column address decoder, as shown in Figure 2.37.

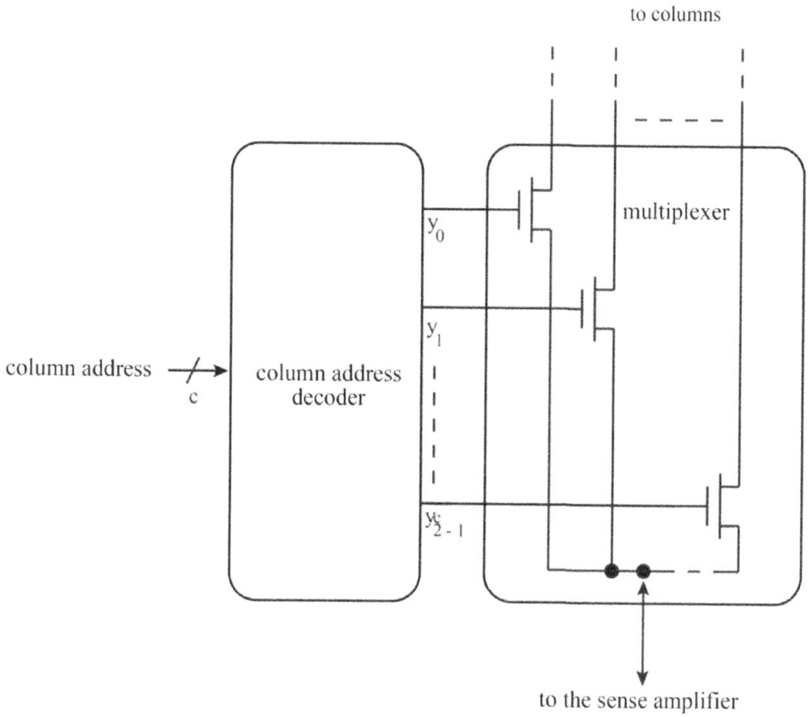

Figure 2.37. *The column selector*

When there is only one read/write system as, for example, in a 64 Ki-word SRAM, there are two implementation solutions depending on whether the SA and the write buffer share (see Figure 2.38(a)) or do not share (see Figure 2.38(b)) the data columns.

Tree decoding allows the decoding and multiplexing functions to be combined, as shown in Figure 2.39, which presents a four-to-one tree decoder-based column decoder (four-input pass-transistor-based column decoder). The number of components is thus reduced to a minimum. However, the delays induced by the structure (stacked transistors) increase quadratically.

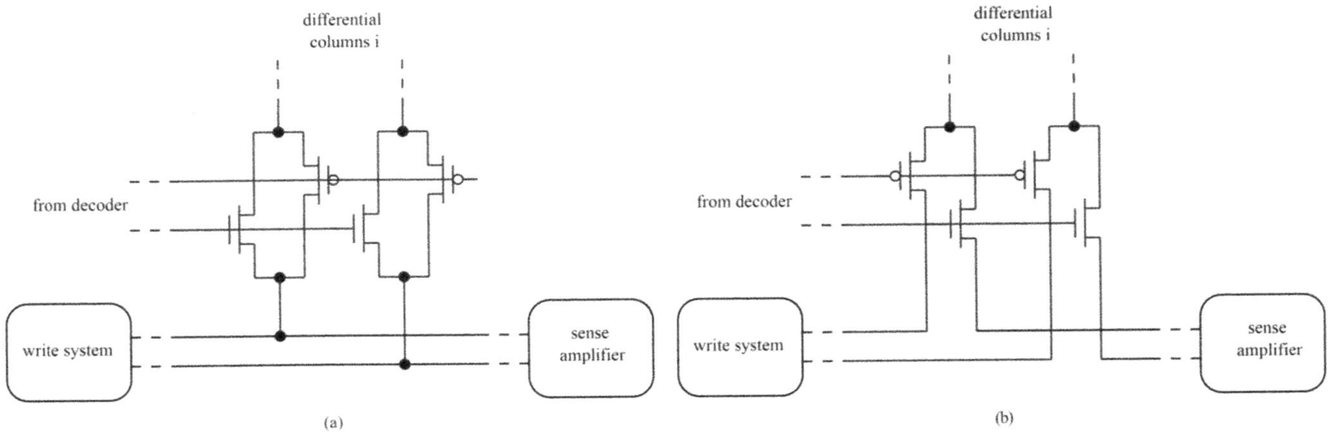

Figure 2.38. *The column selector in context with (a) or without (b) sharing of data columns*

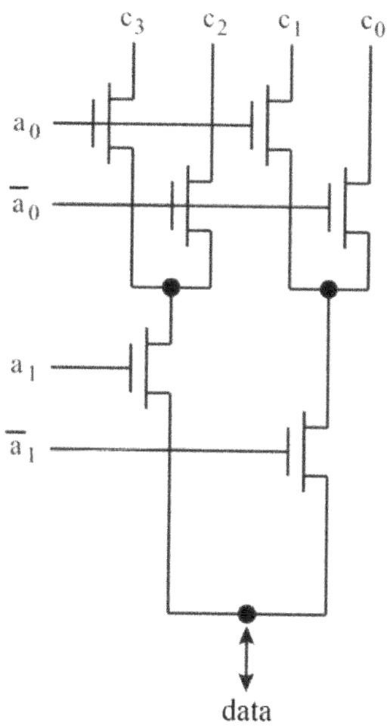

Figure 2.39. *Tree decoding and multiplexing*

2.2.8. *The sense amplifier*

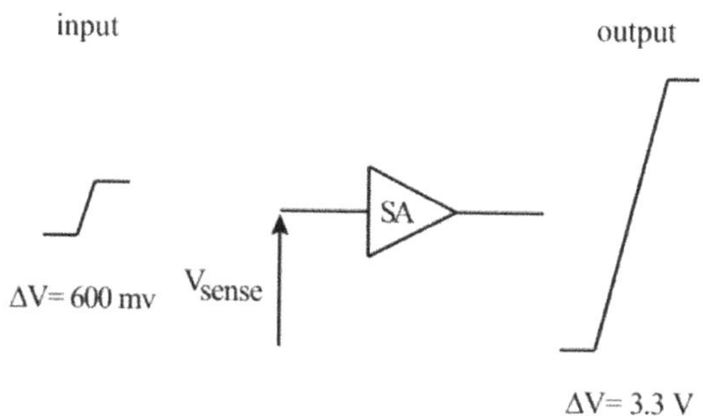

Figure 2.40. *Role of the SA*

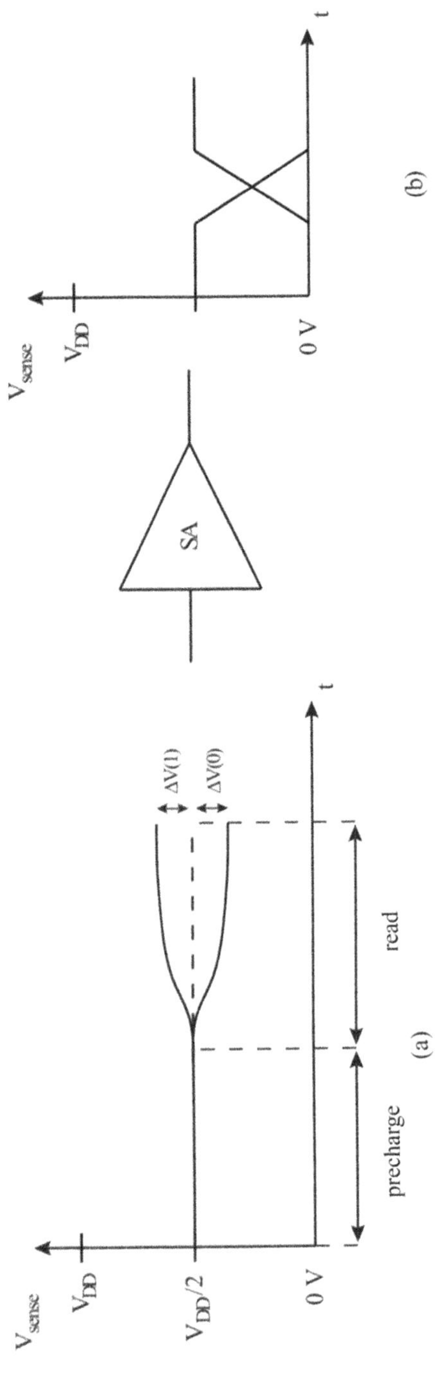

Figure 2.41. *Function of the sense amplifier (amplitude scale not followed)*

The sense amplifier, as its name suggests, serves to amplify the amplitude of the signal read from the selected cell (on the order of hundreds of mV) to make it compatible with the logic levels V_{DD} and Gnd of the peripheral logic (see Figure 2.40). Figure 2.41(a) shows the evolution of the SA input voltage. At the output (b), the voltage is saturated. This is a first approach. In fact, in the case of DRAM, the SA is connected in parallel to the bit lines. The two timing diagrams are then combined (see Figure 2.47 for an example).

The selected cell is connected to a column with high capacitance, and switching times are long due to input impedances (RC product). Two approaches are possible: either it is an amplifier with a single input connected to the single data column (see Figure 2.42(a)), or a differential amplifier is used (see Figure 2.42(b)). In practice, only the second solution is used for its robustness, as common-mode noise is eliminated. When the cell delivers only the normal form, as is the case for a DRAM cell, it is possible to use a differential amplifier (see Figure 2.42(c)) with one input connected to a reference potential. This is the case for the dummy cell architecture (see Volume 3 dedicated to DRAM). In the case of destructive read-out (DRO), as in DRAM, it is necessary to regenerate the information read from the memory cell. This is an auxiliary function of the sense amplifier. A final function for certain models, such as the differential amplifier, is to isolate the memory array from the I/O system.

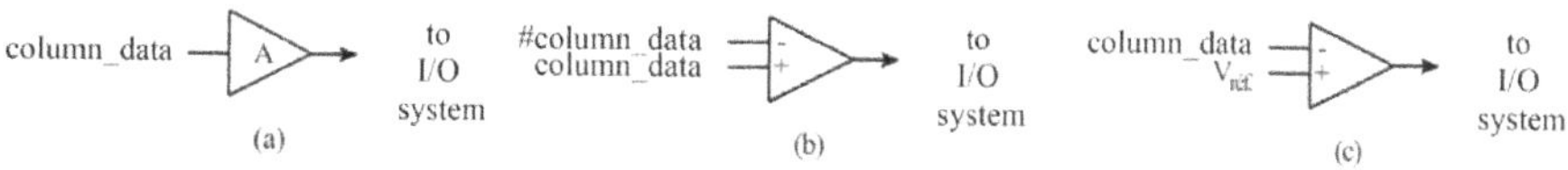

Figure 2.42. *Different solutions for reading the memory cell*

The basic model is the latching-type sense amplifier (rarely called a flip-flop sensor). It is composed of two cross-coupled latches, as shown in Figure 2.43(a). The feedback has positive gain. The I/O logic subsystem is connected directly to the columns or to the drains of the cross-coupled latches. Figure 2.43(b) shows the corresponding transistor circuit diagram (role of transistors T_3 to T_6). However, there is also an inverter (role of transistors T_7 and T_8) that amplifies the read signal and isolates the amplifier from the I/O logic system. It also converts the differential output to a single-ended output (differential to single-ended converter). A single-output system is called single-ended, meaning single or asymmetric output, as opposed to a differential system.

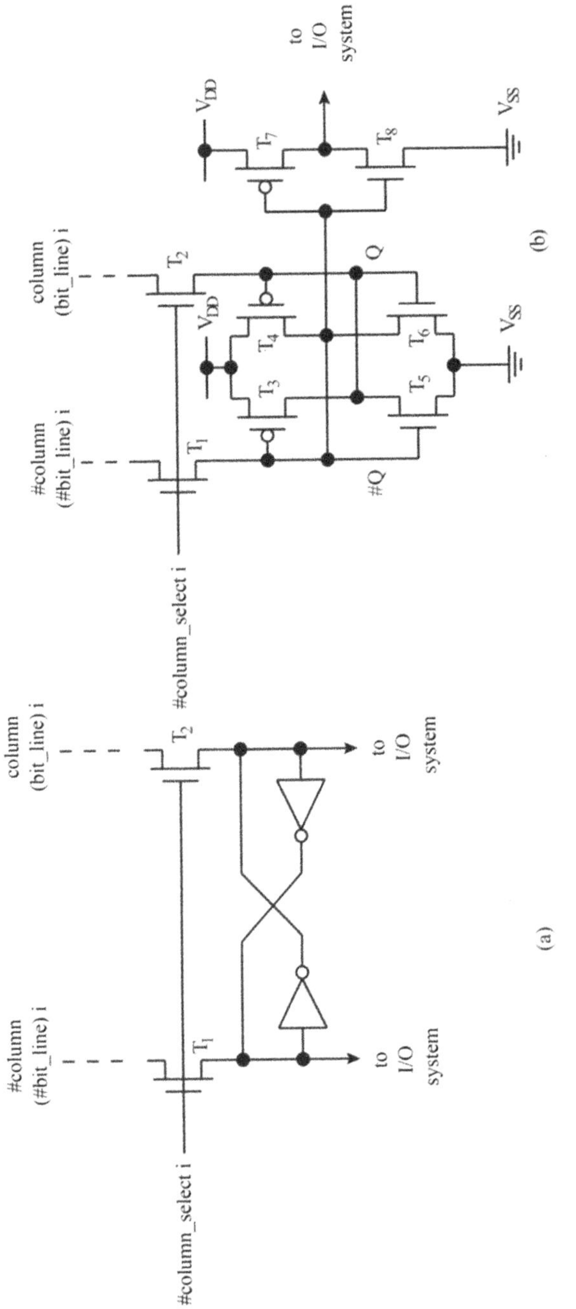

Figure 2.43. *The static version of the latching-type sense amplifier*

The evaluation times (bitline sensing delay) and amplification of the information have a non-negligible duration. They must be minimized. To achieve this, the sense amplifier must be fast. A bipolar technology is often used. The consequences are significant power consumption and a larger silicon area than with unipolar technology, mainly CMOS. To reduce this current consumption, it can be put into a power-down state. Figure 2.44 shows an example of an SA with power control. The SA is only useful during a read cycle. Moreover, during this cycle, it can be disconnected after the state is stored by the I/O stage (useful operating time equal to 50% of the cycle time). This is the role of transistor T_7. Transistors T_5 and T_6 are controlled by the same signal (disconnection). An inverter (T_8 and T_9) isolates the SA from the downstream logic stages.

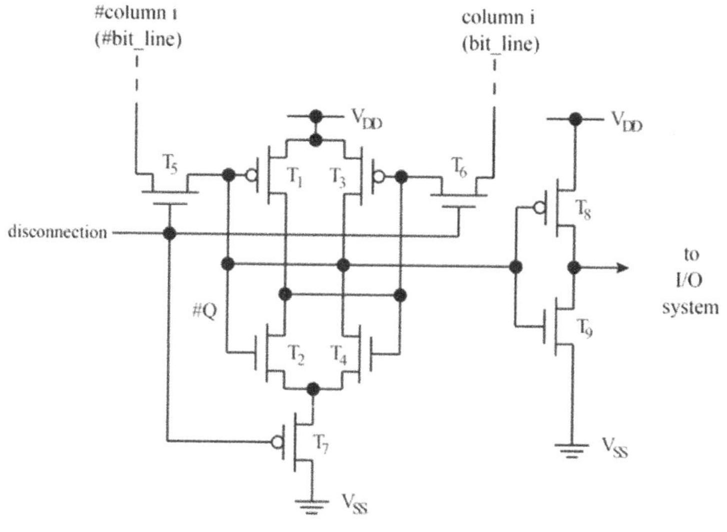

Figure 2.44. *The sense amplifier with power control*

There are obviously static and dynamic versions. Figure 2.45 shows the dynamic version, also called clocked SA. The columns are precharged to a voltage close to the switching point of the amplifier. Transistors T_1 and T_2 are the core of the amplifier. Two transistors are responsible for precharging (T_3 and T_4). Transistors T_5 and T_6 set up as transmission gates, balance the two branches of the amplifier. The standard output inverter (T_8 and T_9) isolates and logically adapts the read signal. The advantage lies in lower power consumption and reduced switching times compared to the previous classical structure. For more details on the operation, see Lynch and Boll (1974).

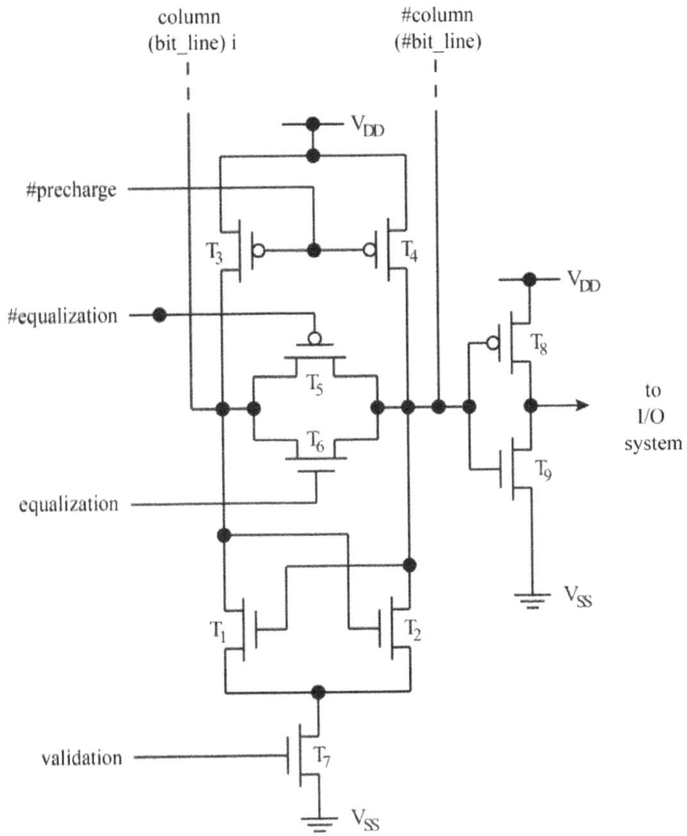

Figure 2.45. *The dynamic version of the latching-type sense amplifier*

The differential amplifier eliminates common-mode noise because it performs a subtraction of the input signals. It also provides better sensitivity. The order of magnitude of a differential signal is a few hundred mV. Figure 2.46 shows its basic diagram. Transistors T_1 and T_2 are the loads for the other two transistors. Since the outputs are complementary, the conduction of T_3 is opposite that of T_4.

Two switching thresholds may exist to reduce the SA response time (bitline sensing delay) while avoiding possible output oscillation. This is then a sense amplifier with an input stage of the Schmitt trigger type (see section 3.4.3 of Darche (2004)). Ochii et al. (1985) described such an approach.

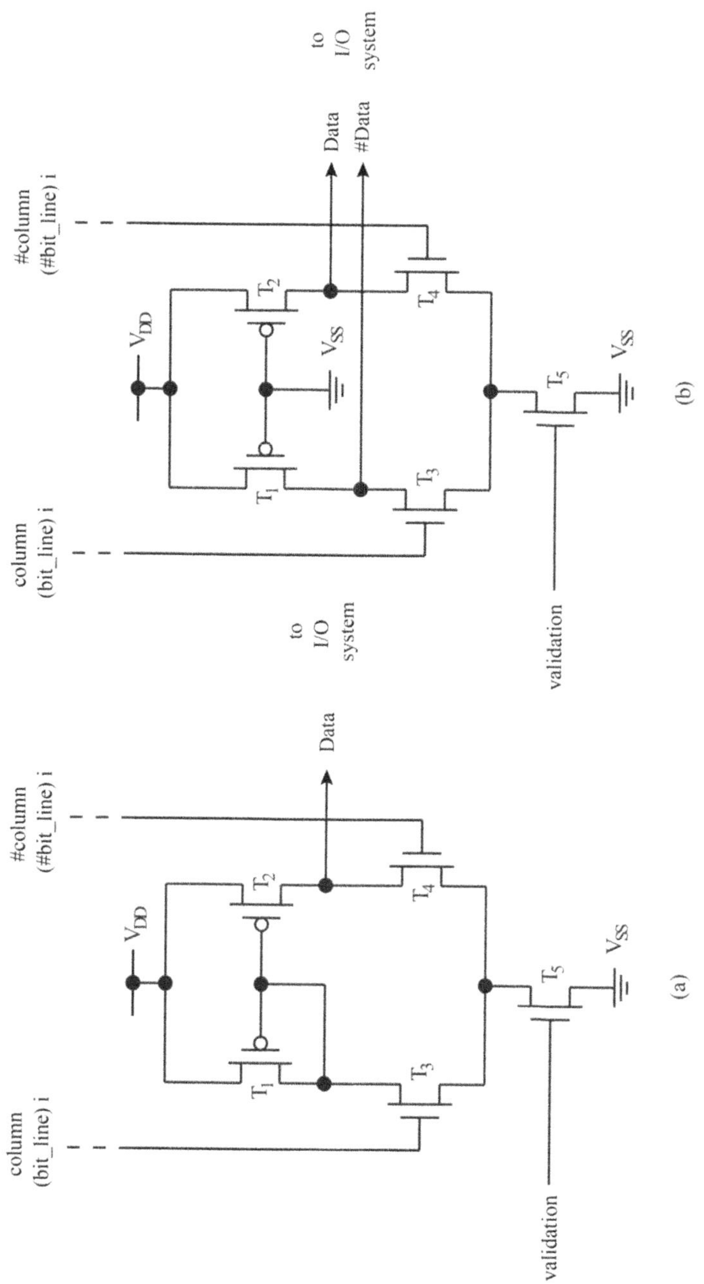

Figure 2.46. *Basic circuit diagrams of the differential amplifier*

The amplifier must be sensitive and have a high voltage gain. The storage density is directly linked to the sensitivity of the read system (Heller et al. 1976). Indeed, the more sensitive it is, the smaller the memory cell can be in the case of a DRAM. The number of cells per column for a given area can therefore increase. But reaching an output voltage close to the supply voltages (rail-to-rail) will depend on the amplifier's gain, its slew rate and the output load. It may then be necessary to use a two-stage system (dual-stage SA) composed of a differential preamplifier (sense preamplifier or SPA), generally with differential output, followed by the classic differential sense amplifier (see Figure 2.47). DiMarco et al. (1994) proposed an example of this type of approach.

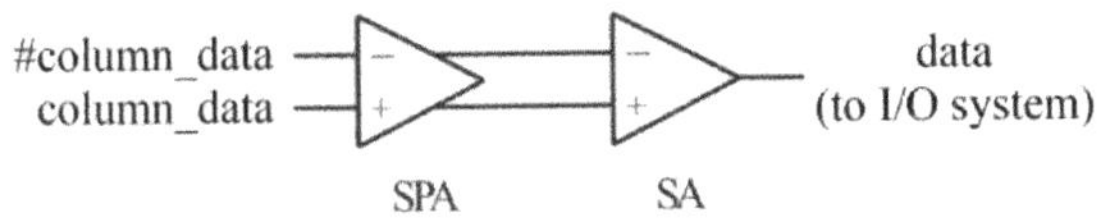

Figure 2.47. *Two-stage amplification chain*

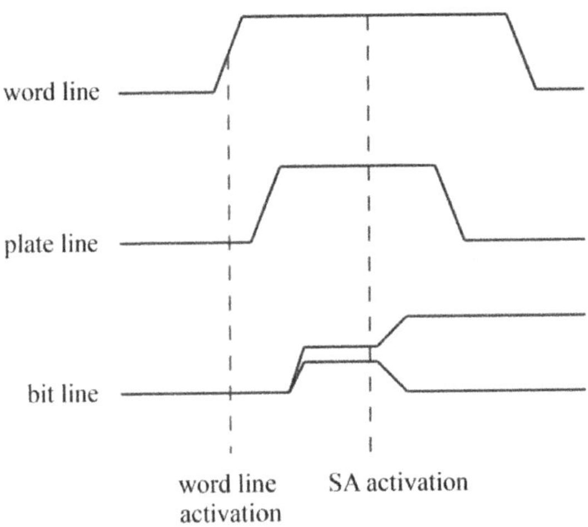

Figure 2.48. *Simplified read timing diagrams according to the step-sensing scheme (time axis (abscissa) not shown)*

All these techniques operate in voltage mode (voltage SA or V-sense amplifier). The problem is the parasitic capacitances of the columns and the high input impedances that limit the slew rate. To improve switching times, current mode has been used (current SA or I-sense amplifier). Moreover, certain emerging technologies such as MRAM (magnetoresistive RAM, see Volume 6) must use this mode.

In the case of a destructive read-out (DRO), as is the case for DRAM or FRAM (ferroelectric RAM, see Volume 6), it is necessary to regenerate the information read from the memory cell. This is an auxiliary function of the sense amplifier. Figure 2.48 shows an example of a read operation.

Various column topologies have been devised to make reading less sensitive to differential-mode noise, especially for DRAM. They will be detailed in Volume 3.

2.2.9. *The write circuitry*

The advantage compared to a read operation is that a write operation handles electrical signals of greater amplitude, even maximum amplitude. Figure 2.49 presents a basic write circuitry. The inverter buffers amplify the data in both its normal and complementary forms. Two transistors allow connection to the columns.

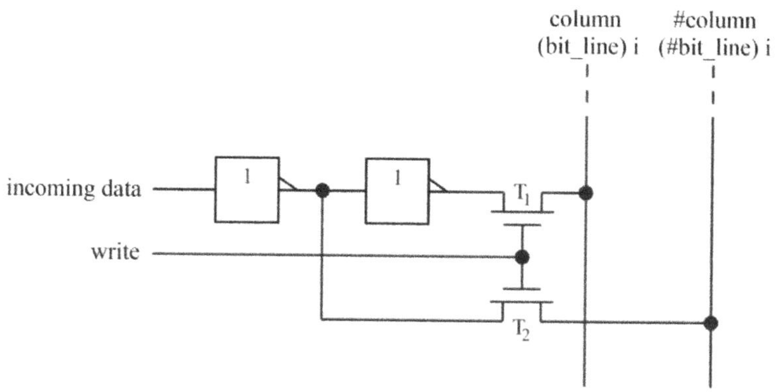

Figure 2.49. *A basic write circuit*

2.3. Conclusion

This chapter has presented the main functional blocks that make up a semiconductor memory.

The next chapter presents more specific functional blocks such as phase- and delay-locked loops and specific power supply systems for a semiconductor memory.

3

Additional Functional Blocks

This chapter details more specific functional blocks than those described in the previous chapter. These include phase-locked and delay-locked loops, as well as power supply systems. These circuits appeared with synchronous models and electrically reprogrammable memories.

3.1. The phase-locked loop

The phase-locked loop (PLL) enables the generation of a signal whose frequency is a multiple of that of a reference signal and which is in phase with it. Figure 3.1 shows its basic structure. The phase comparator calculates an error signal that controls the oscillator. This signal corrects any frequency offset between the output clock signal and the frequency reference.

The drawback of this component is its high and constant power consumption, even when the memory is idle.

3.2. The delay-locked loop

The delay-locked loop or DLL is an analog or logic circuit that compensates for the time skew (time delta) that may exist between a reference signal and an output signal by equalizing the phase between the two. Like its counterpart, the phase-locked loop, the output clock signal is locked to the input signal. As shown in Figure 3.2, it consists of a variable delay line, a phase comparator (PC) or phase detector (PD), and a circuit that converts the delay into a control command for the delay line.

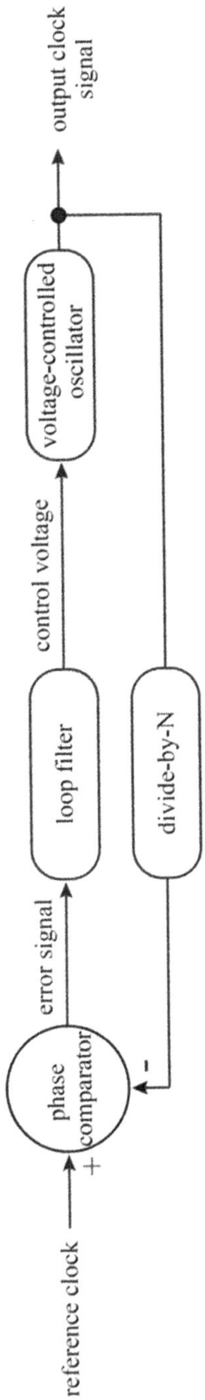

Figure 3.1. *Basic structure of a phase-locked loop*

The delay value is increased or decreased, respectively, using the Inc and Dec signals. It thus allows a phase shift of a signal, but with fixed steps. A logic circuit solving the problem of this phase shift is called a clock-deskew buffer. It is essential for the latest generations of synchronous memories with cycle-based communication (DDR3 SDRAM for double data rate 3 synchronous dynamic random access memory; see Volume 4) and packet-based communication (Rambus DRAM and others; see Volume 5) to solve the clock-skew problem. Schnell (2000) details the reference patent. The drawback of this component is its high and constant power consumption, even when the memory is idle

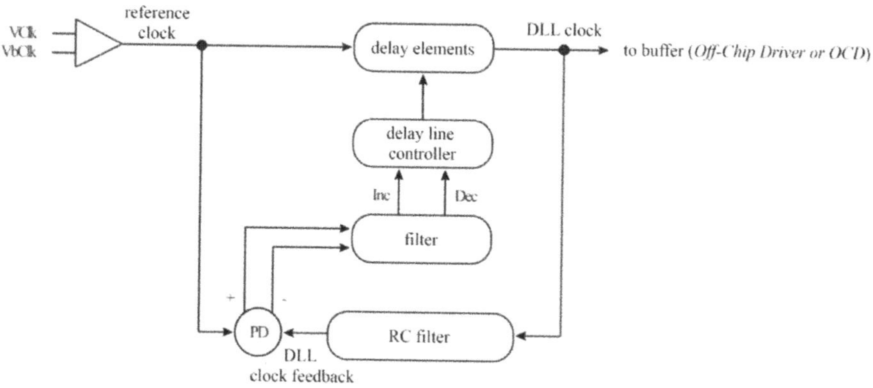

Figure 3.2. *Block diagram of a delay-locked loop*

3.3. Internal voltage generators

Internal voltage generators (on-chip voltage generator) enabled a technological advance by eliminating multiple internal voltages. Today, they are becoming increasingly important because different parts of the chip have different power supplies. They come as down-converter or up-converter voltage converters, with possible polarity inversion (voltage inverter). Depending on their function, they must be able to supply a higher or lower current, with or without output current regulation. First, we identify the substrate-bias voltage generator, which delivers a negative voltage V_{BB} (bulk supply-voltage) to control PMOS (positive channel metal–oxide semiconductor) transistors. The voltage up-converters are mainly used to overcome the threshold voltage $V_{GS(th)}$ of MOS transistors and to generate the programming voltage (programming power voltage) V_{PP} for flash EEPROM (flash electrically erasable programmable read-only memory or FEEPROM; see

Volume 6) non-volatile memories. Thus, for DRAM, the wordline boost circuit allows the memory cell capacitor to be charged to the maximum voltage, i.e. the supply voltage V_{DD}, by overcoming the threshold voltage of the switching transistor.

3.3.1. *Wordline boost circuit*

When a MOS transistor operates in switching, the maximum or minimum voltage, depending on the type of transistor, is linked to the threshold voltage $V_{GS(th)}$. When an NMOS (negative channel MOS) switches the V_{DD} voltage, the maximum output voltage will be $V_{DD} - V_{GS(th)}$. For a PMOS model switching the ground (Gnd), it will not drop below $V_{GS(th)}$. To solve this problem, from the 64 Kib generation onward, a line amplifier is added at the output of the row address decoder, which shifts the control level to the supply voltage (full swing) in the NMOS case. It is powered by a voltage V_{DH} higher than the circuit's supply voltage V_{DD}. Figure 3.3 shows a solution with a level shifter that drives a line amplifier (driver). The high voltage is applied to the power input V_{DH} (voltage drain high side).

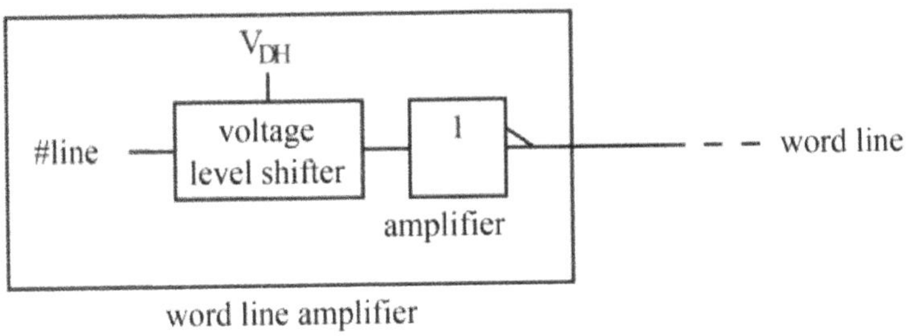

Figure 3.3. *An example of a wordline boost circuit*

Figure 3.4 shows a typical circuit diagram of a voltage up-converter. When transistor T_3 conducts, capacitor C_{boot} is charged to $V_{boot} = V_{DD} - V_{GS(th)} - V_{OL}$ via transistor T_1. When T_3 turns off, T_2 raises the output voltage V_{DH} to a voltage at V_{DD} thanks to the charged capacitor, and the V_{G2} voltage is shifted by V_{DD}. This capacitor is implemented as a transistor. C_{p_gate} is the parasitic capacitor between the gate and ground. This setup allows the threshold voltage $V_{GS(th)}$ to be bypassed. This initially adopted technique is called "bootstrapping from the source", and the associated memory circuit is called a wordline bootstrap driver. Another bootstrapping method is to use a MOS varactor (Joynson et al. 1971, 1972). Boonstra et al. (1973) explains the operation of one implementation.

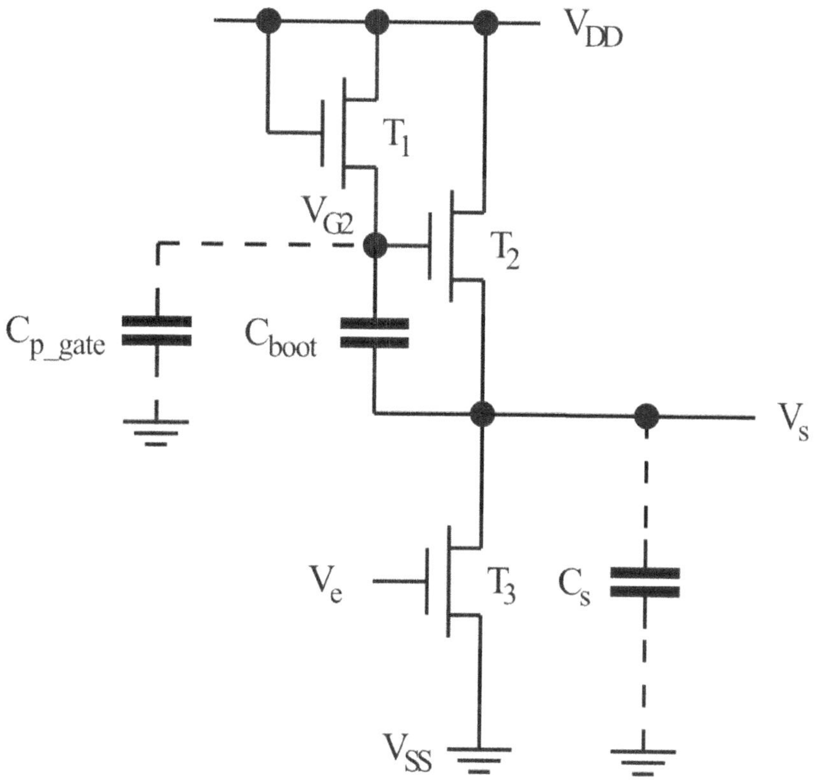

Figure 3.4. *Bootstrapping technique*

The bootstrapping coefficient r is defined by:

$$r = \frac{C_{boot}}{C_{boot}+C_{p\_gate}} \quad [3.1]$$

To solve the symmetrical threshold voltage issue for NMOS transistors in CMOS (complementary MOS) technology, Figure 3.5 shows the standard circuit diagram of a true rail-to-rail level shifter, i.e. without voltage drop at the extremes of the voltage swing caused by the threshold voltage $V_{GS(th)}$. Tan and Sun (2002) describe a low-power version.

Modern line drivers use a multi-stage charge pump (Brugler and Jespers 1969) associated with a voltage regulator (see, for example, Gillingham et al. (1991)), hence the name charge pump converter. The noise related to column coupling is reduced by half.

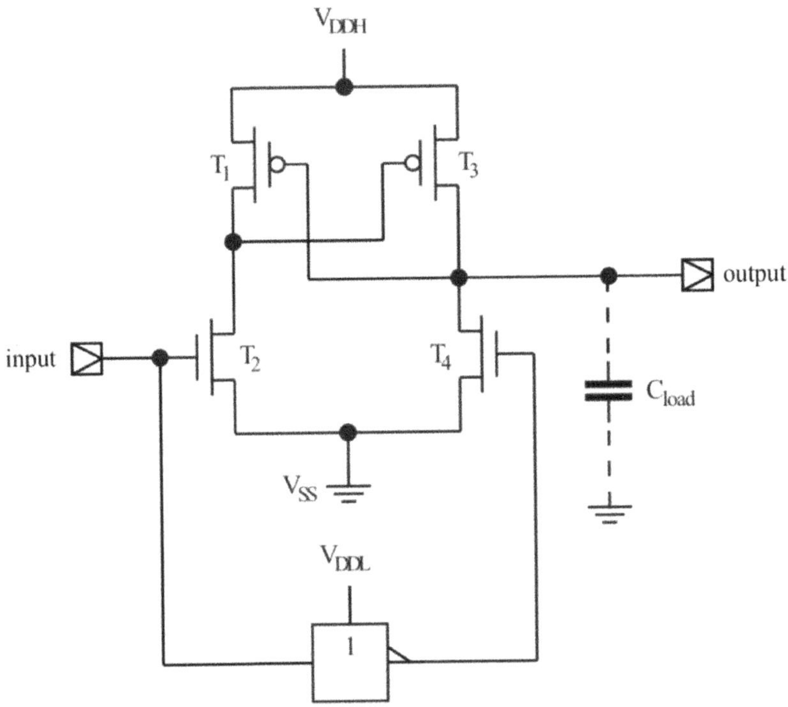

Figure 3.5. *Rail-to-rail level shifter*

3.3.2. *Mid-V_{DD} generator*

This subcircuit generates a voltage $V_{DL} = V_{DD}/2$ for column precharge (data-line precharge) and for powering one plate of the cell capacitor. Precharging at mid-supply voltage (mid-V_{DD}) reduces current spikes due to a voltage swing cut in half and helps reduce the total current consumed by the chip. By halving the supply voltage, the dielectric thickness of the DRAM cell's storage capacitor could be doubled. Other advantages are described in Taylor and Johnson (1985a, 1985b). This technique appeared with the 4 Kib generation of DRAM. One technique involves short-circuiting a differential line that has a complementary state (i.e. one at V_{DD} and the other at V_{SS}), thereby sharing the total charge. This happens after the signal is restored when reading a DRAM cell, for example, or during differential column precharge, with one at V_{DD} and the other at 0 V (V_{SS}) (Foss and Harland 1975). The industry's generalized approach is to use a voltage regulator. Figure 3.6 shows the basic circuit diagram.

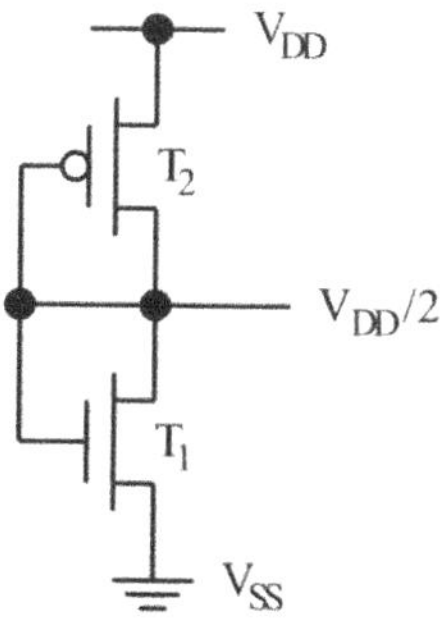

Figure 3.6. *Basic circuit diagram of a divide-by-two voltage divider*

3.3.3. *Internal voltage regulators*

Memories need to generate voltages generally lower than the supply voltage, both positive and negative, in order to reduce feature size, improve reliability and lower power dissipation. Reducing the consumed current allows the memory to be used in portable systems (battery-operated RAM; see section V2-6.2.2). However, the designer must improve the signal-to-noise ratio (SNR). These voltage regulators are characterized by high output current. They can also be current-regulated, as in converter no. 3 in Figure 3.7, to control the charge current of data lines.

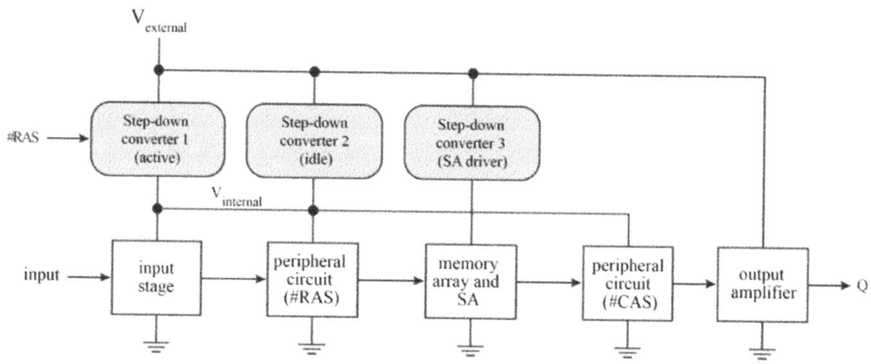

Figure 3.7. *Voltage conversion system (Fujii et al. 1989a, 1989b)*

These converters now use the charge pump technique (Brugler and Jespers 1969).

3.4. Implementation

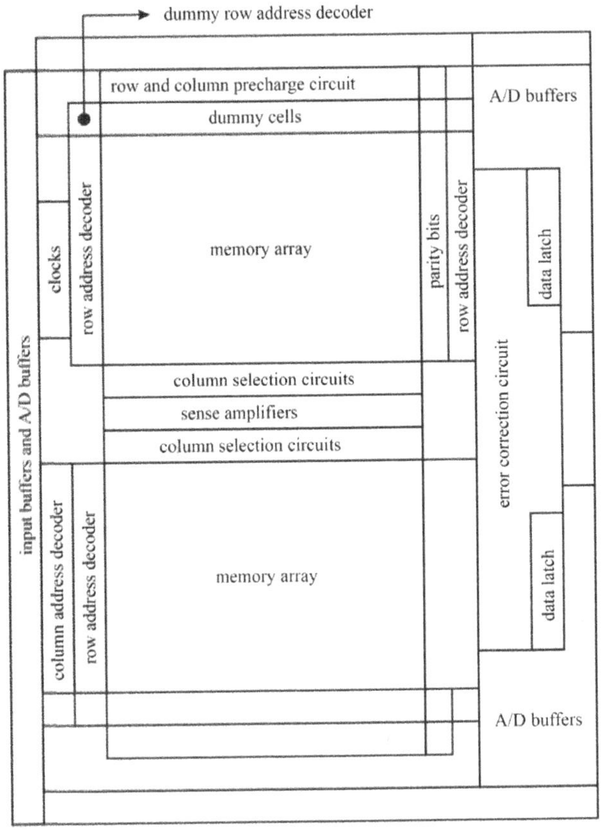

Figure 3.8. *Topology of a ROM chip (based on Davis (1985))*

The area required to implement an element is measured in terms of the normalized area (minimum feature size) F^2, which depends on the lithography used and the design rules. The first description of a memory cell was given by Igarashi et al. (1966). It was an associative memory, not a random-access memory. Its description is found in Volume 7. Figure 3.8 shows an example of a read-only memory layout inspired by Davis (1985). Two memory arrays can be distinguished, each surrounded by its row address decoder and column selection circuits. They share the sense amplifiers (in the center) and the column address decoder (on the left). At the periphery, the I/O circuits (latches and electronic buffers) can be seen. An innovative feature is the presence of an error detection and correction unit (see section 6.4). Furthermore, the manufacturing yield is directly linked to the chip size.

The larger the area, the lower the yield. Research therefore aims to offer maximum performance and functionality for an acceptable manufacturing yield. Redundancy techniques for components or systems, activated by laser (Smith et al. 1981) during test phases, are implemented to improve yield.

The manufacturing technologies used are those of transistors, as grouped in Figure 3.9. They can be unipolar or bipolar. Bipolar technologies mainly use saturated transistor logic such as TTL (transistor transistor logic; see section 2.3.2 of Darche (2004)), which was the first industrial standard, and non-saturated transistor logic, represented by ECL (emitter coupled logic; see section 2.3.3 of Darche (2004)). The advantage of combining manufacturing technologies is to benefit from the strengths of both. For example, Suzuki et al. (1989) detail an implementation where ECL is used for I/O and decoding stages, while the core remains in CMOS for its low power consumption. Gallium arsenide (GaAs) can be used for specific applications such as space. An example can be found in Takano et al. (1987). Bipolar and especially CMOS memories, such as logic components, are sensitive to junction breakdown and electrostatic discharges (ESD for electrostatic discharge). More implementation details are given in Itoh (2001).

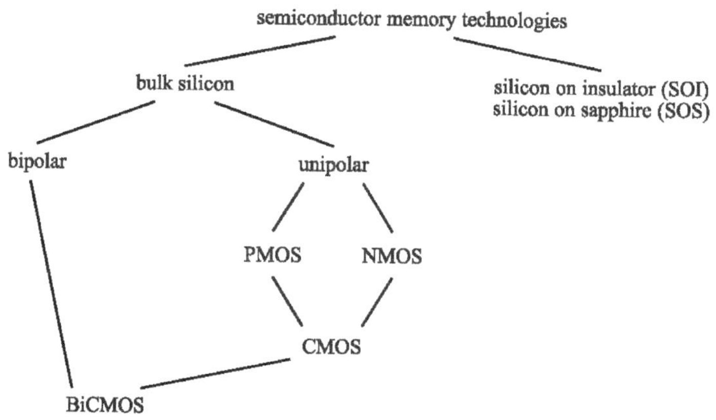

Figure 3.9. *Simplified classification of microelectronic technologies for semiconductor memory manufacturing*

Manufacturing technology is important. Switching from a 250 nm feature size (1997) to 180 nm (1999), for example, reduces the area by about 50%, with the side of the chip square decreasing by about 30%. DDR5 SDRAM is manufactured using 10 nm technology (Kim et al. 2019, 2020).

3.5. Conclusion

This chapter has presented specific functional blocks such as phase-locked and delay-locked loops and the specific power systems of high-speed semiconductor memory.

The next chapter presents techniques for improving performance such as bandwidth or latency.

4

Advanced Internal Organization

To improve memory performance such as bandwidth or access time, it is necessary to increase either the data format size *n* or the internal operating speed. To achieve this, modular internal organizations such as block partitioning (or memory sub-zones) and banking have been introduced. Furthermore, to respond to the evolution of computer architectures toward parallelism, it became necessary to parallelize operation requests using multithreaded architectures. These approaches are described in this chapter.

4.1. Data format expansion

To expand the data format from 1 to *n* bits, the number of columns selected for an address A becomes *n*. The resulting bandwidth increases by a factor of n. These columns may be adjacent or distributed, among other reasons due to issues related to noise and propagation delay. They may also come from separate blocks (see section 4.2). We can mention John (1996), who proposed the VaWiRAM (variable width random access memory), a component with a reconfigurable format.

4.2. Block partitioning

The increase in memory size, even though integration advances continuously reduce the size of a memory cell, results in an increase in the capacity of lines and especially columns. This leads to increased access times. Moreover, column current accounts for more than 50% of total consumption. To reduce these drawbacks, the memory area can be partitioned into memory sub-zones called "blocks" or planes (also known as a sub-array, or section), by dividing the total number of columns $n_{tot\_columns}$ by K, the number of blocks.

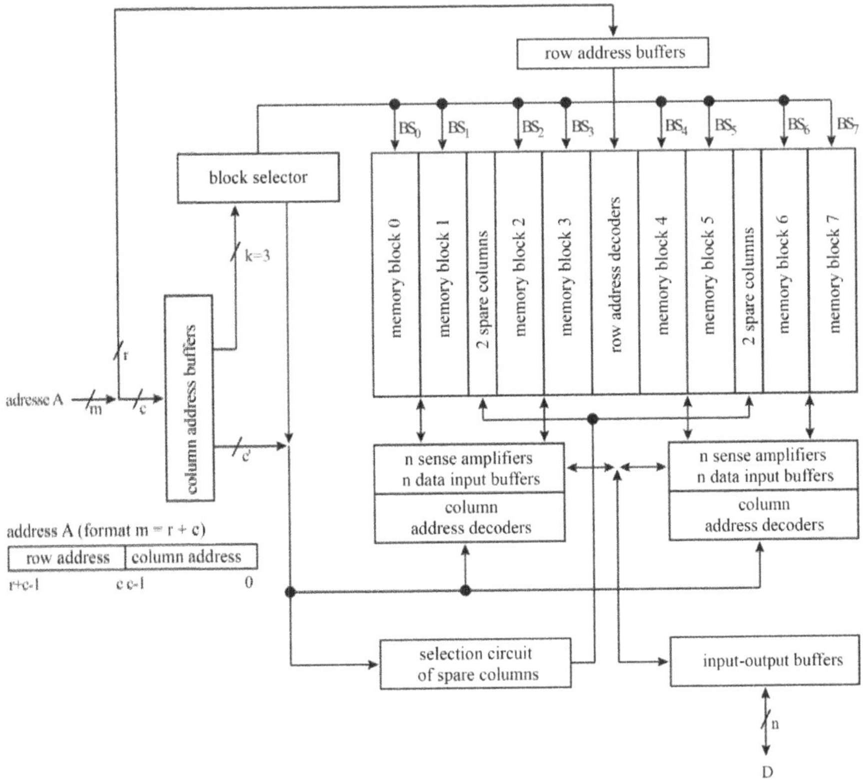

Figure 4.1. *Coincidence-based selection with K (= 8) memory blocks (r = 8, c = 5, and n = 8)*

This justifies the second name of this architecture, which is literally the "divided wordline structure" (DWL) (Yoshimoto et al. 1983). A block is a sub-memory area with its (post-)column address decoder, its sense amplifiers (one per column) as applicable and, if required by the memory type, its write system. The block address (Z-address) is stored and decoded by the associated address decoder (block decoder or Z-decoder) to select a given block K_i. The row address decoder is shared by all blocks or, if the number is large, by a group of blocks. Yoshimoto et al. (1983) describes an example of 32 Ki × 8-bit SRAM organized with 8 blocks of 256 rows and 32 columns (see Figure 4.1). Some of the address lines are used to select a block. The first consequence is a reduction in current consumption, both static (DC current) and/or dynamic (AC current) (Ochii et al. 1982). This hierarchical approach (hierarchical memory architecture) helps to reduce the length of the connections and thus decrease parasitic capacitances and reduce power consumption by activating only one block at a time during access. Power supply current spikes are also reduced. The second advantage is that the row selection time is reduced, as the row length is shortened and thus its total capacitance. The third advantage is lower sensitivity to alpha particles (see section 6.4) since the active area of the memory zone is reduced (= one block).

Address A thus breaks down into three parts: the highest-weight part for selecting the row, the middle part for selecting the block and the lowest-weight part for selecting the column within a block (see Figure 4.2). If blocks exist, then for coordinates, X and Y always represent the row and column coordinates, respectively. Z represents the coordinate of the relevant block.

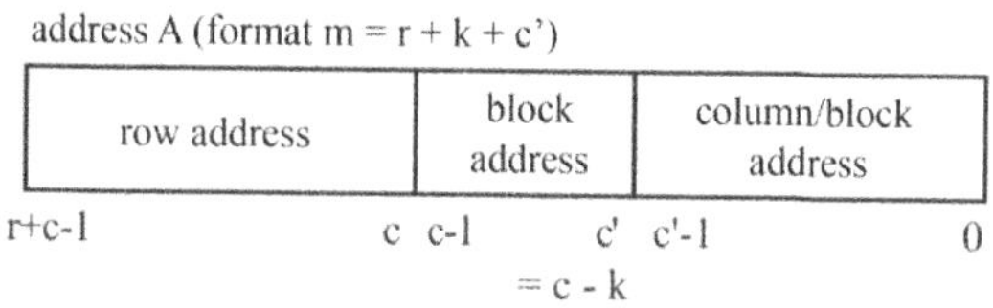

Figure 4.2. *Decomposition of an address into row, block and per-block column sub-addresses*

4.3. Bank partitioning

The company Mosys (Monolithic System Technology Incorporated), inventor of the bank concept, named the corresponding component multibank dynamic RAM (MDRAM) and intended it for graphics applications (Hsu 1998). It was a competitor to multiport video memories (VRAM, video RAM and WRAM, window RAM; see Volume 7). As shown in Figure 4.3, a (internal) bank is the integration of complete memory modules with the internal replication of external bus signals, hence the presence of electronic buffers. It is therefore distinguished from a block by the integration of control and input/output (I/O) systems. For more information on internal structure, see Przybylski (1995) and Leung et al. (1997). It was used in the Nintendo GameCube.

Access time depends on the length of rows and columns. The idea of multibank memory is to divide memory into small independent memories or banks (memory bank). Their size is 32 KiB, and their number ranges from 16 to 64. All banks are connected to an internal bus that is linked to the component's exterior by a simple signal repeater or transceiver (see section 3.4.2 of Darche (2004)). In more advanced organizations, an internal controller manages the access policy. A controller associated with a FIFO (see Volume 7) buffer is responsible for ensuring timing (see Figure 4.4). Ayukawa et al. (1998) propose a control scheme for this type of memory.

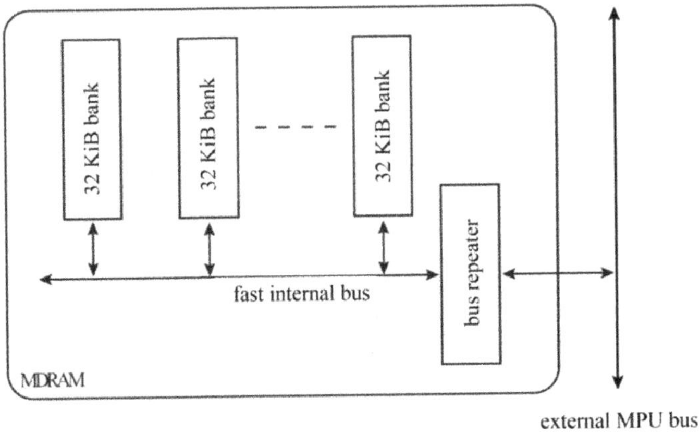

Figure 4.3. *Organization of a Mosys MDRAM*

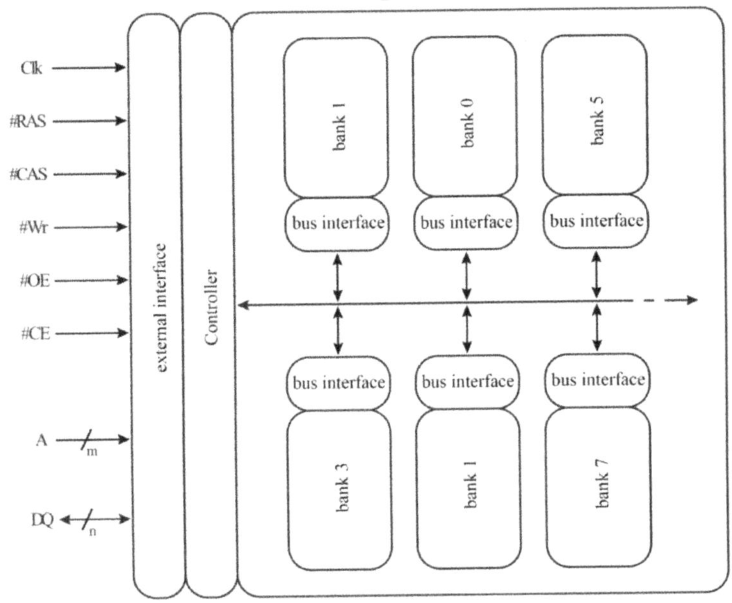

Figure 4.4. *Multibank architecture*

Access to the bank is the same as a classic access. The address is a triplet (bank, row, column). Figure 4.5 presents the simplified state diagram of operation.

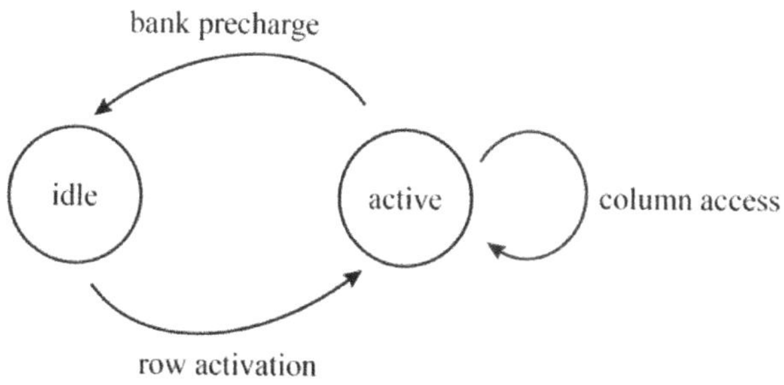

Figure 4.5. *Bank access state diagram*

A single-bank architecture is structurally limited in terms of burst mechanism. Only one row is active at a time because there is only one row of sense amplifiers. Furthermore, with multiplexed addressing, the row address cannot be sent during the burst. With multiple banks, it is possible to overcome this limitation. To optimize the command bus bandwidth, several banks can be kept open simultaneously and read and write operations can be carried out in some banks while others are open or closed. Access to the banks is performed in parallel. Access to data is then done by selecting the bank. This approach improves both latency and throughput. If there are $B = 2^b$ banks, the improvement is by a factor B (speed-up factor) after the initial latency of the first access. It is a scheme of internal interleaving (interleaving technique, explained in section 5.2.4) with a high interleaving degree.

Along the same lines, to enable prefetching, the multibank approach is a solution as shown in Figure 4.6. Several banks are activated and provide a word which a multiplexer selects. Only the first access takes the maximum access time t_{acc} (see Chapter 1 of Volume 2); the following ones have access time corresponding only to the selector's switching time.

In the case of DRAM, dividing the memory area into banks also helps reduce the total number of refresh cycles (see Chapter 3 of Volume 3) by a factor equal to the number of banks, since refreshing occurs in parallel. From an energy standpoint, activating only one bank at a time also helps reduce power consumption. This drawback of peak and average current consumption overhead was addressed by the JEDEC (Joint Electron Device Engineering Council Solid-State Technology Association) standard of DDR2 (see Volume 4). Buses can also be separated. This approach is well suited for concurrent access as in parallel architectures. On the downside, the controller is more complex to design. Moreover, in an embedded version (see Volume 7), a multibank approach can become a bottleneck. To overcome it, Ogawa and Horowitz (2001) propose a wave-pipeline-type data bus to maximize bandwidth.

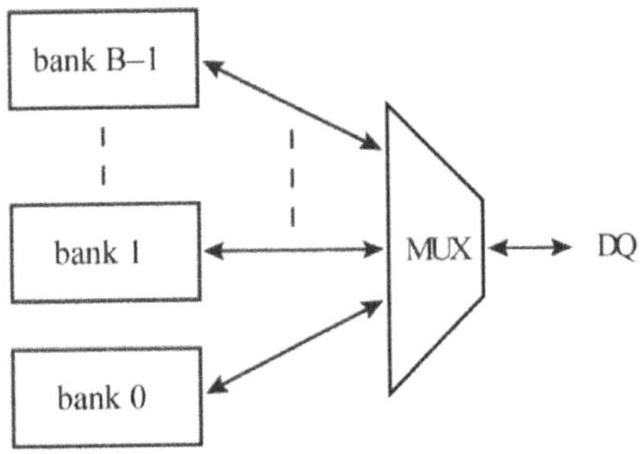

Figure 4.6. *The multibank approach*

A similar concept is BRAM or block RAM in the field of programmable logic (see Chapter 4 of Darche (2004)). It refers, for reasons of silicon efficiency and performance, to hardcore[1] memory blocks, i.e. real blocks (see Embedded Memory section of Volume 3), in some FPGA (field-programmable gate array, see section 4.3.2 of Darche (2004)) models available for use.

4.4. Multithreaded architectures

Huge electronic advances have been made in interfaces, and today, data rates of several Gb/s per I/O pin over copper links are achieved. But despite functional and structural improvements such as the page mode used by DRAMs (see Chapter 4 of Volume 3), functional partitioning (pipelining) and prefetching, used notably by synchronous DRAM (SDRAM for synchronous DRAM; see Volume 4) or the multibank approach (see previous section), the memory core faces a timing wall. It must comply in particular with timing constraints such as $t_{CC(min)}$, the minimum time between two column accesses in the same row for a read or write; $t_{RC(min)}$, the minimum time between two row activations in the same bank; or $t_{RR(min)}$, the minimum time between two row activations in different banks. These times strongly limit the component's throughput by constraining the command rate. Moreover, the I/O data format of the memory subset increases, following the processor data path format, with a 64-bit format becoming standard. As shown in Figure 4.7, the memory module receives all signals, possibly stored and redistributed after amplification by a register, for access to a full word. Access to a cell occurs in several steps: activation, one or more operations on the cell (read or write), and precharge. Activation consists of enabling the bank by selecting

1 In contrast to the term softcore, which is a logical description in a hardware description language or HDL, such as VHDL (VHSIC hardware description language), and which is synthesizable.

a row of cells. Their content is stored by the sense amplifiers (latch sense amplifier (SA)). Reading or writing takes place in the SA row. The precharge step transfers the SA data back to the row's cells and precharges the columns to prepare for another row access or for a refresh. These steps are triggered by sending a command: respectively, ACTIVATE, READ or WRITE, and PRECHARGE. The entire memory module is selected by a single chip enable signal (#CE), even if the required data format is smaller than the I/O width, resulting in maximum power consumption.

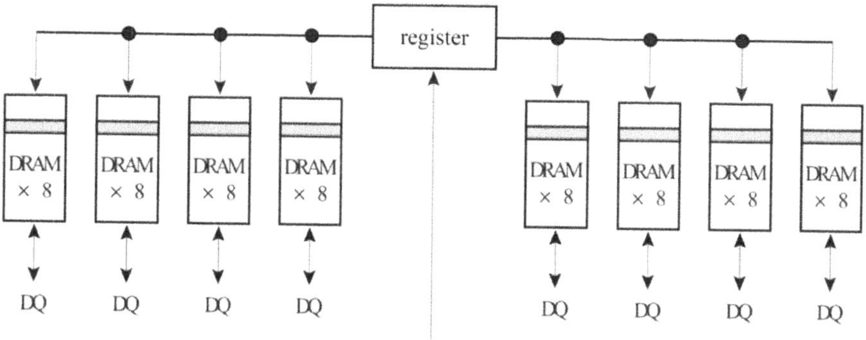

Figure 4.7. *Standard access to a DIMM-type module*

But many applications, especially in graphics, do not require such a format (Ware and Hampel 2005). Ware et al. (2006, 2007) gives an order of magnitude for these times with t_{CC} = 5 ns, t_{RC} = 40 ns and t_{RR} = 10 ns, which we will use in the following examples. Note that activating rows in different banks is less time-consuming than within the same bank due to column management logic – precharge, address decoding, read, and sensing and latching.

Moreover, the memory subset must adapt to new multicore architectures (CMPs, chip multi-processors) which, as the name suggests, have several cores (commonly two to eight), i.e., independent processors sharing only the last-level cache, L2 or L3 (see Volume 8). So, the degree of access parallelism must be increased. In operating systems (OS), a thread or lightweight process is a subdivision of a task or (heavyweight) process that allows increased parallelism. Applied to our domain, the term thread refers to the possibility of parallelizing operation requests. It is a subdivision (segmentation) of a memory access. There are several variants depending on whether the concept applies to the component itself or to the rank (also called module). These are threading (process segmentation) at the device level (device-level threading) and threading at the module or rank level (module-level threading).

For the first, the basic idea is to reduce the access granularity of columns and rows to increase data access parallelism. The classic transfer mode will be called "single-threaded mode" (single-threaded data transfer or ST mode) as opposed to the new mode called "microthreaded" (microthreaded data transfer or MT mode). The concept's inventor, Rambus, naturally calls it microthreading. As shown in Figure 4.8(a), a t_{CC} time classically allows access to a data burst DQ in format *n*. To increase column access granularity, this access must be split both temporally and spatially. Thus, in the microthreaded version (see Figure 4.8(b)), the external data path DQ in format *n* will be divided into two, each data sub-path A or B being assigned to a column access (spatial partitioning). Moreover, time t_{CC} will also be split and assigned to different column accesses (temporal partitioning). The request rate is then multiplied by up to 4. This partitioning applies either to the same bank or to different banks.

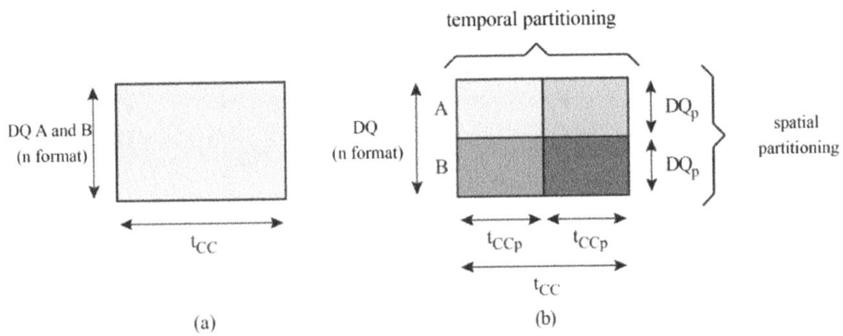

Figure 4.8. *Comparison between classic column access mode (a) and microthreaded mode (b) (Ware et al. 2006, 2007)*

Let us place ourselves in the context of a multibank architecture with a data format *n* of 16 bits. In a classic access, called single-threaded here, an external request (throughput of 0.8 Gb/s per link), also called a command or instruction, such as a bank open or close, a read or write access request (request path RQ in Figure 4.9) breaks down into internal operations such as row activation, column access or column precharge executed in logic pipelines. The three aforementioned timing constraints must be respected, which limits the memory throughput (see Figure 4.9). In this example, 16 bits are delivered per pin in 5 ns, resulting in a bit transport interval t_{bit} of 0.3125 ns or a throughput of 3.2 Gb/s per DQ pin. To achieve this, after a command to access a row (i.e., activation of the corresponding bank), two commands to access the open page (row *z*), here reads of columns *a* and *b*, are received. After an access latency, the data is output in the form of two successive bursts of 32 bytes. A precharge request ends the bank access, which is then deactivated. The striped periods are available for access to other banks.

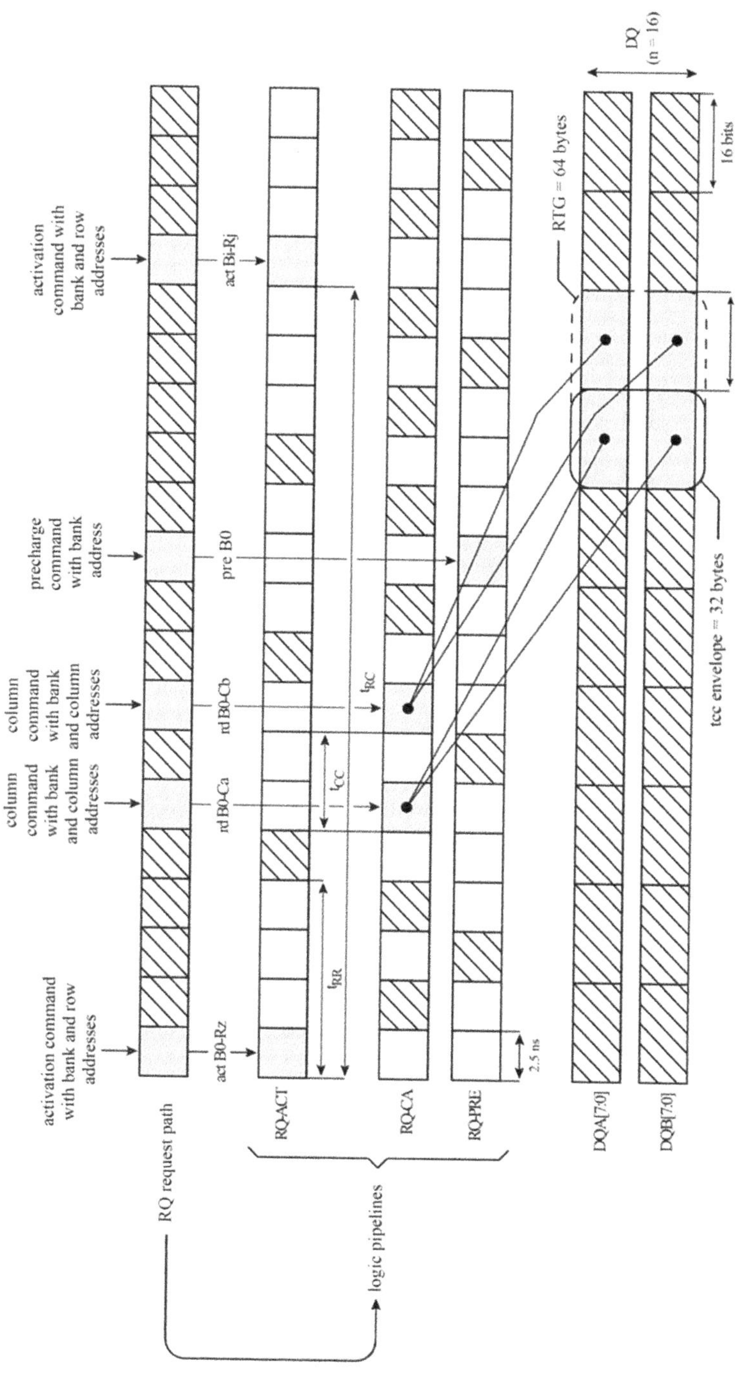

Figure 4.9. *Timing diagrams of internal pipelines in single-threaded mode in the case of two successive reads (according to Ware et al. (2006, 2007))*

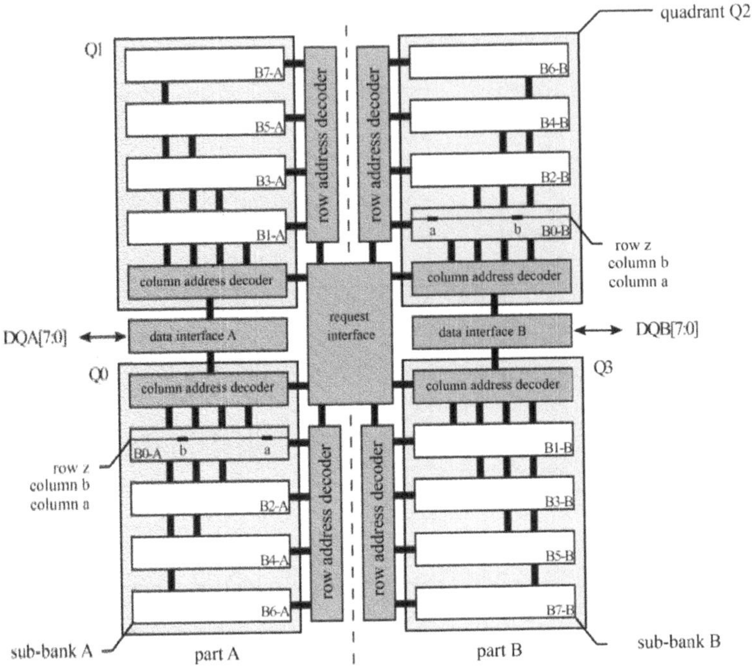

Figure 4.10. *Simplified functional organization of a multibank memory*

The memory core corresponding to these timing diagrams is that of Figure 4.10. It is a model with eight banks. Each bank is divided into two independent half-banks, A and B, operating in parallel. The sub-banks are grouped into quadrants Q_0 to Q_3. The first two are assigned to part A of the I/Os, the other two to part B. Even-numbered quadrants contain even-numbered sub-banks, and odd-numbered quadrants contain odd-numbered sub-banks. This subdivision into sub-banks A and B means that the number of columns in a bank is thus divided by two. In the developed example, only one bank was activated (grayed bank B0) and two columns *a* and *b* per sub-bank were accessed in read.

Figure 4.11 shows the previous functional organization operating this time in microthreaded mode. The subdivision into independent quadrants Q[3:0] and into two I/O interfaces A and B enables a temporal and spatial partitioning, respectively, of the t_{CC} interval. It is worth noting that each quadrant has its own address decoding logic, thus allowing for the future autonomous operation of the quadrants. In the following example, two banks will be activated.

Figure 4.12 shows an example of microthreaded operation with temporal partitioning of accesses for both banks B0 and B1 (shaded with variation). The previous time intervals are now divided by two. The result is a doubling of request throughput (1.6 Gb/s per link) and I/O throughput (6.4 Gb/s per pin). Note that this doubling of throughput is not achieved by doubling the format of the internal data paths of the memory, which remains 128 bits here. The banks are activated successively with alternating even/odd numbering. The times t_{CC} and t_{RR}, respectively, are divided into two periods t_{CCp} and t_{RRp}, respectively (temporally staggered MT transaction). This makes it possible to insert an additional column access command within one t_{CC} period. Precharge commands close the banks.

We will call this mode MT 2 × 2, indicating a microthreaded mode where two column addresses are sent per t_{CC} for two different banks. More generally, we will speak of an x-way × *y*-bank mode, with *x* indicating the number of column addresses per temporal envelope t_{CC}.

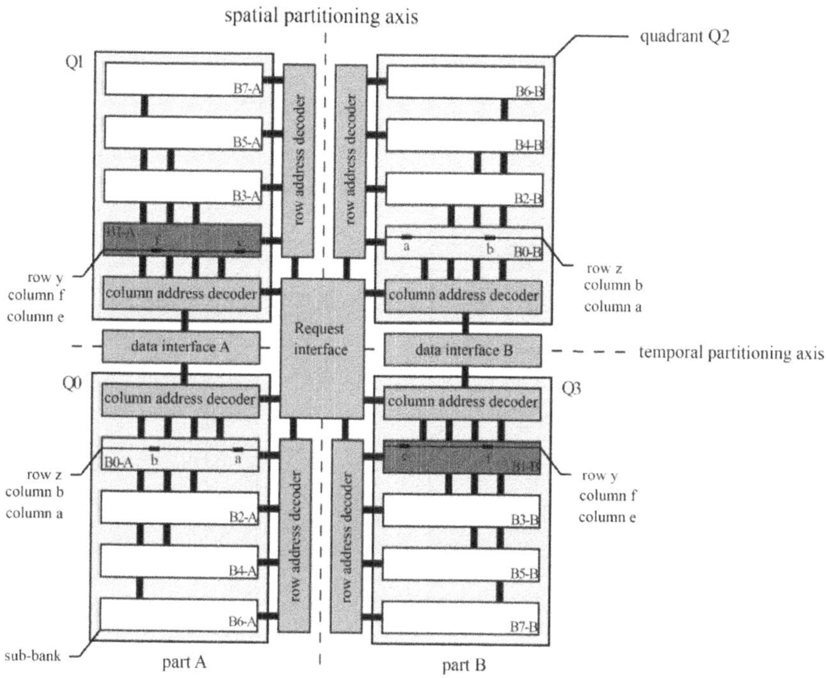

Figure 4.11. *Simplified 2 × 2 microthreaded functional organization (according to Ware et al. (2006, 2007))*

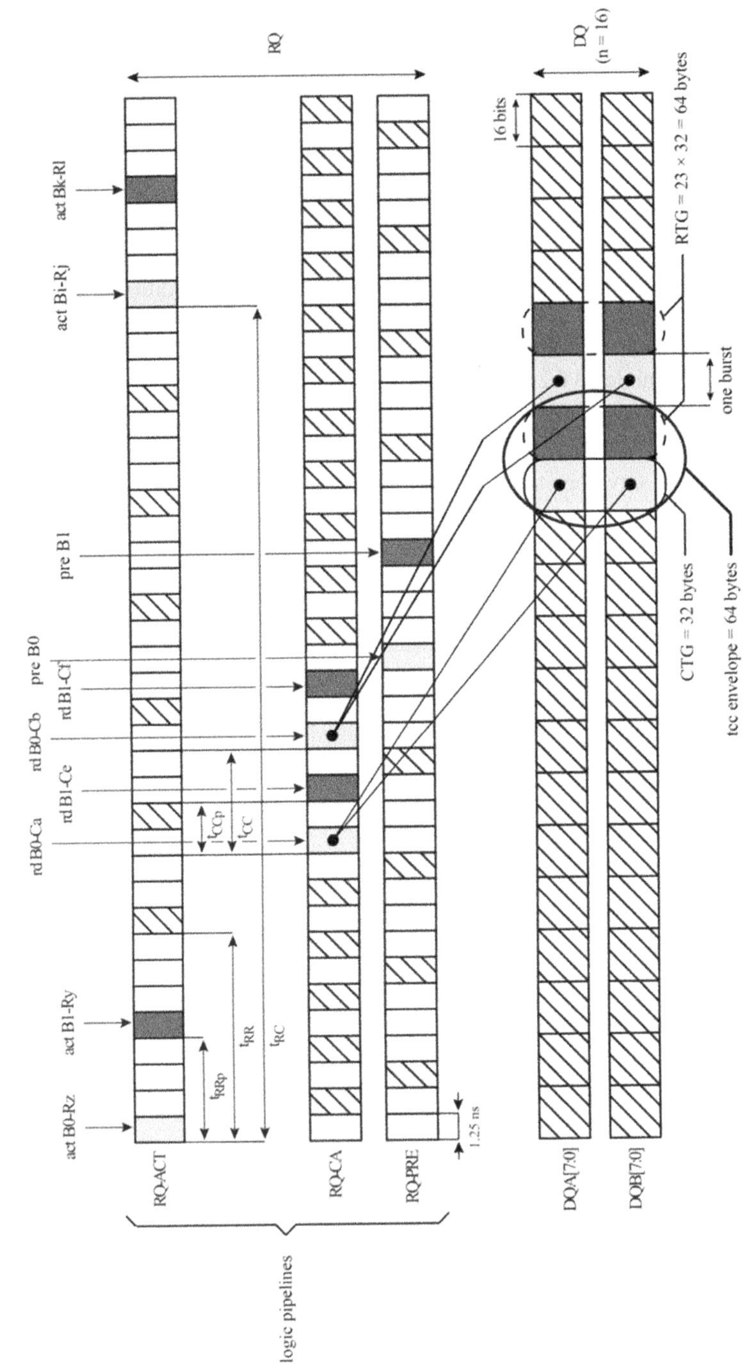

Figure 4.12. *Timing diagrams of internal pipelines in 2 × 2 microthreaded mode with temporal partitioning in the case of reads (according to Ware et al. (2006, 2007))*

Figure 4.13 shows the breakdown of characteristic times to enable microthreading. From these times, it is possible to define, for all the modes studied in this section, the row transaction granularity (RTG), the column transaction granularity (CTG) and the t_{CC} envelope. The row transaction granularity is the amount of information accessed during a t_{RR} duration in ST mode or t_{RRp} in MT mode. The column transaction granularity is the amount of information accessed during a t_{CC} duration in ST mode or t_{CCp} in MT mode. The t_{CC} envelope is the total amount of information accessed during this duration. These are measured in bytes

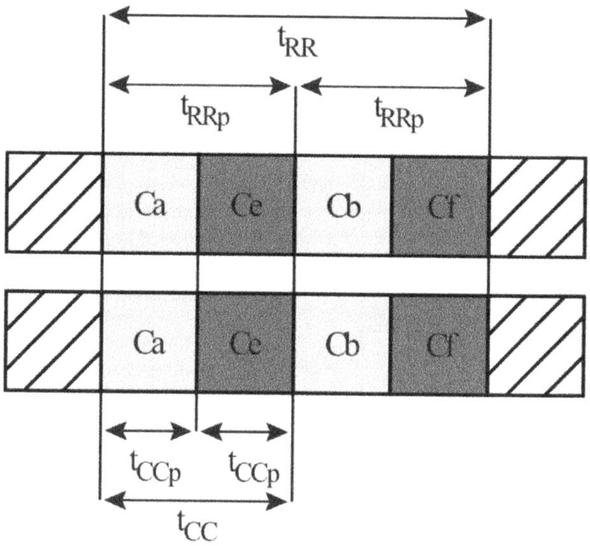

Figure 4.13. *Breakdown of characteristic times in microthreaded mode*

Figure 4.14 presents the other aspect of microthreading, which is spatial partitioning. This becomes possible when the data path width is divisible into multiple sub-paths, here named A and B, themselves divisible into DQA/B[7:4] and DQA/B[3:0]. The time t_{CC} is spatially subdivided to allow two concurrent accesses, but still with the constraint of alternating even/odd banks to avoid access conflicts. Each data byte is delivered as two quartets distributed across I/Os A and B (link-staggered MT transaction).

The functional organization in Figure 4.15 performs a spatio-temporal partitioning of accesses corresponding to the following timing diagrams. Two banks will be accessed, two columns per sub-bank.

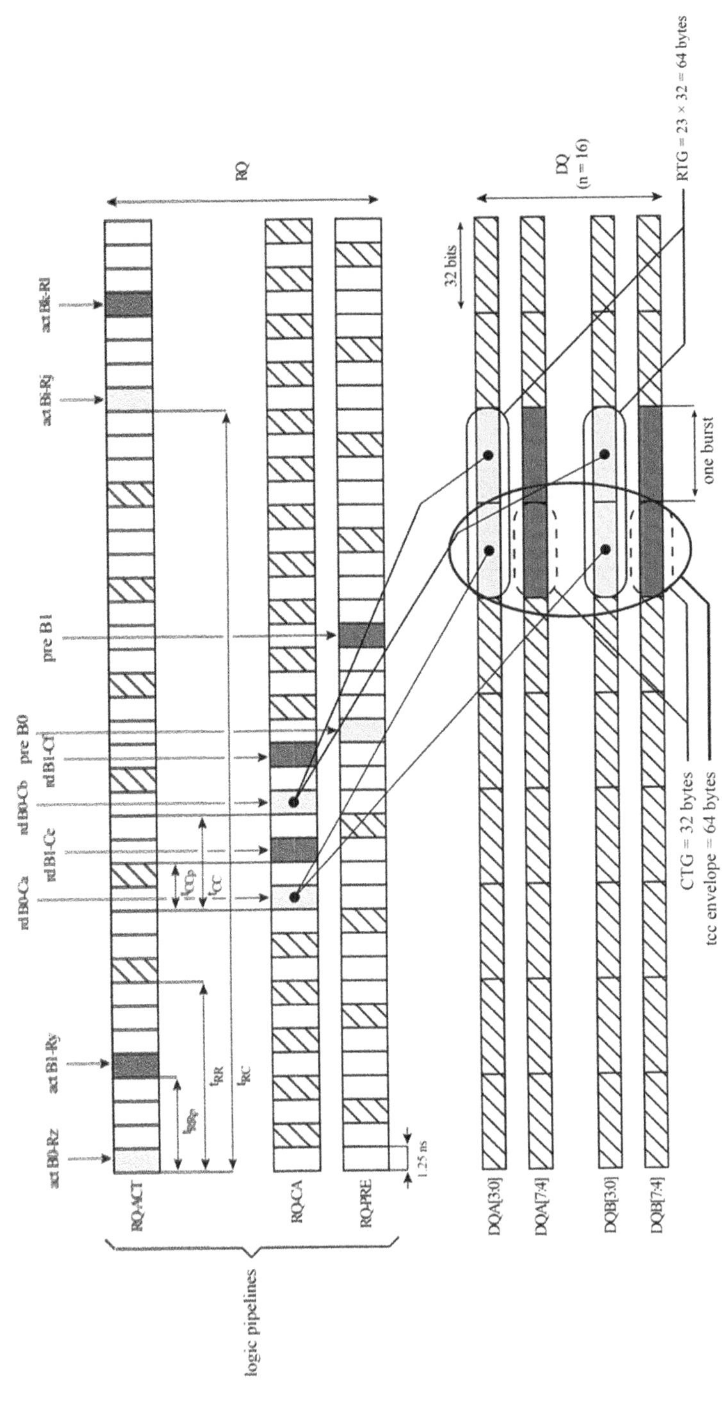

Figure 4.14. *Timing diagrams of internal pipelines in 2 × 2 microthreaded mode with spatial partitioning in the case of reads (according to Ware et al. (2006, 2007))*

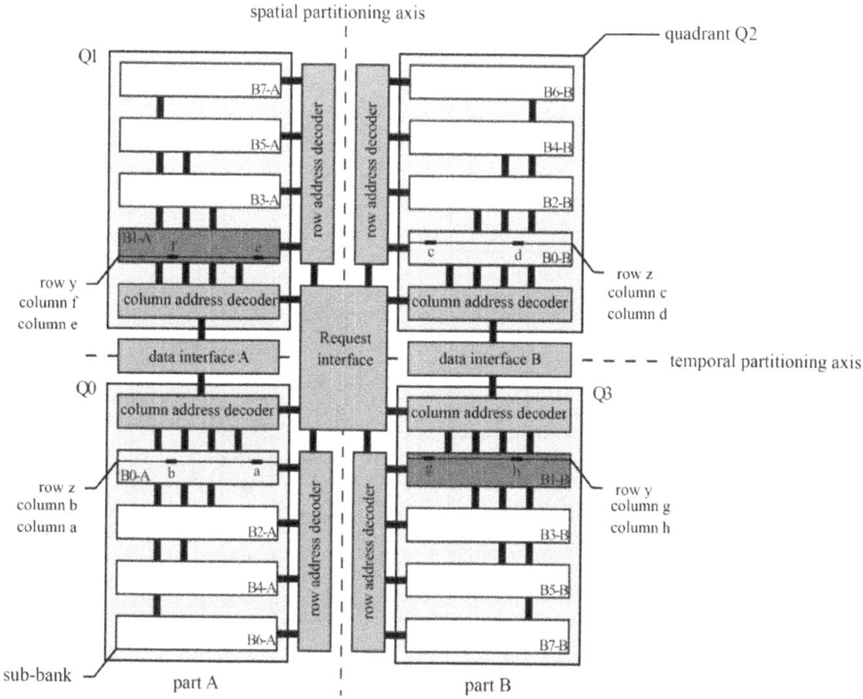

Figure 4.15. *Simplified 4 × 2 multithreaded functional organization for an example of microthreaded reads (according to Ware et al. (2006, 2007))*

In Figure 4.16, for each access command (reads), two concurrent column addresses are provided, always with the constraint of alternating between even and odd bank ownership (temporal partitioning).

The read data are sent, depending on their origin, to I/Os DQA or DQB (spatial partitioning).

Compared to Figure 4.12, the number of accessed columns doubles per t_{CC} period. This mode is called "MT 4 × 2 mode" (four requests per t_{CC} period).

The internal organization of a memory operating in MT 4 × 4 mode is shown in Figure 4.17, except that the 16 sub-banks become 16 separate banks, independent of their operations.

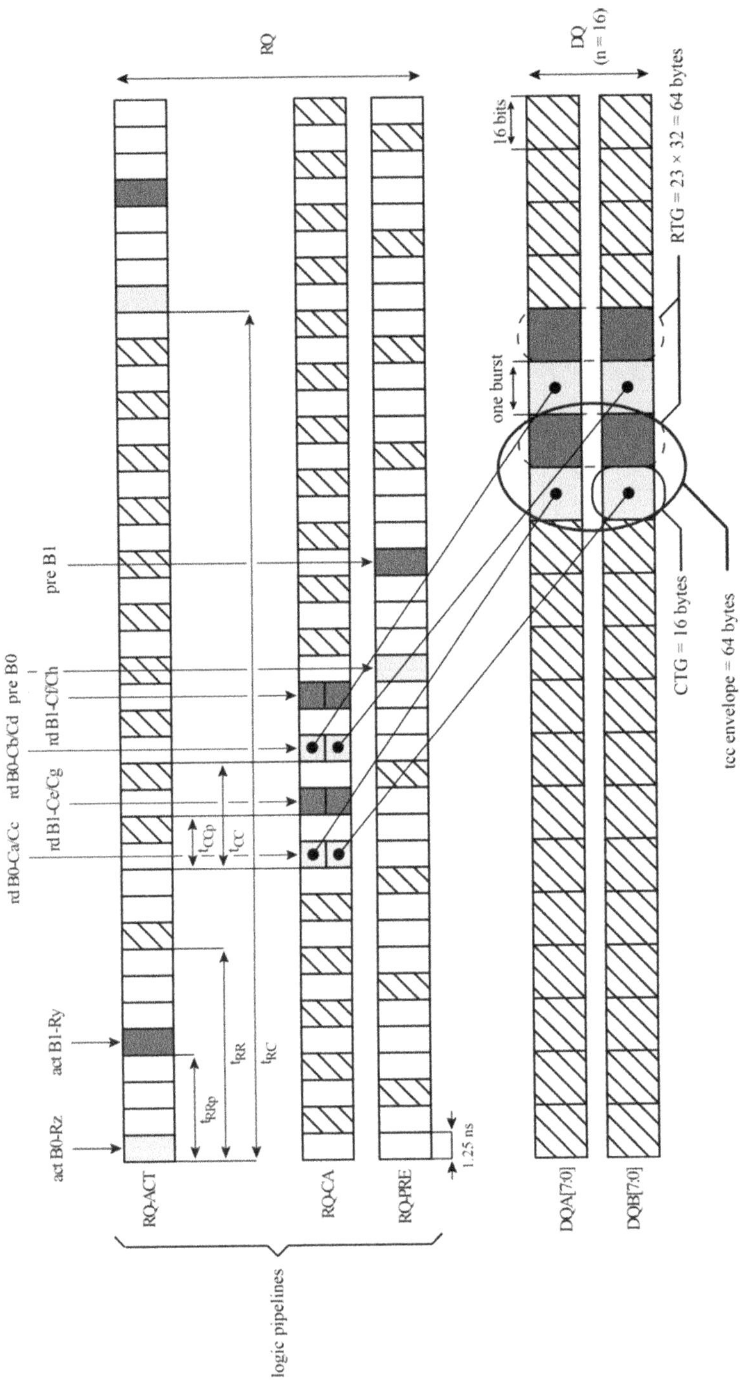

Figure 4.16. *Read timing diagrams with internal pipeline details in 4 × 2 microthreaded mode (according to Ware et al. (2006, 2007))*

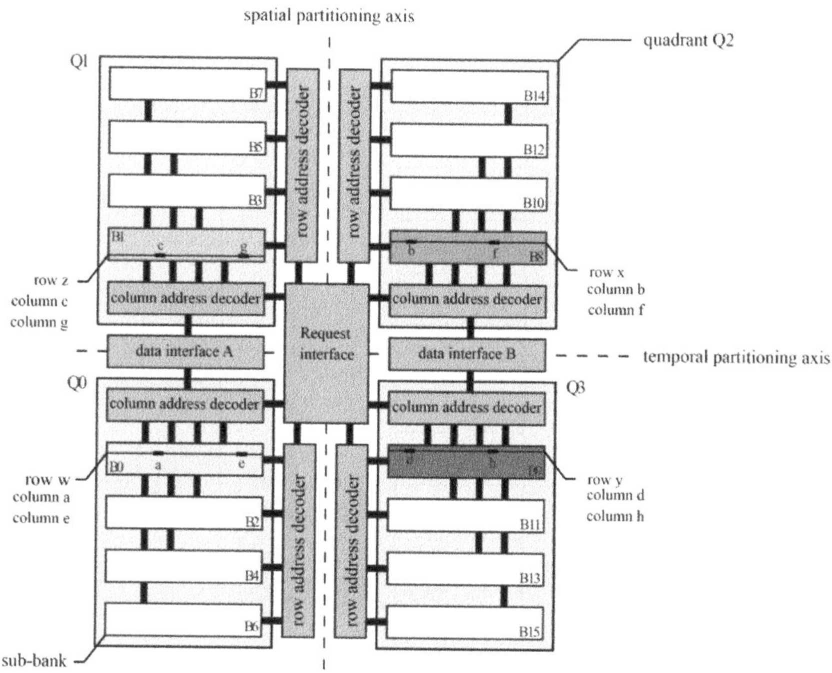

Figure 4.17. *Simplified 4 × 4 multithreaded functional organization (according to Ware et al. (2006, 2007))*

Figure 4.18 shows a read from two columns in each of these four banks. In this mode, t_{RR} is divided into four t_{RRp} periods. The order of bank activation does not matter since they are independent.

In summary, the microthreading technique doubles the output data rate compared to a conventional memory (ST mode), and this without changing the operating speed of the memory core. It increases access granularity by offering smaller-format data ($n/2$) and by allowing many more column access commands to be issued compared to conventional access (referencing SDRAM). The access rate in microthreaded mode is two to four times smaller with this architecture. The command bus utilization rate thus increases, resulting in better performance than SDRAM. Power consumption is also lower since only the involved components are active. This mode therefore helps reduce processor or core wait time in parallel architectures.

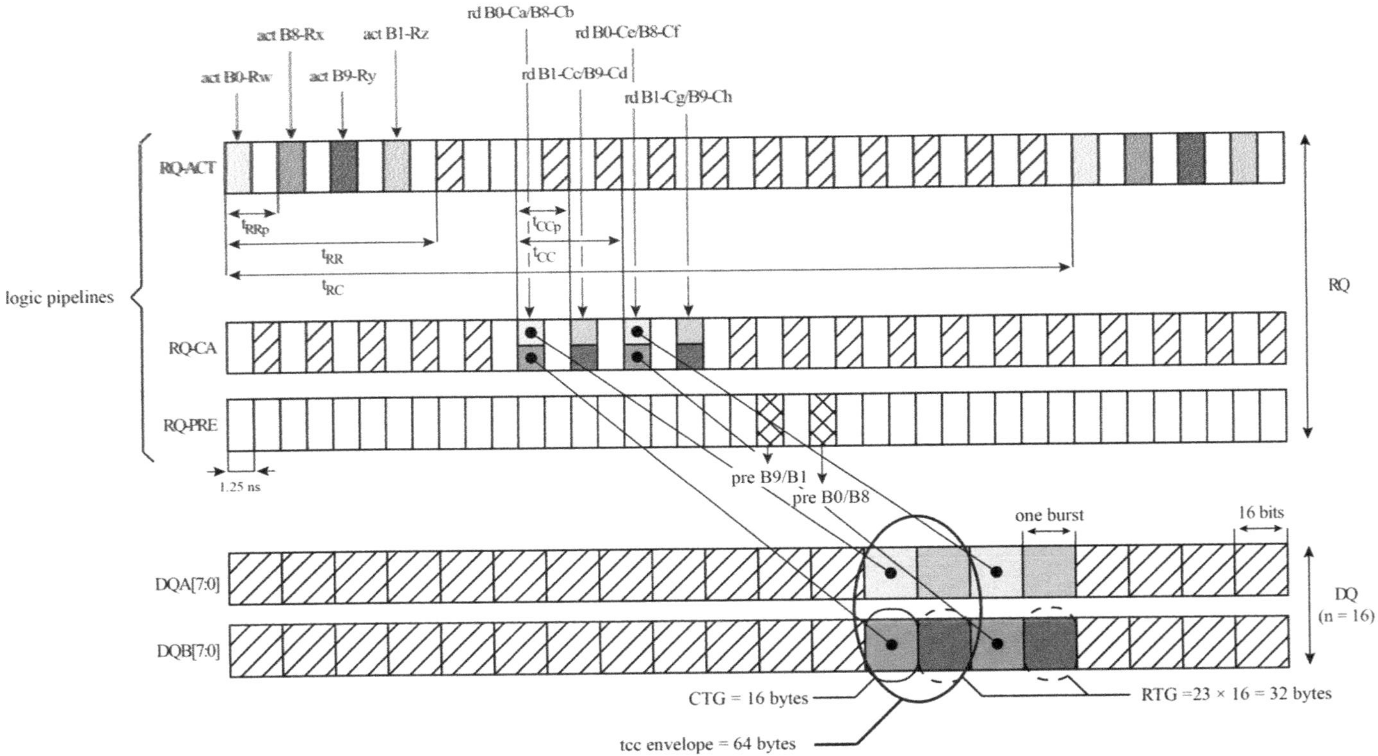

Figure 4.18. *Timing diagrams of internal pipelines in 4 × 4 microthreaded mode for a series of reads with spatio-temporal partitioning in the case of reads (according to Ware et al. (2006, 2007))*

The modifications to be made to a component for this functionality are minimal and concern more the interface than the core itself. However, the quadrants must operate independently, which requires integrating the row and column address decoders into each quadrant. Table 4.1 summarizes all the data related to the various granularities defined above. Volume 5, dedicated to packet-based memory, details the access operation.

	Characteristics		
Modes	RTG (bytes)	CTG (bytes)	Envelope t_{CC} (bytes)
ST	64	32	32
MT 2 × 2 (temporal partitioning)	64	32	64
MT 2 × 2 (spatial partitioning)	64	32	64
MT 4 × 2	64	16	64
MT 4 × 4	32	16	64

Table 4.1. *Summary of granularity sizes according to operating modes*

For the second approach[2], the basic idea is to split the rank into two. The equivalent approach is the dual-channel module, which, however, requires an even number of modules. Module access becomes parallel. In a dual-channel module, the module is divided into two independent parts, each with its own data, control/command and address buses[3] (see Figure 4.19).

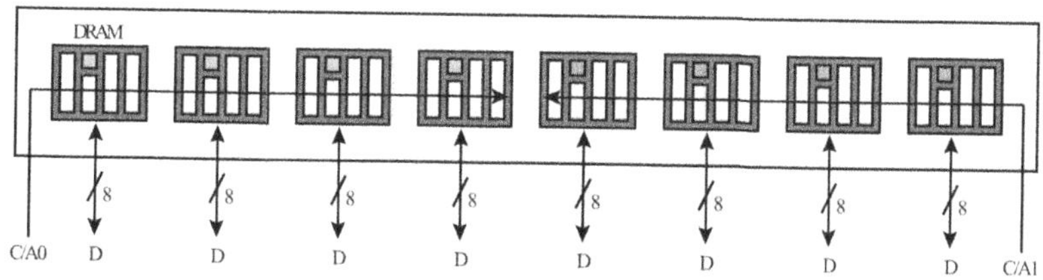

Figure 4.19. *Data access in a dual-channel module (according to Giovannini et al. (2009))*

2 For topic consistency, this paragraph was placed here but should be in the next section (see section 5.2).

3 We will use, to refer to certain buses, the abbreviations C/A or CA for command/address and C/C/A or CCA for command/control/address.

Zheng et al. (2009) propose an equivalent idea with the decoupled DIMM. Ahn et al. (2009a, 2009b) further propose an equivalent idea with the MCDIMM (multicore DIMM).

It consists of subdividing the rank (rank subsetting) into two subsets called VMDs (virtual memory devices). Each physical component has its own DQ data path. But the memory rank receives commands sequentially from a master via a common bus. After a register, a demultiplexer distributes these to the relevant memories via an individual bus (see Figure 4.21). This approach makes it possible to limit the number of packages activated for accesses smaller than that of a conventional rank.

With the threaded module, all memories share these buses (see Figure 4.20), unlike the previous proposal.

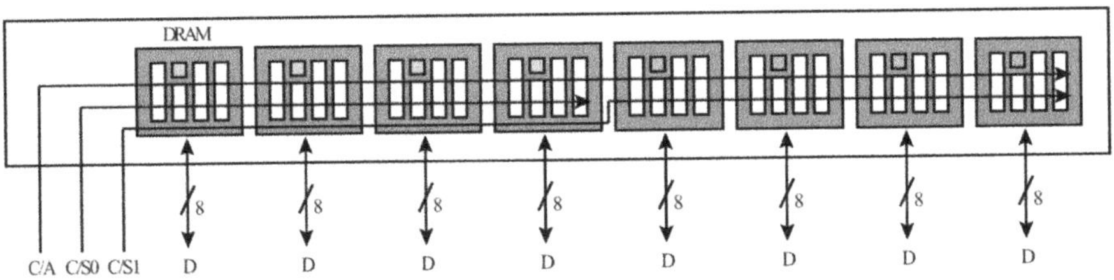

Figure 4.20. *Data access in a threaded-type module (according to Giovannini et al. (2009))*

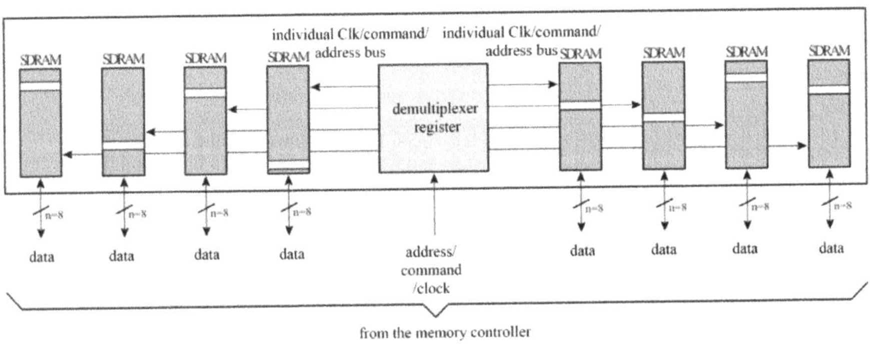

Figure 4.21. *Internal connection of the MCDIMM*

4.5. Conclusion

Apart from increasing the format, all these approaches divide the memory area (component or rank) into subsets to increase command and data throughput by accessing information in parallel. They thus reduce unnecessary data fetching (overfetch) by lowering dynamic power consumption. The presented approaches are implemented in industrial components such as static and synchronous dynamic memories.

The next chapter presents the external aspects of a memory system.

5

External Aspects of a Memory System

First, this chapter examines the classic techniques for interfacing a semiconductor memory, such as buffering and address decoding. To meet access constraints, specific interfacing techniques such as serial interfaces and multiple access ports are then explained.

In the second part, the issue of improving system performance in terms of latency and throughput is addressed. Various applicable approaches are detailed, such as increasing the data width and capacity as well as addressing techniques such as interleaving and offsetting.

5.1. Interfacing

Interfacing consists of linking two systems from both logical and physical perspectives. At the logical level, this may involve the communication protocol. At the physical level, it is necessary to adapt the signals electrically, temporally and logically.

After describing these control signals, this first section presents signal conditioning and address decoding. The concept of a port is then introduced.

5.1.1. *Basic control signals*

When a memory provides or receives data in format n, it is said to be of width n (n-wide format). Thus, a class of memories with a data interface in formats of

1, 4, 8, 16, 32 and 64 bits is called, respectively, bit-, nibble-[1], byte-, word-, double word- and quad word-wide. When the memory is accessed with a parallel address for data format $n > 1$, it is called "wide input/output" (wide I/O). Figure 5.1 summarizes the input/outputs of a generic asynchronous memory inspired by a static random access memory or asynchronous SRAM (static random access memory) (see Volume 2). The #CE signal is used to select the package. In the case of a read-write memory (RAM), an operation command must be added. Since reading and writing are mutually exclusive and to save a pin on the package, since connections have a non-negligible cost, there is usually only one signal named (R/#W) or more simply #WE, with writing arbitrarily active at logic low. The OE signal enables data output during a read. The data input D and data output Q may be separated (separate (data) I/O or SIO; Figure 5.1(b)), but more commonly, they are combined (common (data) I/O or CIO; Figure 5.1(a)). The benefit of separating I/Os is the absence of bus contention. This type of interface is used, for example, by the QDR SSRAM (quad-data-rate synchronous SRAM; see Volume 4).

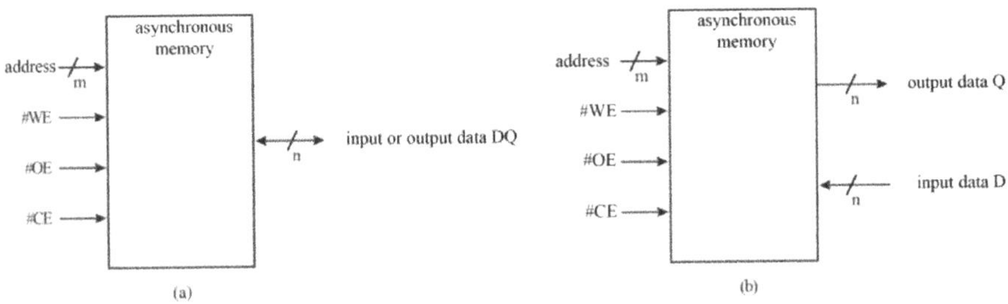

Figure 5.1. *Logic diagram of a common-access (a) and separate-access (b) asynchronous static RAM*

The VHDL code (VHSIC (very high speed integrated circuit) hardware description language; see Darche (2002)) to synthesize the interface of a generic RAM with formats $n = 8$ bits and $m = 16$ is given below:

```
entity memory is port (
A: in std_logic_vector(15 downto 0);
#OE: in std_logic;
#WE: in std_logic;
#CE: in std_logic;
```

1 Here, this term means format n = 4 bits. It should not be confused with one of the access modes of dynamic random-access memory (dynamic RAM or DRAM) with the same name (nibble mode), which involves accessing four contiguous bits (see Volume 3).

```
DQ: inout std_logic_vector(7 downto 0);
); end memory;
```

Its operation can be described by the truth table in Table 5.1. When the chip select is active (#CE = 0), the memory responds to any access request from the processor or a controller. The #OE signal controls the data output buffer. When the chip is not selected, or if it is and the output enable signal is not active, the Q output is in high impedance.

#CE	#OE	#WE	Operation	I/O
0	0	1	Read	Q
0	1	1	Read	Q = Z
0	X	0	Write	D Q = Z
1	X	X	Standby	Q = Z

X = don't care condition.

Table 5.1. *Truth table for the operation of a generic RAM*

The address can be time-multiplexed (multiplexed address) to limit the number of pins. This means the address is split into a row address and a column address, sent one after the other. This is the case with dynamic RAM or DRAM (see Volume 3). Otherwise, the operation is called non-multiplexed (non-multiplexed operation).

Access can be asynchronous or synchronous. In the latter case, an external clock signal is required, hence the synonym for asynchronous mode is "unclocked mode". A synchronous interface allows access to another memory cell during read while the data from the current cell is on the output. During write, it allows new data to be entered while a write is in progress. This approach reduces wait times.

Some memories may have an internal format that is a multiple of a byte, but the interface remains in byte format. In the case of a 16-bit memory, a signal called BHE (byte high enable) selects the most significant byte (MSB) or the least significant byte (LSB) using an internal multiplexer. When this signal is active, address line a_0 selects the desired byte. This operating principle can of course be extended to higher formats using other address lines. The truth table in Table 5.2 describes the operation.

BHE	Address line a_0	Selection
1	0	LSB
1	1	MSB
0	X	Write

X = don't care condition.

Table 5.2. *Byte-mode access for a memory with higher format (n = 16 bits)*

5.1.2. *Signal conditioning*

An important role of the internal bus interface is signal conditioning, which includes amplification, filtering, storage, protection and isolation operations.

Buses have limited fan-out (i.e. current driving capacity; see section 3.6 of Darche (2021b)) and fan-in capabilities (see section 2.2.1 of Darche (2004)). This means that it is not possible to connect an unlimited number of logic gates. An amplifier or electronic buffer (buffer or driver) must be inserted to regenerate the electrical signal and reduce parasitic capacitances. When the buffer is bidirectional (necessary for the data bus), a transceiver must be used.

Some signals must be temporarily stored during an exchange with the microprocessor or MPU (microprocessor unit). This is the role of a latch or non-latching register (see Figure 5.2). When there is a risk of electrical conflict (when several outputs are connected to the same input (bus)), only one output must be activated at a time. Special logic types must then be used, such as open-collector, open-emitter or open-drain logic, or three-state logic, the third state being the high-impedance state (see Chapter 2 of Darche (2004)). The high-impedance state makes it possible to isolate a logical subset of a bus, for example.

The two important functions are signal protection and adaptation. The outside world (from the perspective of the interface) is hostile. Electrostatic discharges are one example. But there are also electrical surges, linked for instance to signal propagation on a transmission line (see section 4.1 of Volume 2). Therefore, sufficiently powerful and fast overvoltage and undervoltage limiting components must be used. The electrical-, timing- or signal-type characteristics (edge or level) may differ from those used internally. That is the role of the adaptation stage. For example, a pulsed signal can be converted into a level signal, the electrical impedance can differ, etc. Sometimes, control signals can or must be logically combined to be used. For instance, read and write signals can be combined into a single signal (state signal or edge-triggered command), or conversely, a read/write signal can produce two separate signals, one for reading and one for writing.

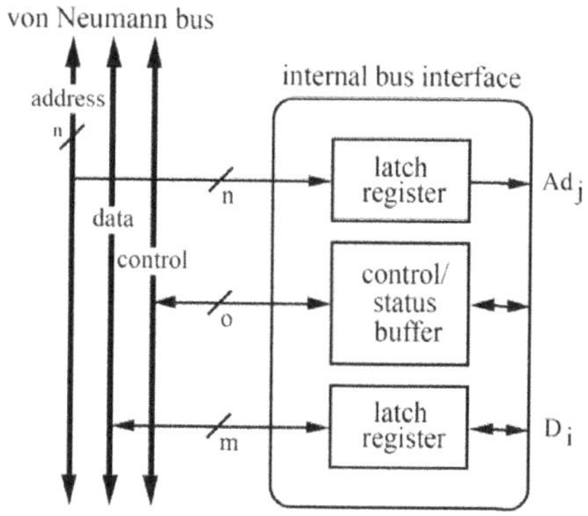

Figure 5.2. *Amplification and storage*

Once the signal is amplified, stored and adapted, it can be used by the same subsystem, for example, for address decoding, or by other subsystems (controller and external interface).

Electrical (i.e. galvanic) isolation is never required for a memory.

5.1.3. *Address decoding*

External address decoding is functionally identical to its internal counterpart (see section 2.2.6).

An address decoder[2] is a combinational logic operator. At the input of this operator is the address bus (or a part of it, $m' \leq m$) and control lines (o) such as address valid or clock. At the output, the address decoder provides one or more selection signals for the controller (or chip or device), generally named CS_k (for chip select), CE_k (for chip enable), G_k (for gate), sometimes E_k (for enable), as well as one or more register selection signals RS_l (register select). The presence of several selection signals (index k) for a single controller, even though only one signal is needed, is justified by the simplification of address decoding.

2 Do not confuse address decoder and logic decoder, even though a logic decoder (see section 2.4.2 of Darche (2002)) can be used for address decoding.

Several design options are available; for example, simple combinational operators (i.e. logic gates) can be used to synthesize a specific logical decoding function from the logic equation (see Exercise E2.5 of Darche (2002)), or a complex operator can be used, such as a logic decoder (see section 2.3.6 of Darche (2002)), a comparator, or even a ROM (read-only memory). Figure 5.3 shows the first case. When three address lines from an address bus are connected to a three-to-eight logic decoder, one output Y_i out of 2^3 ($i \in [0, 2^3 - 1]$) is active at the same time. When we have the combination ($Ad_4 = 1$ (LSb for least significant bit), $Ad_5 = 0$, and $Ad_6 = 1$ (MSb for most significant bit)), output Y_5 is active, here at the logic low level. Once the controller is selected, it always uses an internal logic decoder to select one register among 2^n. The register addresses usually follow one another. The least significant address lines are connected to the register selection inputs RS_l (if there are 2^n registers, then $l \in [0, 2^n - 1]$). This first approach requires decoding all addresses to avoid ghost addresses. If the addressing capacity is large, the number of components can be high.

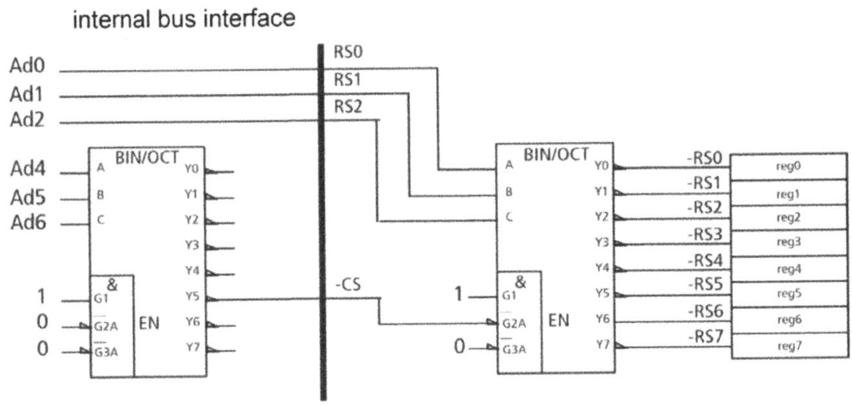

Figure 5.3. *Decoding by logic decoder*

The comparator-based solution allows generating a selection for a single address or a given set (see Figure 5.4). It presents the same drawback as before. The main interest of this solution lies in the ability to choose a selection threshold using the comparison outputs (possibly by combining them).

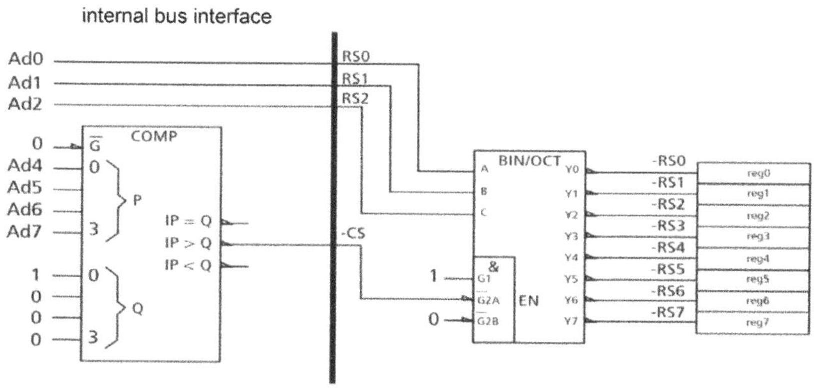

Figure 5.4. *Decoding by a logic comparator*

The final option is to write the logic equation of the decoding function and implement it in discrete or integrated form (programmable logic circuit or memory) using simple logic operators. Figure 5.5 shows the second suggestion, where each memory cell in the decoding memory contains a minterm[3] of the function.

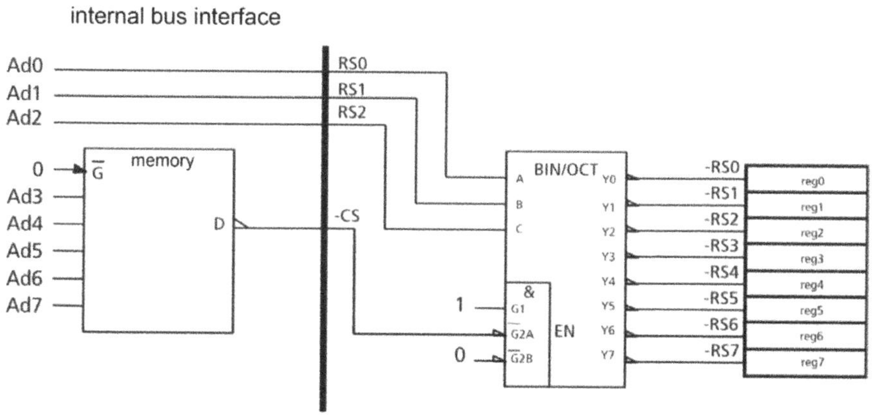

Figure 5.5. *Decoding by ROM*

The use of a comparator allows programming the base address by modifying the binary data used for comparison. This does not mean it is impossible with other

3 A minterm is a p-term (logical product (AND) of logical variables) of degree n (Boolean function of n variables). See section 1.4 of Darche (2002).

solutions, but in the case of a full logic equation solution, for example, configuration lines for the address must be added. To conclude this topic, it is also possible with these complex operators to logically combine decoding outputs so that an element is selected by more than one address. If necessary, the selection signals can be combined with other signals, such as a read–write signal or an address valid signal.

The address decoder makes it possible to select sets of addresses. If the least significant addresses are used, the addresses will be sequential. If there is a one-to-one correspondence between the address space and the set of selections, the decoding is said to be complete or absolute. Otherwise, it is a case of incomplete or ambiguous decoding with the presence of ghost addresses, which occurs when not all address lines are included in the logical decoding function before simplification. Take the example in Figure 5.6. Let there be a 4-bit address bus (n = 4) and a controller with one register to select. If the decoding function only considers address lines Ad_2 to Ad_0 the controller is selected for two addresses 2^{n-1} apart, for example, 7 and 15. If it is lines Ad_3 to Ad_1, it responds to two consecutive addresses, for example, 0 and 1.

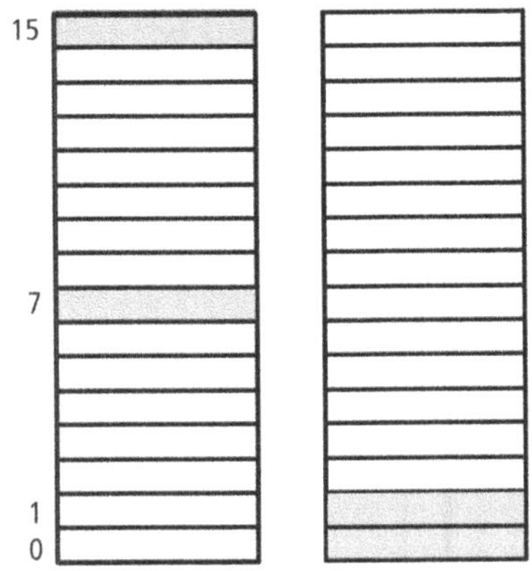

Figure 5.6. *Example of ghost addressing*

If it does not pose a problem (complete addressing not required and no address conflict with other present or future entities), this solution is then of interest because it saves logic operators and thus hardware components or chip area. The type of approach is chosen with the goal of simplifying the hardware, provided that it does not, of course, interfere with the specification and operation.

5.1.4. *Serial interfaces*

Accessing data in parallel offers many advantages such as fast data access. However, it is expensive technologically because it requires an integrated circuit package with a large number of pins and parallel buses – one for data and one for address – sized, respectively, according to the data word width n (one wire or copper trace on a printed circuit board (PCB) = one bit of the word) and the address width m, which occupy surface area on a PCB. Some applications do not require high-speed access, and cost is the main criterion. This is the case, for example, with televisions. Accessing information from time to time, such as the frequency of a channel, can be done sequentially. Serial access allows the bus width to be reduced. To access memory, the address A of the data and the command word (read or write), and possibly the data D (in the case of a write), must be sent via a serial bus. In response, an acknowledgment may be sent with data if it is a read. Serial-access memory (SAM) is a conventional memory, meaning internally organized in parallel, but the interface is of serial type (see Figure 5.7).

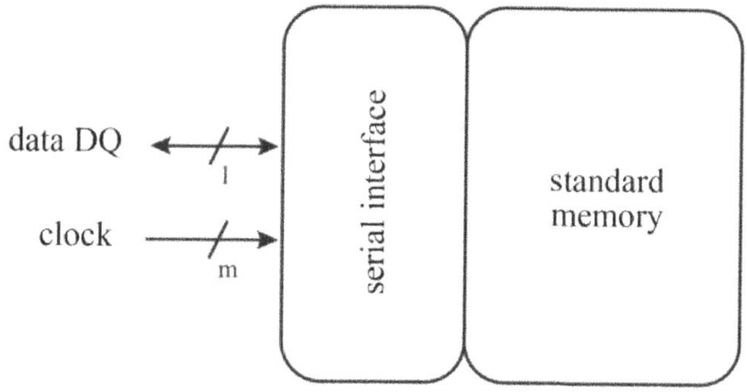

Figure 5.7. *Block diagram of a synchronous serial interface memory*

Several serial buses exist, such as the I²C (Inter-Integrated Circuit) bus from Philips (see section 8.2.3 of Darche (2003)), the Microwire™ bus from National Semiconductor and the SPI™ (Serial Peripheral Interface) bus from Motorola.

Table 5.3 summarizes some of their characteristics. The number of connections may be fixed or depend on the number s of slave nodes connected to the bus.

	Interfaces			
Characteristics	I²C	Microwire™	SPI™	eSPI
Initiator	Philips	National Semiconductor	Motorola	Intel
Number of connections	2	3 + *s* slave(s)	3 + *s* slave(s)	4 + (1 or 3)
Clock frequency (MHz)	0.1/400/1/ 3.4/5	0.25/1/2	21	20/25/33/50/66

Table 5.3. *Main characteristics of some serial buses for memory*

5.1.5. *Multiple-access memory*

Some applications, particularly those managing I/O for printing and display, for example, need to temporarily store or share information between multiple actors during an exchange, this data being stored in shared memory. The hardware solution is to have a memory with multiple inputs and outputs, also called ports, hence the name multiport memory (multiport memory or MPM) or MPRAM for multi-ported RAM. The DRAM version is naturally called MPDRAM (multiport DRAM). It belongs to a family of memories called specialty memory, also known as application-specific memory (ASM, application-specific memory). Access is also called a port. The port is generally referenced by an uppercase letter (A, B, etc.) by JEDEC or a number. There are dual-port memories (DPMs or DBMs, double-buffered memories), triple-port RAM and quad-port RAM. The dual-access model is the most common.

Figure 5.8 shows different configurations of a quad-port memory. A port can be bidirectional or unidirectional. In the latter case, only one operation is possible: read or write. The first diagram (see Figure 5.8(a)) shows a data path switch with temporary storage (buffered switch). The middle one (see Figure 5.8(b)) allows duplication of a data path (redundant data mirror). The last one (see Figure 5.8(c)) mixes data paths.

Van Sas et al. (1993) shows the difference in circuit diagram between a standard SRAM cell (see Figure 5.9(a)), an SRAM with differentiated input/output (single-buffered memory or SBM, Figure 5.9b) and a double-buffered memory (DBM; Figure 5.9(c)).

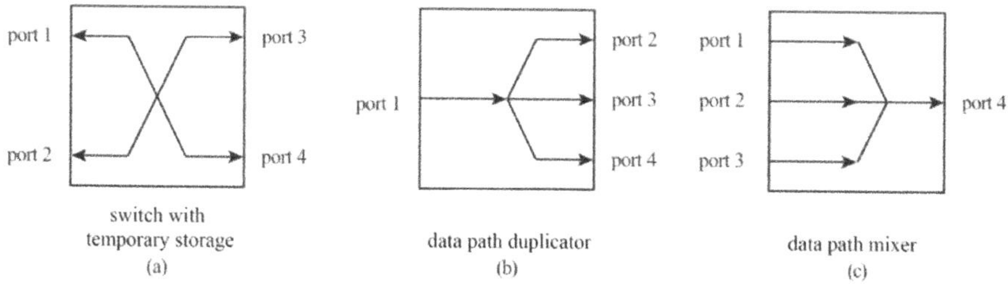

Figure 5.8. *Different configurations of a quad-access memory*

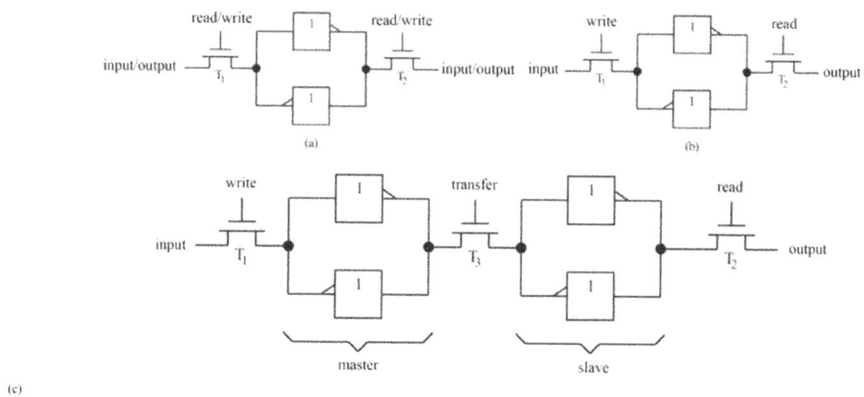

Figure 5.9. *Electronic difference at cell level between three types of memory (according to Van Sas et al. (1993))*

Two commercial examples are QDR SSRAM and NetRAM (network RAM). The QDR version has separate clock signals (K and #K and C and #C) for each unidirectional write and read port. NetRAM has separate bidirectional ports and a common clock signal (Clk).

These shared-content memories are used in communication interfaces (especially networks), data acquisition and playback interfaces with processing generally by a digital signal processor (DSP), and bus bridges. They are also used in video interfaces under the name VRAM (video RAM; see Volume 7). Video memory is a combination of a RAM and a SAM (serial-access memory) with separate ports. In a display interface, it is inserted between the controller and the digital-to-analog converter (DAC; see section 3.5.1 of Darche (2003)) for the analog version or the external interface for the logic version. That is why it is also called dual-ported video RAM. It can also appear as a set of 116 32-bit registers inside a microprocessor such as the SPARC (scalable processor architecture) V9 with ten read ports and four write ports as described (Asato et al. 1995).

Figure 5.10 presents a functional view[4] of a DPRAM (double port RAM). Around a conventional organization are added a double input–output logic and an arbiter responsible for managing concurrent accesses. The memory core is an SRAM (not shown).

Concurrent reads from the same memory cell (i.e. at the same time) pose no problem. However, for concurrent writes to the same cell, only one actor must be allowed access to the memory. It is necessary to have access arbitration logic, also called busy logic, composed of common address detection logic and a cross-coupled arbitration latch. The first element, based on a logic comparator, determines which side to authorize, and the second grants the effective permission to communicate to that side. Wyland (1988) described such a device.

A variant to ensure atomic write access is the semaphore, a mechanism that guarantees atomic access to a resource. It was invented by Dijkstra (1965). The concept is directly inspired by the semaphore used in naval or land transmissions of information from the 18th century. It is a protected variable that restricts access to a resource, here the memory.

Figure 5.11 presents a hardware implementation of a binary semaphore that controls access to the industrial memory IDT7005 from the company IDT. The two D flip-flops store the access requests, and an RS flip-flop acts as the arbiter. After the lock request, the semaphore must be read to know whether the request was granted. The binary data comes from line D_0 of the data bus. Addressing comes from lines A_0 to A_2 of the address bus. This component has eight such devices.

4 The diagram of the functional organization is not the layout of an actual implementation. Its purpose is to aid understanding and, in particular, to show the different relationships that exist between the logical subsets and the data (datapath) and address (address path) paths. See section 3.2.2.1 of Darche (2021a).

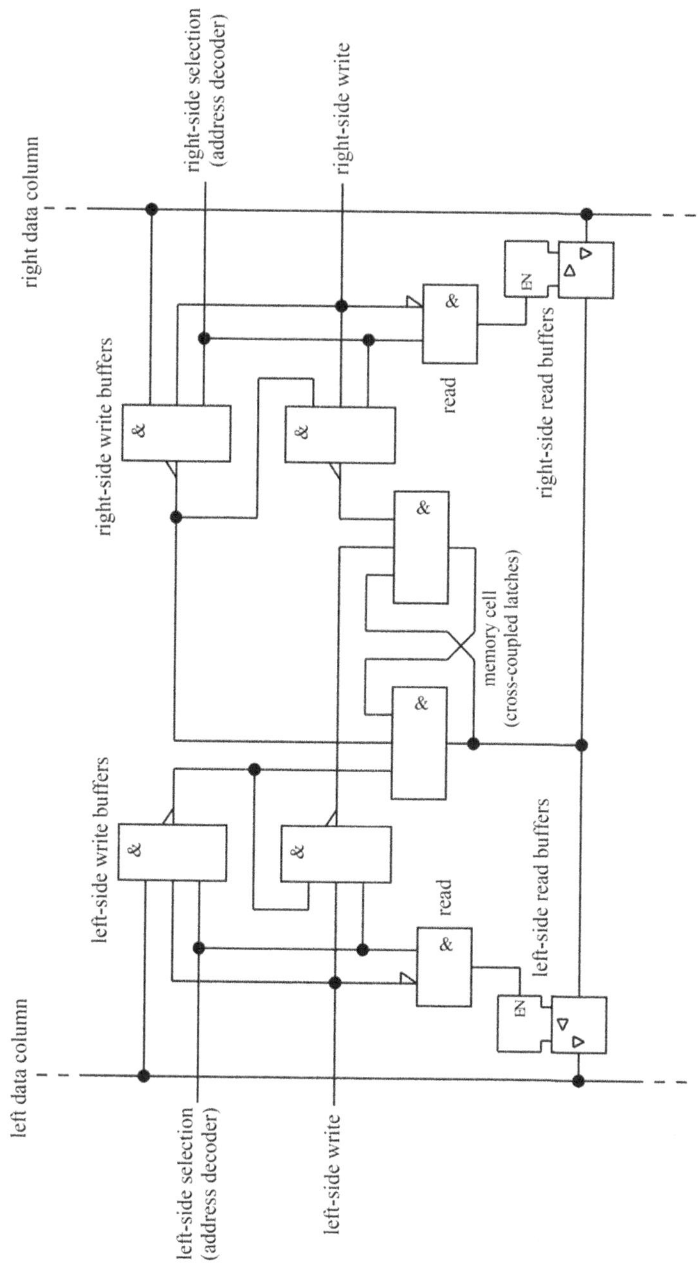

Figure 5.10. *Logic for dual access to a memory cell*

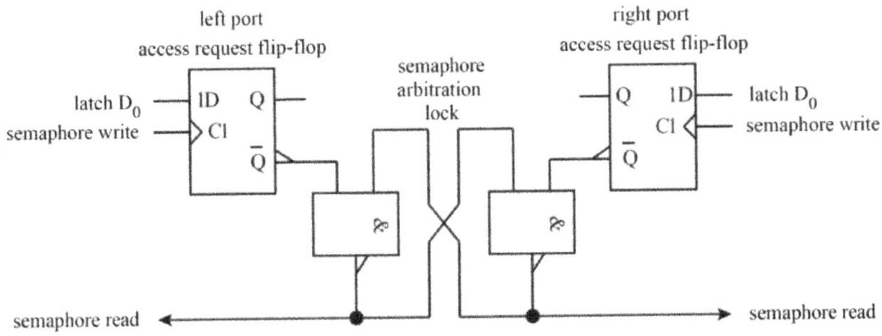

Figure 5.11. *Semaphore for atomic access to memory*

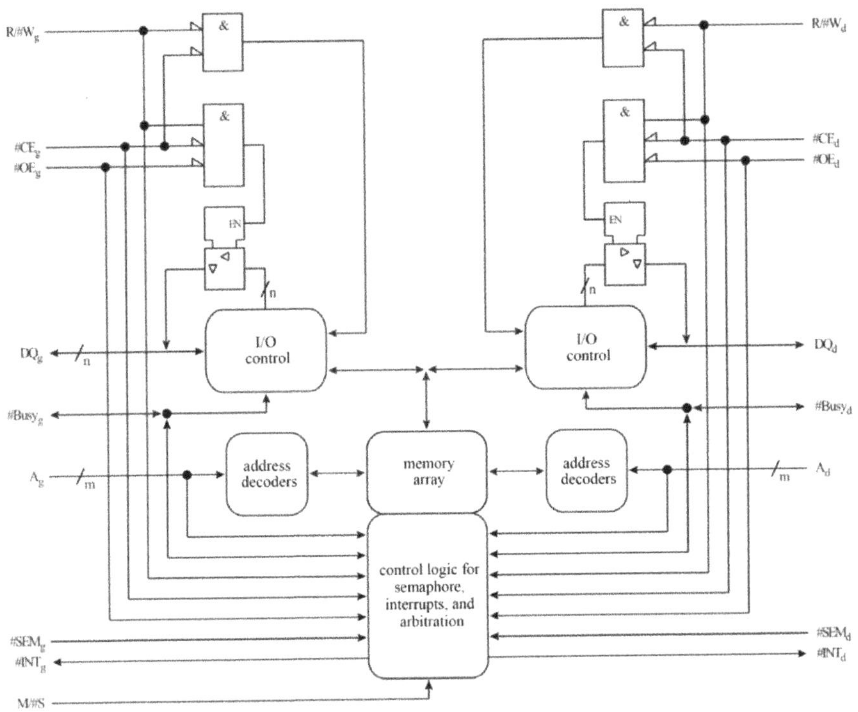

Figure 5.12. *Internal organization of the dual-access memory IDT7005*

This component has other interesting operating modes such as a mailbox (message center), access conflict management logic (busy logic), data width expansion capability and semaphore flags. The first function allows a message to be sent from one port to the other by generating an interrupt request to inform the receiver that a message has been sent. To do this, the last two locations are reserved for message storage. The main disadvantage is that two addresses are blocked for this use, while communication via semaphore is transparent. The busy logic manages simultaneous accesses in hardware by allowing only one port and alerting the other by activating a busy signal. The component can operate as master or slave, thus allowing parallelization of data I/Os.

Figure 5.12 shows the details of this memory combining these two logic subsets. It has two memory ports with independent access (address, control and DQ lines separated). The #SEM signal enables the semaphore. The #INT signal is the interrupt indicator (INTerrupt). The M/#S signal configures a memory as master or slave in an extended architecture by directing the #Busy signal (an output if master, an input otherwise). The #Busy signal indicates the occupation of the other memory port. It is possible with external logic to expand the data format or capacity of the memory.

A "transparency" function allows the information to pass through (pass-through feature) without being stored. Figure 5.13 shows the block diagram of a NetRAM. Note the presence of registers containing the start and end buffer addresses, hence the name PAM (pointer-addresses memory).

Multi-access reading poses no problem. In other cases, a protocol must be defined. For the CY7C1301A, reading is done prior to writing in the case of a simultaneous read–write request. If two write requests occur simultaneously, only one is allowed. For a simultaneous write request, only one is performed.

Several implementation approaches are possible. True multiport access is when read or write operations are independent (true multiport memory). It is possible to use the banked approach (see section 4.3) or similar, such as BRAM (block RAM), with the "banked" version (banked multiport memory architecture) having as many input/output ports as banks. It allows high I/O throughput through interleaving (see section 5.2.4.). Also worth mentioning are the stream-buffered memory architecture, streaming multiport memory architecture or multi-pumping, with p buffered input/output ports and a single memory, and the replicated version (replicated multiport memory architecture) with one write port connected to p independent memory zones, each with a read port. All memories store the same information. The version with a cache, or cached multiport memory, associates a single-port memory with a cache to serve requests. Volume 7 on specialty memories will detail their organizations.

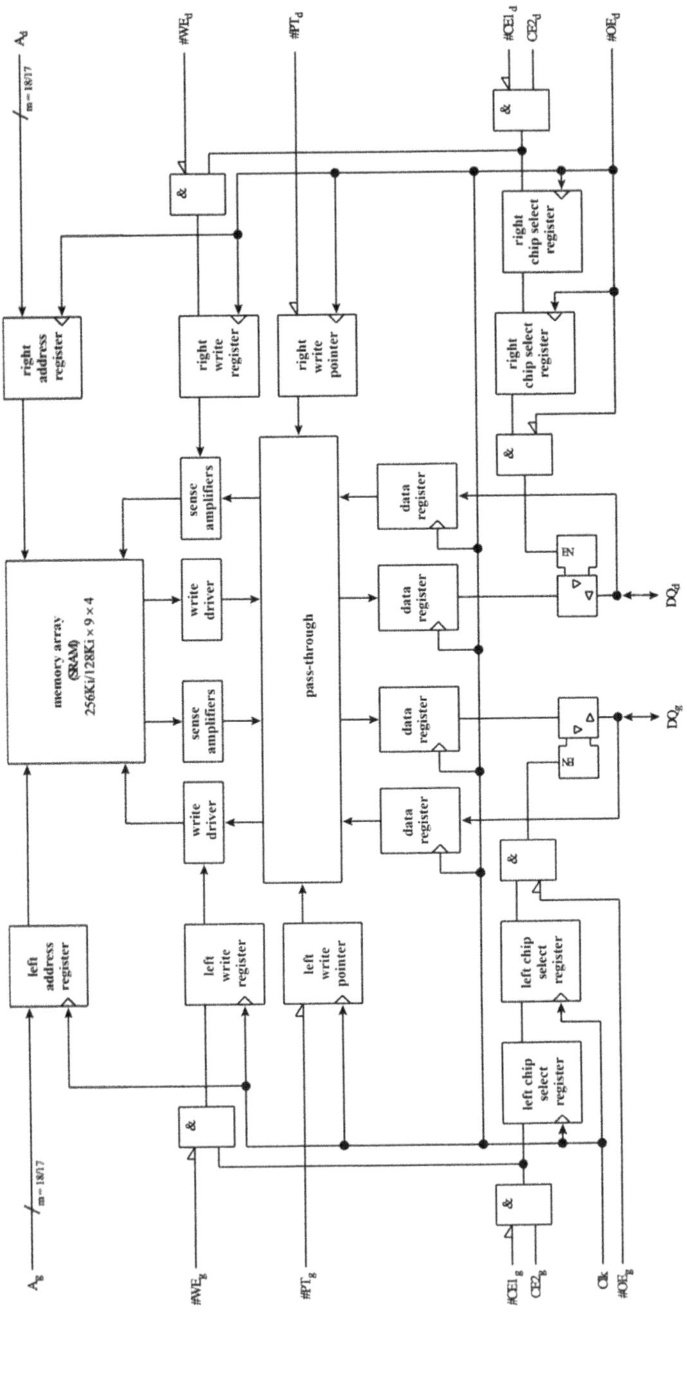

Figure 5.13. *Functional organization of a NetRAM referenced as CY7C1301A (Cypress Semiconductor Corp.)*

5.2. External performance improvements

Manufacturers offer generic components with fixed format, timing and electrical characteristics and interfaces. The designer may wish to adapt the memory format to that of the computer's data path. Its latency must also be adapted to that of the processor or, at least, be as small as possible. Moreover, in some applications such as multimedia, it is necessary to provide the highest possible data throughput.

5.2.1. *Data width increase*

If a single component is not enough to achieve the desired format *n*, it is possible to externally extend it (width expansion) by assembling several memory data I/Os, while the address lines are shared. Figure 5.14 gives an example of assembling *n* memories M_i ($i \in [0, n - 1]$) with 1-bit format to extend the subset to *n* bits. These *n* memories are now soldered on a small PCB, the whole called a "memory module" (see Volume 2). This module then behaves as a single memory with format *n*. The idea can be pushed further by using a main memory with data width greater than the processor's, for example, $2 \times n$ for an *n*-bit processor. In this case, bandwidth is doubled. In the general case, it is multiplied by a factor *k* if the format is equal to $k \times n$.

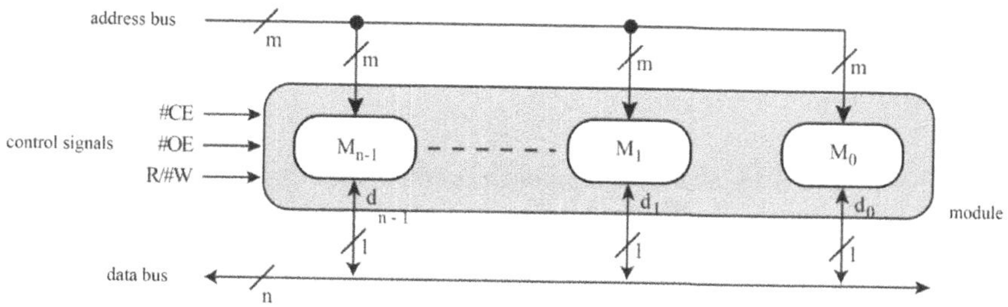

Figure 5.14. *Grouping of n 1-bit format memories to increase data width to n bits*

Examples include the synchronous graphics RAM SGRAM GDDR5 (JEDEC 2009), which has a data width of 128 bits per channel.

Widening the data format requires more traces on the PCB. This trace density causes routing issues and electromagnetic compatibility (EMC) problems in particular.

5.2.2. *Capacity increase*

A single memory is generally not sufficient to reach the main memory capacity, requiring multiple chips (depth expansion). Using them in parallel forces the designer to connect them via a bus. Figure 5.15 presents an example. Each chip is selected via a #CE selection signal generated by an address decoder or a subset of it in the case of tree-based decoders to limit hardware (HW). The output is controlled by a shared output enable signal #OE. The address for each memory chip has format m', with the relation $m = q + m'$.

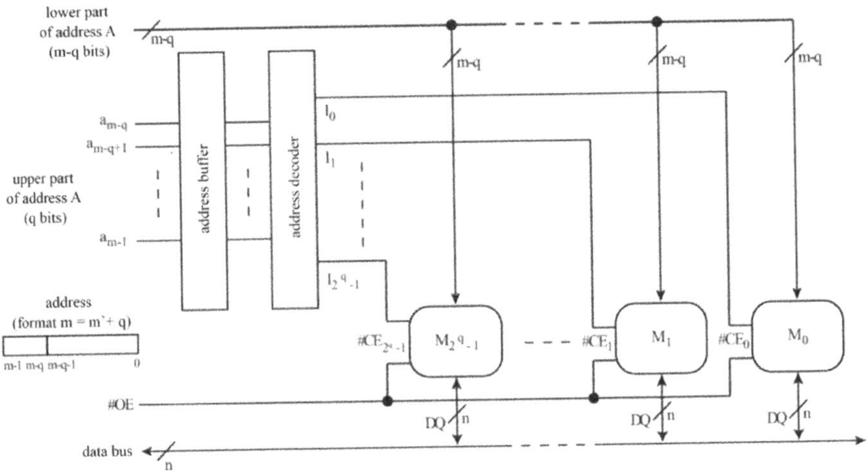

Figure 5.15. *Standard connection of memories on a data bus*

Poppendieck and Desautels (1977) study other memory expansion techniques based on memory mapping such as associative mapping, index mapping, base register and bank switching.

5.2.3. *Rank organization*

By combining the two previous concepts, data width and capacity increase, we obtain an assembly called a "rank" as opposed to an internal "bank". It could also be called an "external bank". The rank organization has its own data, control and address buses. It requires more complex management electronics than interleaved memory. The memory controller is more complex to design, since it must handle refresh, read and write for several ranks. This organization is very efficient in multiprocessor systems because accesses can be parallel (space-multiplexed parallel memories). A memory module (see Volume 2) contains one or more memory ranks. The address at the synchronous dynamic memory (SDRAM for synchronous DRAM) system level (flat mapping) is broken down as shown in Figure 5.16. If there is no gap, it is called a continuous address range; otherwise, it is a discontinuous address space.

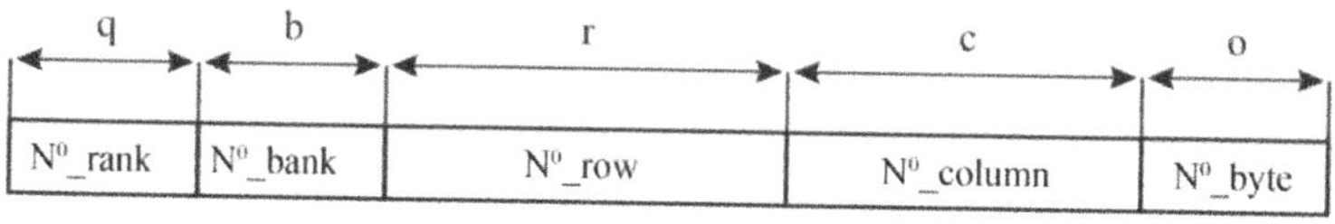

Figure 5.16. *Address breakdown at the SDRAM-type memory module level*

The problem to solve is how to compute the rank address and word address within that rank. Let there be a set of Q ranks of size $L = 2^l$ memory words. How can the mapping be done between the physical address A (continuous address range) provided by the processor without a memory management unit (MMU; see Volume 9) or from its output and the memory system address in the form (module number, address in the module), in the simplest way to implement and compute without creating a memory hole? This mapping can be computed in software or done in hardware. The details of the calculations are given in section 5.2.4.

5.2.4. *Interleaving and address offset*

Let us now use the two previous concepts to achieve interleaving. We consider a uniprocessor context; parallel architectures are studied in a later volume. Single-access memory with access time longer than the processor cycle time limits I/O performance. This problem is not new, as it existed already in the 1970s with pipelined and multiprocessor architectures. The concept of interleaved memories is a solution to this problem. Another term is stripping. Primary memory is divided into independently accessible sections (ranks). Memory address interleaving consists of sharing part of the address across multiple memory chips or modules, each distributed among one of $B = 2^b$ external banks (memory bank) or ranks of size $2^{m'}$ ($m = b + m'$). The number of external banks B, i.e. the number of independently accessed ranks, is called the interleaving degree E. The minimum number of ranks is two. There are in fact several interleaving methods. The two main ones are high-order interleaving and low-order interleaving. The terms low and high orders refer to the *b* bits of an address used for bank selection.

The first method (high-order interleaving (Rau 1979)) uses the high-order address bits as rank selectors, while the low-order bits are common to all modules. The memory space is divided into B consecutive banks. This is spatial interleaving.

The downside is poor performance for consecutive access. It resembles the capacity increase discussed in section 2.4.2.

The second method (low-order interleaving; see also Hennessy and Patterson (1994)) is the inverse of the first method. This is the principle used in the PC (personal computer). An address A is mapped to bank no. A modulo 2^b. The address A' in the selected bank is equal to A div 2^b. Access is therefore performed in parallel. Reading by the master is done sequentially. Data selection is then done using a decoder that selects the output of one of the banks using the output enable signal, as in the example in Figure 5.17 or using a multiplexer if all memory outputs are active. The latter solution is more efficient but consumes more current since all memories are selected. The chip enable signal #CE is common to all memory modules. Note that compared to Figure 5.15, the address fields have been reversed. This selection principle is similar to that of a hard disk drive (HDD), where, once the arm is positioned on a cylinder, the requested track is addressed by selecting one of the heads. There can be up to 256 external banks, as is the case in supercomputers (Raghavan and Hayes 1990).

We see that address *m* is split into m' high-order bits and *b* low-order bits (m = b + m'). The m' bits address $2^{m'}$ memories in parallel, and the *b* bits select one piece of data among 2^b. Figure 5.18 gives the example of a four-way interleaving (b = 2). Successive addresses are evenly distributed across memories. There is therefore a uniform distribution of the address space. This scheme is called sequentially interleaved memory (SIM). The memories can operate in parallel.

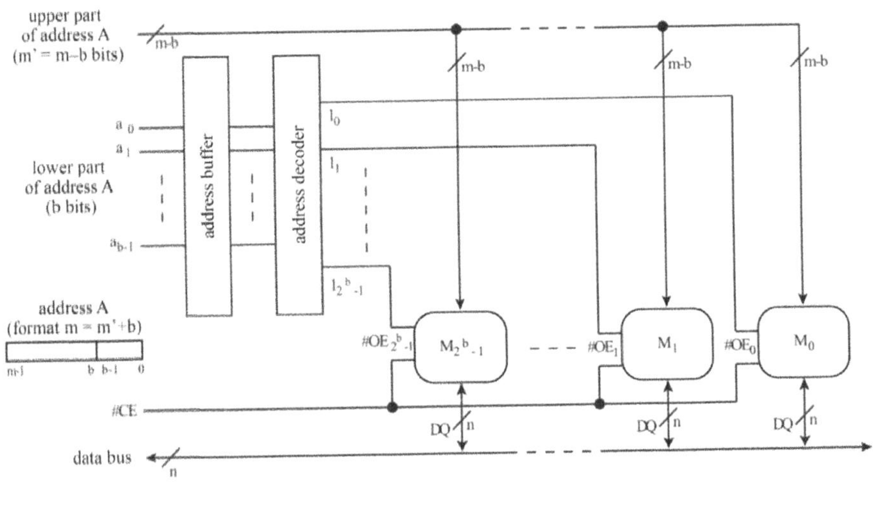

Figure 5.17. *Low-order interleaving of memories*

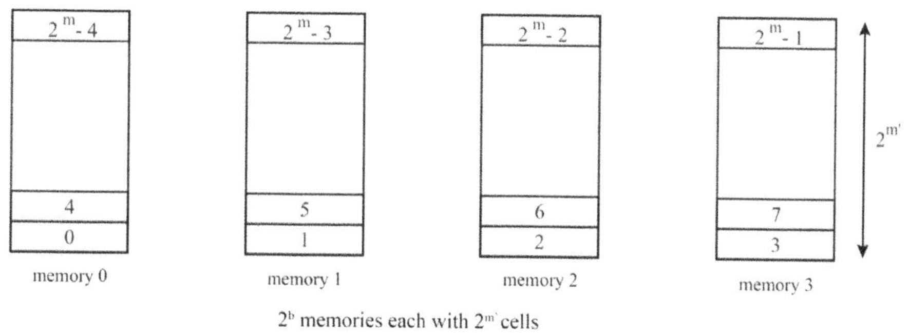

Figure 5.18. *Distribution of addresses in each interleaved memory (four-way interleaving)*

Figure 5.19 shows the timing distribution of accesses during reads in this memory. Access lasts several CPU (central processing unit) cycles. The banks operate in parallel. This is therefore a time-multiplexed access interleaving (time-multiplexed parallel memories (Seznec and Lenfant 1994)). Latency decreases for contiguous accesses without crossing boundaries. It also increases the subset's bandwidth since the base cycle time t_c of a memory is divided by E (= 2^b) in the best case. We thus have the throughput equal to:

$$\text{peak throughput}_{\text{interleaved mode}} = \text{throughput}_{\text{non-interleaved mode}} \times E \qquad [5.1]$$

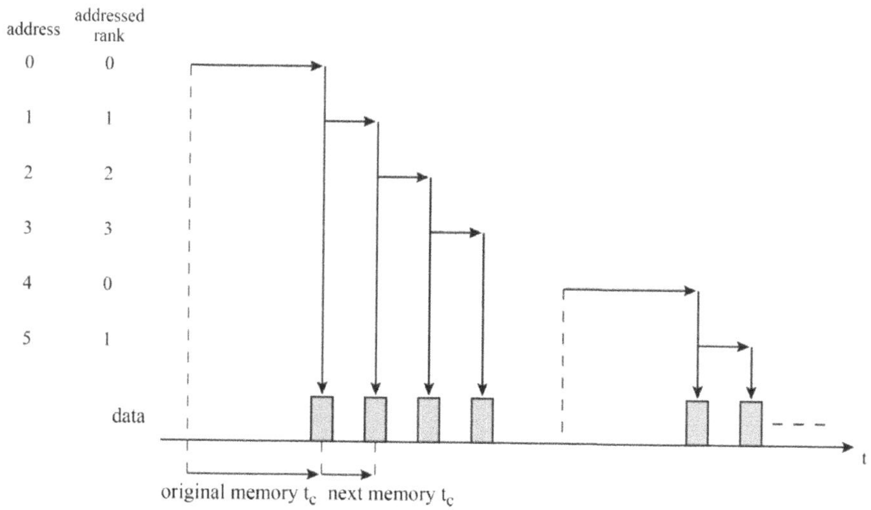

Figure 5.19. *Timing distribution of read accesses in interleaved memories*

In the case of dynamic RAM, dividing the memory area into external banks also reduces the total number of refreshes by a factor equal to the number of banks since they occur in parallel. If several ICs or banks are needed to achieve a given total capacity, this technique is therefore preferable to width increase.

Since address distribution is uniform, the solution is optimal for storing sequentially addressed data, i.e. sequential access to information. However, performance degradation is observed for certain address patterns. An example is when the address gap is a multiple of the number E of banks. The information is stored in only one bank and interleaving is then useless, with the cycle time being that of a single bank. This is the worst case. This performance loss is due to the regularity of values. In any case, transfers larger than 2^b memory words, aligned or not, lead to performance loss.

Poor performance is expected for interleaved addressing with addresses that are multiples of the number of banks. The need for integer division makes implementation significantly more complex. One solution would be to use interleaving and skewing. The memory skewing scheme described by Kuck (1968) consists of shifting the address distribution at each sweep of all the banks. As shown in the example in Figure 5.20, the first five addresses (starting at 0 for address and bank number) are distributed incrementally across the five banks. Then, a shift of two for the starting bank number is applied for the next five, etc. The shaded area marks the start of addresses for each row. The exact name is "two-way skewed five-way interleaving scheme".

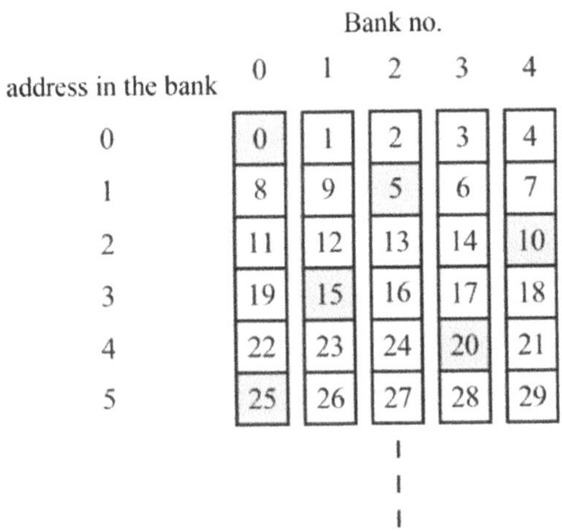

Figure 5.20. *Distribution of addresses in each skewed memory (four-way skewing)*

The general case is an interleaving of E banks with storage skewed by step P (P-way skewed E-way interleaving scheme). The formulas to compute all parameters are:

$$\text{address in bank} = \text{address A div E} \qquad [5.2]$$

$$\text{bank number offset} = (\text{address in bank} \times \text{P})\text{modulo E} \qquad [5.3]$$

$$\text{bank number (or module index)} = (\text{address A}) + \text{bank number offset modulo E} \qquad [5.4]$$

Skewed interleaving was studied by Harper and Jump (1986, 1987), who showed that a step of one (P = 1) was better with interleaving than without it. Figure 5.21 gives an example with E = 8 banks (skewed-storage eight-way interleaving scheme). Using relations [5.2]–[5.4] with P = 1, the following three formulas compute all parameters of this configuration:

$$\text{address in bank} = \text{address A div E} \qquad [5.5]$$

$$\text{bank number offset} = \text{address in bank modulo E} \qquad [5.6]$$

$$\text{bank number (or module index)} = (\text{address A} + \text{bank number offset })\text{ modulo E} \qquad [5.7]$$

address in the bank \ Bank no.	0	1	2	3	4	5	6	7
0	0	1	2	3	4	5	6	7
1	15	8	9	10	11	12	13	14
2	22	23	16	17	18	19	20	21
3	29	30	31	24	25	26	27	28
4	36	37	38	39	32	33	34	35
5	43	44	45	46	47	40	41	42
6	50	51	52	53	54	55	48	49
7	57	58	59	60	61	62	63	56

Figure 5.21. *Skewed storage interleaving with right banks*

It could be considered to use a prime number of banks (Lawrie and Vora 1982) to improve memory bandwidth (prime memory system (PMS) approach). Figure 5.22(a) shows an example of prime degree interleaving with seven banks prime degree seven-way interleaving), which can be compared with standard interleaving at E = 8 banks (see Figure 5.22(b)). The following two formulas compute all addressing parameters for the prime degree seven-bank interleaving scheme:

$$\text{address in bank} = \text{address A div E} \quad [5.8]$$

$$\text{bank number} = \text{address A mod E} \quad [5.9]$$

The following formulas compute all addressing parameters for the standard eight-bank interleaving scheme with $m = 7$ bits and $b = 3$:

$$\text{bank number} = \text{b least significant bits of A} \quad [5.10]$$

$$\text{address in bank} = \text{m} - \text{b most significant bits of A} \quad [5.11]$$

(a)

address in the bank	Bank no. 0	1	2	3	4	5	6
0	0	1	2	3	4	5	6
1	7	8	9	10	11	12	13
2	14	15	16	17	18	19	20
3	21	22	23	24	25	26	27
4	28	29	30	31	32	33	34
5	35	36	37	38	39	40	41
6	42	43	44	45	46	47	48
7	49	50	51	52	53	54	55
8	56	57	58	59	60	61	62

(b)

Bank no. 0	1	2	3	4	5	6	7
0	1	2	3	4	5	6	7
8	9	10	11	12	13	14	15
16	17	18	19	20	21	22	23
24	25	26	27	28	29	30	31
32	33	34	35	36	37	38	39
40	41	42	43	44	45	46	47
48	49	50	51	52	53	54	55
56	57	58	59	60	61	62	63

Figure 5.22. *Prime-degree interleaving schemes: sequential (a) and seven-bank (b)*

The BSP supercomputer (Burroughs Scientific Processor (Kuck and Stokes 1982; Lawrie and Vora 1982)) used such a memory system. It accepts gaps (1/B of the capacity) as shown in the example in Figure 5.23. The PMS approach may therefore not be optimal.

A solution called PPMS for perfect PMS (Gao 1993) is based on the Chinese Remainder Theorem. It chooses the bank size L and the number B of banks, which are coprime (also called relatively prime). Moreover, B is a prime number and, for implementation reasons, L is a power of 2. Addresses are given by the following formulas:

$$\text{bank number} = \text{A mod B} \qquad [5.12]$$

$$\text{address in bank} = \text{address A mod L} \qquad [5.13]$$

Figure 5.24 shows an example with B = 3 banks of size $L = 2^3$.

address in the bank	Bank no. 0	1	2
0	0	1	x
1	3	x	2
2	x	4	5
3	6	7	x
4	9	x	8
5	x	10	11
6	12	13	x
7	15	x	14

Figure 5.23. *Prime-degree memory system with capacity loss*

address in the bank	Bank no. 0	1	2
0	0	16	8
1	9	1	17
2	18	10	2
3	3	19	11
4	12	4	20
5	21	13	5
6	6	22	14
7	15	7	23

Figure 5.24. *An example of a PPMS system (B = 3 and L = 8)*

Another scheme could be the approach using an irreducible polynomial (I-Poly interleaving scheme or polynomial interleaving modulo an irreducible polynomial) to compute the bank index. For example, using the polynomial $x^4 + x + 1$ (polynomial 19; see section 6.7.2.1. of Darche (2000)), this gives Figure 5.25.

Other interleaving policies exist, for example, based on a pseudo-random distribution of consecutive addresses (pseudo-randomly interleaved memories (PRIM) schemes) as proposed by Rau (1991), which uses a function based on an exclusive OR (XOR; see section 2.2.10 of Darche (2002)). An implementation is used by Zhang et al. (2000), which the authors call permutation-based page interleaving. It is detailed in Volume 4. See also Raghavan and Hayes (1990) for more information.

address in the bank \ Bank no.	0	1	2	3	4	5	6	7	8	9	10	11	12	13	14	15
0	0	1	2	3	4	5	6	7	8	9	10	11	12	13	14	15
1	19	18	17	16	23	22	21	20	27	26	25	24	31	30	29	28
2	38	39	36	37	34	35	32	33	46	47	44	45	42	43	40	41
3	53	52	55	54	49	48	51	50	61	60	63	62	57	56	59	58
4	76	77	78	79	72	73	74	75	68	69	70	71	64	65	66	67
5	95	94	93	92	91	90	89	88	87	86	85	84	83	82	81	80
6	106	107	104	105	110	111	108	109	98	99	96	97	102	103	100	101
7	121	120	123	122	125	124	127	126	113	112	115	114	117	116	119	118
8	139	138	137	136	143	142	141	140	131	130	129	128	135	134	133	132
9	152	153	154	155	156	157	158	159	144	145	146	147	148	149	150	151

Figure 5.25. *Irreducible polynomial interleaving scheme defined by $P(x) = x^4 + x + 1$*

In summary, interleaving is simple to implement. Its management is mainly hardware-based. It is very effective, especially for burst access (i.e. sequential access), as in the case of cache (see Volume 9) with banked memory access. In a write-through policy, interleaving the main memory provides significant access time gains. The access time is that of a bank for the first access or when crossing a bank boundary. Otherwise, it equals the output enable time or the selection time of one multiplexer path. However, it does not consider the types of programs to be executed after storage in main memory, nor how the memory is used. First comes the operating system (OS), then the user's applications. Burnett and Coffman (1970) recommend, for example, separating instructions and data at the memory level. Access performance must also consider the spatial locality of the data and its frequency of use (temporal locality; see the cache concept in Volume 8). The interleaving concept is updated in Volume 4, which details its implementation with

SDRAM. The access policy, i.e. the order of access request sequencing, is important. That is why memory controllers (see Volumes 3 and 4) are beginning to consider it. This policy is inefficient for random accesses. The modulo interleaving policy is difficult to implement, but it offers better performance for sequential and random accesses. The interleaving technique can also be implemented internally. The page access mode (see Volume 3) of DRAM is one example.

5.3. Coupling

Coupling defines the proximity of a memory to a processing element or unit (PE/PU). A directly/tightly coupled memory or TCM is a fast memory with deterministic timing. It has low latency, allowing a processor to avoid slowdowns. Its addressing is standard (i.e. random). It is therefore not a cache. Volume 8 details this type. In contrast, a loosely coupled memory or LCM is shared among multiple masters in a distributed system.

5.4. Conclusion

This chapter presented the external aspects of a memory component or system. It first examined interfacing with a processor. The control signals of a generic component were detailed. The electrical aspect with signal conditioning and the logical aspect with address decoding were discussed. To conclude this first part, the concepts of serial and multiple access were addressed.

The second part focused on improving performance in terms of throughput, capacity and latency. Several techniques external to the component can be implemented, such as increasing the data word size n or the total capacity and organizing in rows. Accessing memory with a word of format $k \times n$ (see section 2.4.1) multiplies throughput by a factor of k. The drawback is a wider memory bus, which occupies more space on a motherboard PCB. The use of external banks (see section 4.3) or rows allows for independent accesses. Each row has its own buses or channels. The memory controller in the case of DRAM is more complex to design, but accesses can occur in parallel. The technique of address interleaving reduces access time and increases throughput.

The next chapter defines additional concepts related to information storage such as framing, storage order, layout and error detection/correction.

6

Additional Concepts

When a memory interacts with an exchange master, i.e. a processor or an exchange controller such as the direct memory access controller (DMA), operating issues can arise.

The increase in the overall information processing format (i.e. data, instruction code and address) has consequences for memory access. The format of various generations of microprocessors (MPU for microprocessor unit) has evolved from the original 4 and 8 bits to 16, 32 and then 64 bits and, for graphics processors (GPU for graphics processing unit), for example, with their VLIW (very long instruction word) architecture, to 128, 192, 256 and 384 bits. Since memory is generally organized in smaller word sizes, this raises the issue of aligning data larger than a byte in primary memory, which is organized in bytes, and the order in which information is stored.

With the increase in total capacity and the reduction in minimum feature size of electronic chips, or simply in harsh environments, such as those involving temperature or radiation, the problem of hardware and software errors has emerged. It thus became necessary to implement first error detection and then correction mechanisms for one or more errors.

This chapter now details these additional concepts related to information storage in memory (alignment, storage order and layout) and its integrity, which relies on error detection and correction (EDAC).

6.1. Data alignment

The problem of alignment can arise when a processor moves from an 8-bit datapath (see section 3.2.2.1 of Darche (2021a)) to a multiple of the byte ($k \times 8$ bits, with k an integer > 1) while its primary memory remains organized by byte. Indeed, if a processor accesses a memory word whose address causes it to straddle two 8k-formatted storage units (example in Figure 6.1), it must perform two memory accesses to retrieve the entire word. This increases latency accordingly. There may also be a consequence during a segment size limit check, reducing the segment size by one word (see Volume 9).

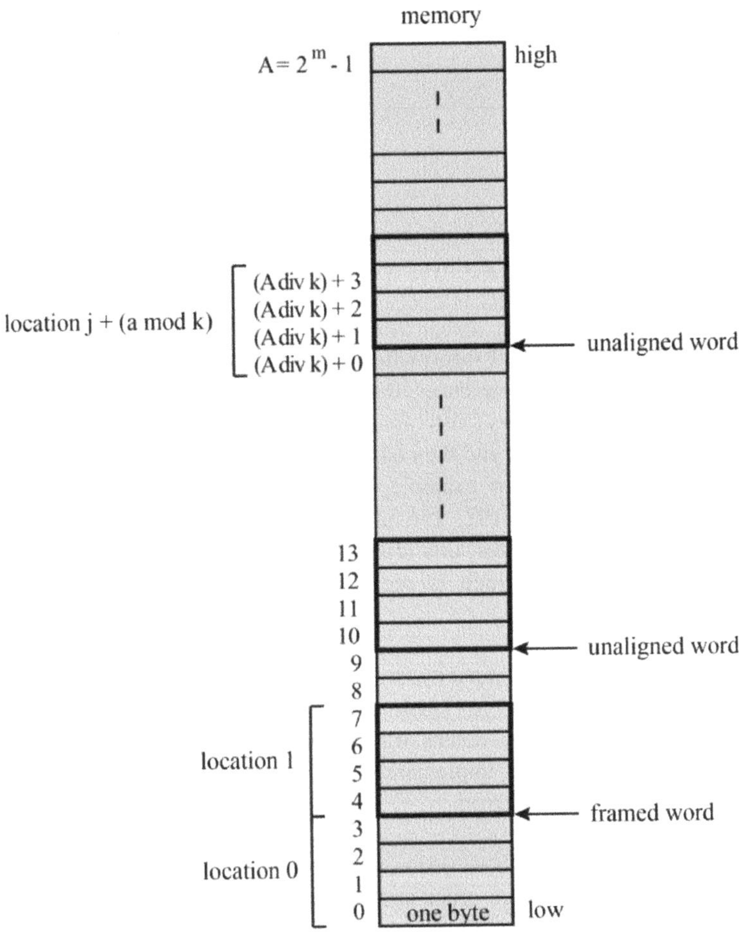

Figure 6.1. *Example of aligning a 32-bit memory word in a memory space organized by byte*

More generally, the alignment problem occurs when information in ($k \times n$) format, with k an integer > 1, is stored in a memory with format n. Alignment is verified by the following equation:

$$\text{address modulo alignment} = 0 \qquad [6.1]$$

Alignment simplifies memory access. One example of use is the MIPS (microprocessor without interlocked pipeline stages (Hennessy et al. 1982)) RISC (reduced instruction set computer, see section 1.2 of Darche (2021c)) architecture. The trade-off is a larger generated code size than in a version with misalignment. A misaligned access of an operand during access may incur an execution time overhead, as with the x86 family. There is also the compilation directive *#pragma align* in the C language, which enforces alignment of the generated machine code.

6.2. Information storage order: a matter of endianness!

There is a hardware-level addressing model that affects the byte storage order in memory, known as endianness. There are two storage methods called little-endian (LE) and big-endian (BE). The origin comes from the book *Gulliver's Travels* by Jonathan Swift (1726). In it, Gulliver lands on the island of Lilliput, where two communities clash over how to crack an egg. The BEs crack the egg at the big end ("It is computed that eleven thousand persons have, at several times, suffered death rather than submit to break their eggs at the smaller end") and the LEs crack it at the small end. These two terms were reused by Cohen (1981) to define the two ways of storing data in memory. BE means the most significant byte is stored first (big-end-first), and LE means the least significant byte is stored first (little-end-first). To begin this study, we consider a byte-formatted memory, noting that the issue arises as early as at the bit level (see last paragraph of this section).

Figure 6.2 shows the two ways to store a k-byte word ($k > 1$) in a byte-formatted memory. If the data format equals that of the memory, the issue does not arise. It is trivially noted that if the format is smaller, the issue does arise (see end of this section).

Let us take several examples. The first (Figure 6.3) is storing a 32-bit word in memory using both LE and BE formats. It would be defined in C as follows:

```
int word_32bits = 0xFE876510u;
```

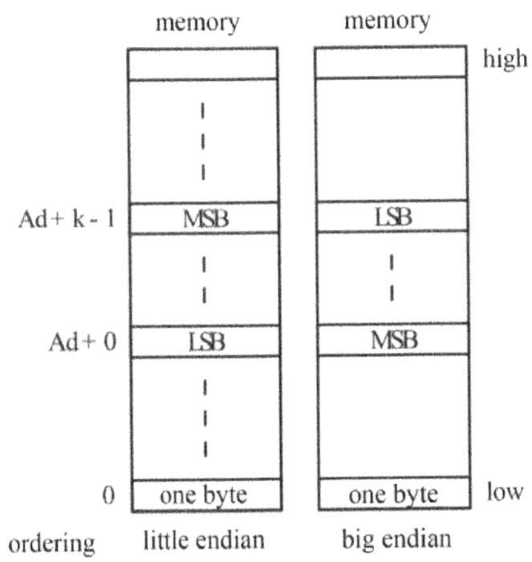

Figure 6.2. *Little-endian and big-endian storage formats*

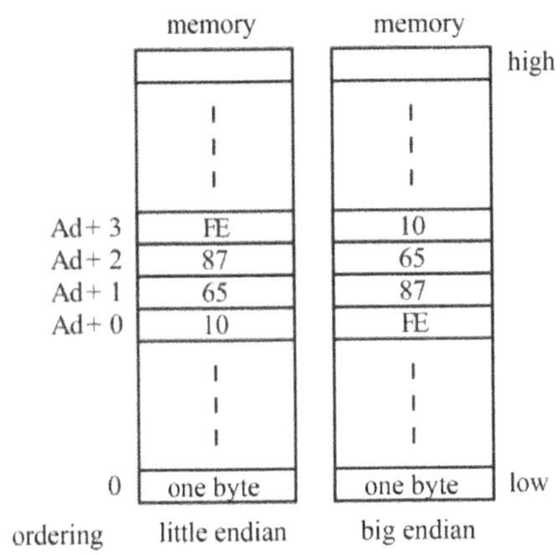

Figure 6.3. *Storing a 32-bit word (FE876510h)*

The second example (Figure 6.4) is a sequence of 8 bytes viewed as a 64-bit word, two 32-bit words and four 16-bit words. The first configuration is declared in C as follows:

```
long word_64bits = 0x1112131415161718u;
```

The next example (Figure 6.5) is splitting the previous word into two 32-bit words using the following C declarations:

int word1_32bits = 0x11121314u;

int word2_32bits = 0x15161718u;

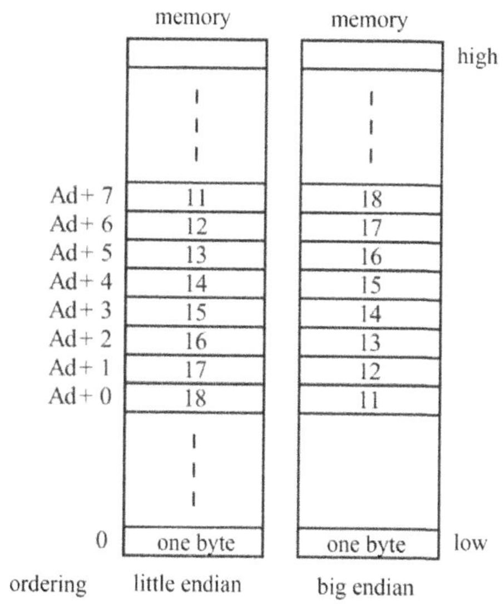

Figure 6.4. *Example of storing with a 64-bit word*

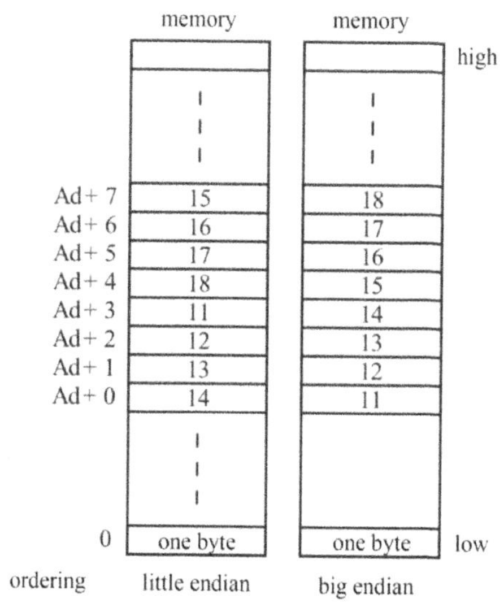

Figure 6.5. *Example of storing with two 32-bit words*

Finally (Figure 6.6), the original word is split into four 16-bit words using these declarations:

```
short word1_16bits = 0x1112u;

short word2_16bits = 0x1314u;

short word3_16bits = 0x1516u;

short word4_16bits = 0x1718u;
```

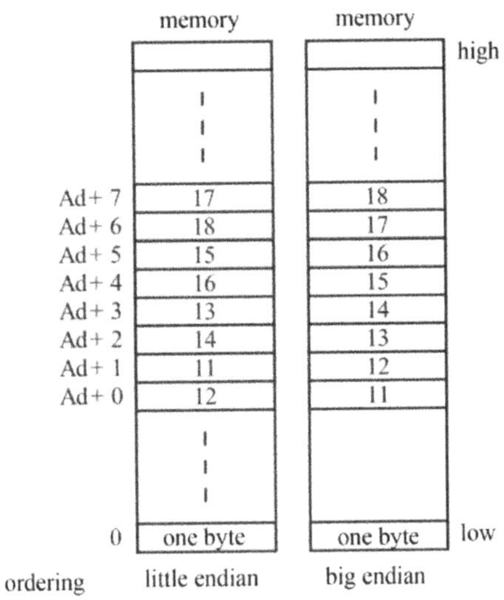

Figure 6.6. *Example with four 16-bit words*

We can observe that, regardless of the format, the left-to-right Western writing order of data is preserved in high-level programming language declarations. The benefit of BE storage is that it stores data in the order it will be read during a memory dump or assembled program, since screen or paper output is done top-to-bottom, with increasing addresses going down. This therefore makes reading easier. Motorola's MPUs (680x ($x \in \mathbb{N}$) and 68K families) operated using this model, as did processors in many computers such as the IBM 360/370 family (Amdahl et al. 1964; Gifford and Spector 1987), the PDP-10 from Digital Equipment Corporation (DEC) (Bell et al. 1978) and many RISC microprocessors such as Sun's SPARC. Intel's 80x86 family MPUs, however, store data using LE order. DEC's PDP-11 computers and the VAX family also used the latter. Computer networking systems also follow this storage model.

These two models coexisted without issue until data exchange was needed between two processors using different modes. The origin of endianness classification stems from the problems caused, as the two models are naturally incompatible. The result is a lack of portability of data and code between two processors using different storage modes. Thus, conversion is necessary, typically at the communication layer. U.S. Patent No. 4956809 (George et al. 1990) offers a solution for transferring files between computers. The network also follows its own standard (network byte order).

Some processors support both storage modes, with a selectable operating mode. They can also automatically perform conversion using specific data-handling instructions. These are called bi-endian (BiE) processors. This is the case, for example, with Motorola's PowerPC family (Becker et al. 1993; Diefendorff 1994). There is a special model called middle endian or mixed endian, with byte orders such as 3-4-1-2 or 2-1-4-3. An example is the 32-bit floating-point model of the PDP-11. It was justified by the fact that this 16-bit machine extended its data format to 32 bits.

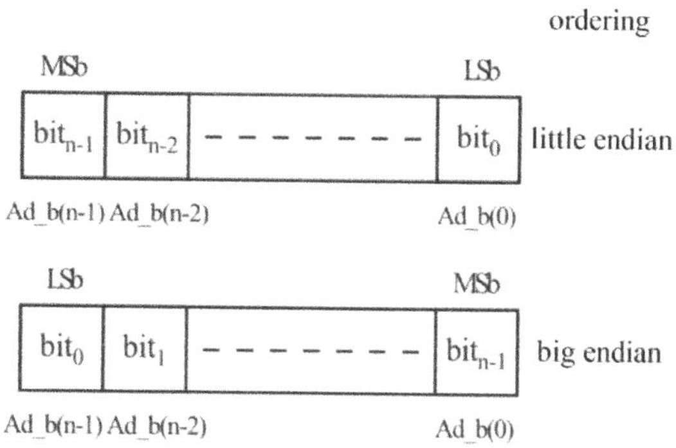

Figure 6.7. *Bit storage order in a word*

To fully explore this concept, we must go down to the atomic unit of information and storage: the bit, as shown in Figure 6.7. LE microprocessors naturally follow this order, since it is standard to represent binary numbers with the most significant bit, or MSb, on the right. The 68K is a BE processor, but its bit order is LE if we follow the official documentation's bit labels! In general, BE processors do not follow their byte order at the bit level. IBM's PowerPC, however, respects BE bit order (meaning bit b_0 is the MSb). But let us not complicate the issue further! Let us stay at the byte level, as IBM reminds us in an application note on the subject (IBM 2000).

Mixed notation involves combining both storage directions, one for the word and one for bit order within the word, as shown in Figure 6.8 (IEEE 1996). To generalize to an n-bit word, LSW and MSW stand for the least and most significant word, respectively.

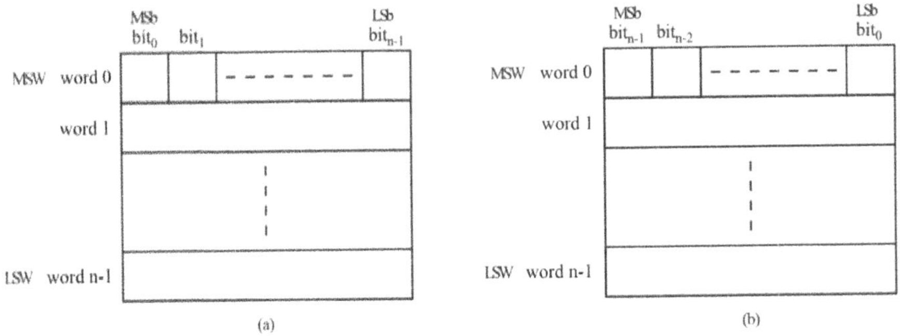

Figure 6.8. *Coherent big-endian (a) and mixed (b) models*

6.3. Memory topography of a computer system

Each computer has its memory map, also called the address map or topography. It is a diagram or list showing all addressable elements in the processor's physical address space. Primary memory obviously occupies the largest range, followed by the BIOS (basic input/output system, see the introduction of Chapter 4 of Darche (2003)). Input/output (I/O) may appear there or have a separate address space (for concepts of space and addressing, see section 2.3 of Darche (2003)).

Figure 6.9 shows that of the PC. In general, for any computer, the bottom of the memory is occupied by the operating system (OS) or kernel with a program area and a data area. Next comes the user area with programs and then data. Memory is then free. The interrupt vector table may be located at the very beginning or end of the microprocessor's address space.

There are generally two BIOSes for the PC: the system BIOS with basic I/O routines and the video BIOS of the graphics card if the graphics controller is not integrated into the north bridge chipset (see section 3.3 of Darche (2021e)).

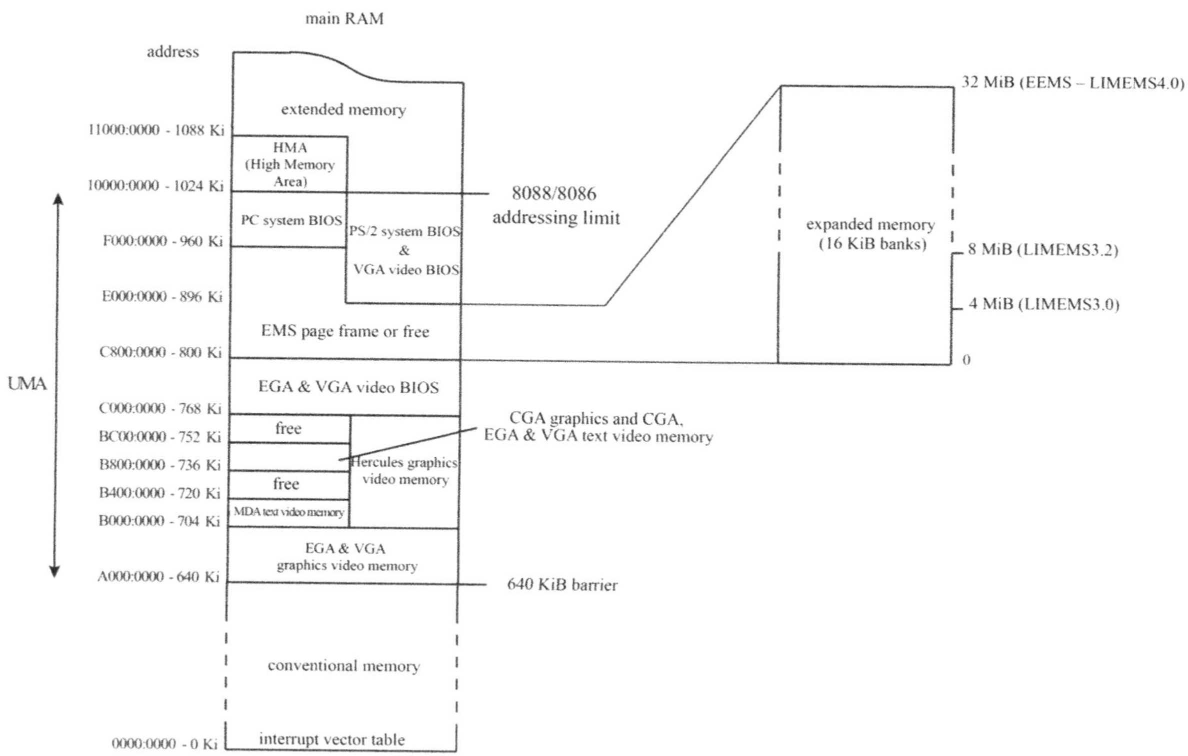

Figure 6.9. *The memory topography of the original PC-type microcomputer (see Volume 5 on microprocessors (2021b and 2021g))*

6.4. EDAC

During manufacturing, memory components can be defective. The increase in chip size or the decrease in design rule dimensions amplifies this situation. An example is a short circuit between a row and a column. Therefore, manufacturers use redundancy techniques to replace defective components. Redundant rows and columns, meaning additional ones (spare wordline or bitline), are implemented and can be activated during testing phases using laser pulses, to replace, for example, a defective line. Horiguchi (1997) detailed these techniques.

In this section, we discuss failures that may occur during operation. Memories can fail and cause hardware faults. Data then becomes corrupted. The cause can be a failure of an internal component, generally a transistor; the failure is then permanent (hard error) with a permanent logical “1” or a permanent logical “0”. The error can be transient (soft error). One cause is an electrostatic discharge or the passage of a high-energy particle from space (high-energy cosmic ray) or an alpha particle from the radioactivity of an earthly material. Cosmic radiation consists mainly of photons, neutrons and protons but also other nuclear particles such as pions and muons. It comes from our Sun (solar cosmic radiation) or distant galaxies (primary cosmic rays). It interacts with Earth’s atmosphere to generate secondary cosmic particles. Terrestrial cosmic radiation is what reaches the Earth (about 1% of primary particles). One of the first studies on cosmic radiation was conducted by Ziegler (1996). Neutrons cause errors in static random access memory (SRAM) and dynamic random access memory (DRAM), but not in flash EEPROM (electrically erasable programmable read-only memory or FEEPROM) or FRAM (Ferroelectric random access memory) (Eto et al. 1998). With the reduction of lithographic resolution λ, DRAM, due to the high capacity of its cell, has better radiation immunity than SRAM. The phenomenon of ionization of dynamic memories by alpha particles was first observed by IBM when its chips were irradiated by their packaging (Ziegler et al. 1996). The consequences can be serious. One example is the Schaerbeek error. During the federal legislative elections held in Belgium on May 18, 2003, a discrepancy of 4,096 votes between voters and registrants was detected in Schaerbeek. The election oversight commission concluded a likely spontaneous and random inversion of the 13th bit of the vote counter ($4,096 = 2^{12}$) (Expert Committee 2003) due to a cosmic ray. Think about the consequences of this type of error in an embedded system (ES) controlling an aircraft or spacecraft (for more technical information, see May and Woods (1979) and Yaney (1979)).

To study these faults, various models exist, the most common being SSF (single-stuck fault). Among others are transition fault (TF), address fault (AF), bridging fault (BF), coupling fault (CF), pattern-sensitive fault (PSF) and dynamic or delay fault (DF) (for more details, see Sharma (2002)).

To avoid or at least minimize these types of errors, one solution is to use an error-detecting code (EDC). Even better, it is possible to correct the error once it is located (EDAC). Indeed, a bit with error is the logical complement of the same bit without error. This is made possible by using an error-correcting code (ECC). To each memory word, additional fault-tolerance information is added. An example of a code that detects an odd number of errors is parity. The PC microcomputer uses it for each word or part of a word in 8-bit format. Its internal memory is also fully tested after a reset by the self-test program called POST (power-on self-test). R.W. Hamming invented a code that corrects one error and detects two (SEC-DED: single-error correcting–double-error detecting code) based on parity (Hamming 1950). With these codes, memory fails only when the number of errors exceeds the code's correction capacity. A selection criterion for these codes is the number of detectable and correctable errors. With the development of mobile systems, a new selection criterion is minimizing power consumption, as presented in Ghosh et al. (2004). For more information on this topic, Chen and Hsiao (1984) presented a review of codes specifically used in memories.

Detection and correction are performed by hardware. The module responsible for this function is called an ECC memory checker or error correction circuit. It is placed in the data path between the MPU, downstream from the cache memory and the main memory (Figure 6.10). A simplified version of the detector is error detection during writing without storing the information in memory, saving memory space. This approach cannot detect internal memory errors. It checks that the data path is not altered. This technique is called "fake parity".

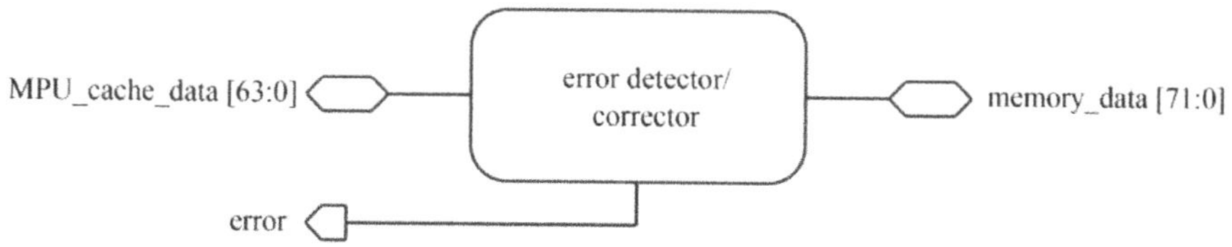

Figure 6.10. *Positioning of the error detector/corrector in a 64-bit data path*

Figure 6.11 shows a parity-based error detector (one bit per byte). During writing, an EDC generator increases the path width by generating a check word. During reading, an error controller checks the data using that word. An error bit is then generated. Read and write signals have been arbitrarily separated for clarity.

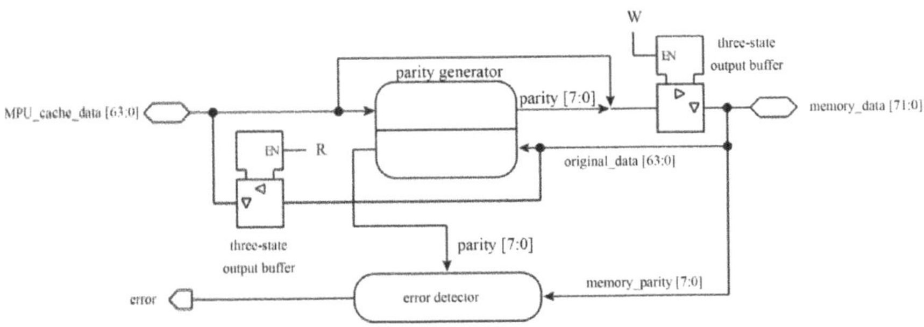

Figure 6.11. *Diagram of an error detector (n = 64)*

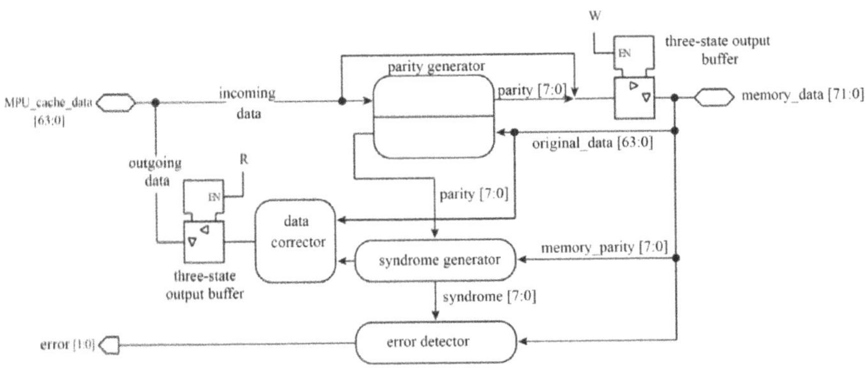

Figure 6.12. *Diagram of an error detector and corrector (n = 64)*

To correct the error, a syndrome generator must be added to the detector to allow data correction (Figure 6.12). The syndrome is the difference between recalculated check bits and received check bits. When a word has no error, the syndrome is the null vector $\vec{S} = 0$. In case of error(s), this vector is not null ($\vec{S} > 0$), and its value identifies the erroneous bits and allows their correction. The error detector, using the syndrome, corrects the bits in error by logically complementing them.

Originally, IBM's PC microcomputer had error detection using odd parity (one bit per byte), unlike Apple's Macintosh. If a memory error occurred, a non-maskable interrupt (NMI, see Chapter 5 of Darche (2021d)) was generated, stopping the computer with an on-screen message "Parity Check Error". This error detection was later abandoned, likely for cost reasons. Today, it is used again, mainly in servers, now with error correction. The detector/corrector is integrated with the SDRAM controller in the PC's north bridge chipset. Alternatively, it can be implemented on the memory module itself. This technology, called Chipkill, was developed by IBM

(Dell 1997). This company offered modules with an embedded ECC controller. The advantage was that it could be inserted in place of a module without error checking. The downside is the added cost since it requires extra integrated circuits specialized in correction, typically four specialized circuits or ASICs (see Chapter 4 of Darche (2004)), and correcting one byte requires four additional bits, meaning 50% more memory capacity for ECC.

The JESD-21C standard (JEDEC 2003) defines the form factor of memory modules (see section V2-3.7). For byte-format modules, there was the 9-bit model for parity only. For 16-bit models, there was the 18-bit model (one parity bit per byte). The move to 32-bit allowed error correction with acceptable efficiency (see Exercise E6.1 and section III-7 of Darche (2000)). The 32-bit family includes 36-bit (four parity bits), 39-bit and 40-bit formats for ECC. For current 64-bit models, there are 72-bit (eight parity bits) and 80-bit models for ECC. It is important to note that the total advertised capacity does not include these extra bits. Only the organization can tell us the type of EDAC. Manufacturer Elpida proposes combining the refresh controller with the error detector/corrector (Super Self Refresh (SSR) Technology).

A memory can integrate an error detector or corrector. For example, a memory chip with parity detection was introduced by Giga Semiconductor, Inc. (GSI) under the name ByteSafe™ SRAM. It includes an extra output #QE (parity error out) that signals a parity error. Being open-drain type, outputs can be paralleled to form a wired-OR (see section 2.3 of Darche (2004)) (for more information, see GSI (2000)). Another example is found in Hidaka et al. (1990), who propose a chip-integrating DRAM and a cache-like SRAM playing the role of cache memory (see Volume 8) under the name CDRAM (cache(d) DRAM, see Volume 7). An EDC (error-detecting circuit) is integrated as shown in Figure 6.13. During a write, from a 32-bit word, a parity byte is generated, and the entire 40 bits are written to memory. This means the data, including any possible errors, is stored. Only during reading is the data corrected if the error count is not too high (here one correctable and two detectable errors) and rewritten to memory

What has been described may suggest that the detection/correction information is stored in memory separate from the data memory. It is possible for memory to store this information in each of its pages (i.e. rows). This solution is called embedded ECC.

When using ECC modules, for economic reasons, it is preferable to use non-dedicated slots to store error detection/correction information. One solution is the use of mass memory units of the RAID type (redundant array of inexpensive disks, see section 7.2.2 of Darche (2003)).

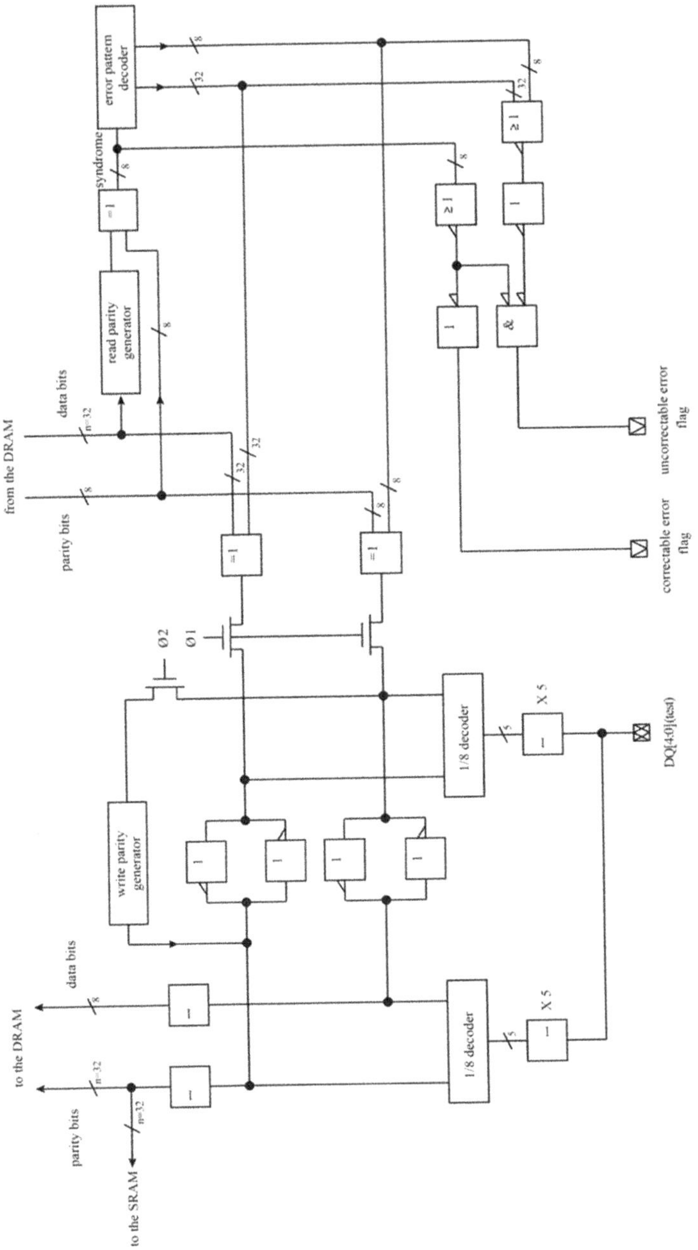

Figure 6.13. *Functional organization of the ECC circuit (according to Hidaka et al. (1990))*

A final and recent example is SGRAM (synchronous graphics RAM) in its GDDR5 (graphics double data rate) version, which integrates an error detector based on a CRC (cyclic redundancy check) code used in the header of an ATM (asynchronous transfer mode) cell. More information is provided in Volume 7.

6.5. Conclusion

This chapter introduced additional concepts such as alignment and the ordering of information in memory. Misalignment had significant performance consequences for MPU generations before the 2000s. EDAC play a crucial role in computing.

Conclusion

This first volume is dedicated to the fundamentals of memory in computers. The first chapter introduces the memory function and its general principles. In particular, both old and current technologies and the characterization of a generic memory are detailed. Then, the functional organization of semiconductor memory is studied in the following two chapters. Chapters 4 and 5 focus on internal and external organizations that improve operational speed. The final chapter addresses additional concepts related to interaction with the processor, such as alignment, ordering of information and memory topography in a system. The final section of Chapter 6 and Appendix 1 provide an introduction to the field of error detection and correction.

Volume 2 studies the static model of asynchronous SRAM (static random access memory).

Appendices

Appendix 1

Introduction to the Field of Error-Detecting and Error-Correcting Codes

A code is an injective mapping from a source set I, made up of objects or information[1] and called the set to be encoded or the source, to a target set C, called the code and made up of binary words. This mapping may also be surjective; the code is then a bijection. Otherwise, the lack of surjectivity is used, particularly in protective codes, to make it difficult to recover the original element. The source alphabet is a set of numeric or alphanumeric symbols (letters, digits, punctuation marks, etc.). The code alphabet is the set of binary symbols. The binary word is called a codeword, and the set C of codewords forms the code. Encoding is the operation that encodes an element from the source set I, and decoding is the reverse operation. Transcoding is the operation that converts one code into another.

The sagittal diagrams in Figure A1.1 show our point in the field of alphanumeric codes, i.e. codes that represent alphanumeric data (lowercase and uppercase alphabetic characters (case), decimal digits and other symbols (punctuation, currency, mathematical symbols, etc.)) in a machine. The subscript indicates the base of the representation, in this case hexadecimal.

Other families of codes exist depending on their domain of use. Numeric or numbering codes are used to represent numbers from different sets ($\mathbb{N}$, $\mathbb{Z}$, $\mathbb{D}$, etc.). The instruction code encodes the instructions of a processor's instruction set (IS, see Chapter 2 of Darche (2021d)). Other codes are suited to more complex information such as sound, image or video. Other families are adapted to the channel, such as codes designed to reduce errors, memory space or communication bandwidth. These include error-detecting and possibly error-correcting codes and information

1 Here, the term "information" is taken in the broad sense. It can represent a datum, an instruction, or an address in the field of microprocessors and memories.

compression codes. Cryptographic codes are used to secure stored or transmitted information. Figure A1.2 shows our discussion.

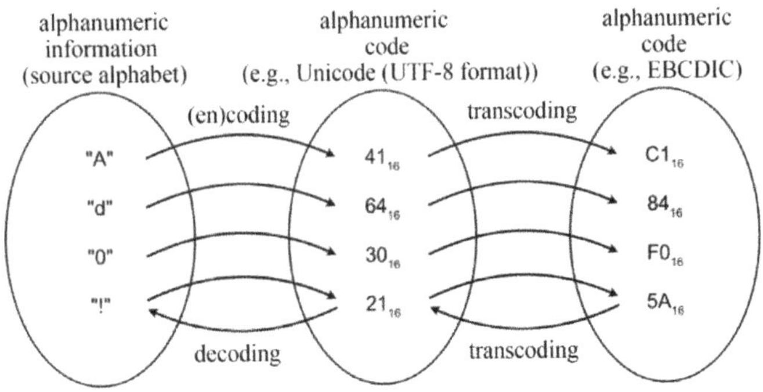

Figure A1.1. *Encoding of alphanumeric information*

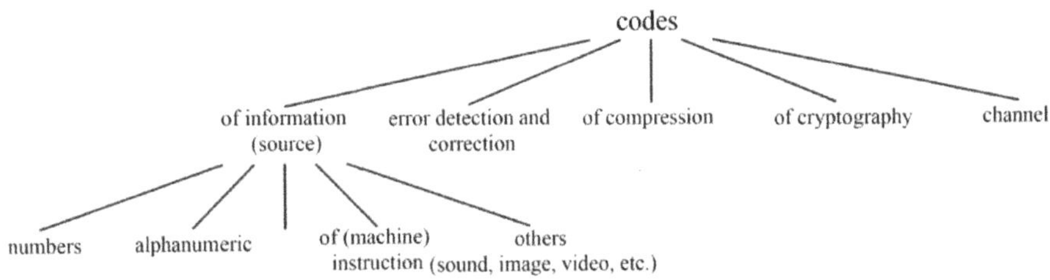

Figure A1.2. *Simplified classification of code families in computer science*

Errors can be introduced during the handling of encoded information. During communication between two entities, for example, between a microprocessor (MPU) and a memory, there may be permanent or temporary disturbances that can cause data transmission errors. Another example is the storage of information in primary or mass memory. A cosmic ray in the first case, or a media defect in the second, can cause one or more errors. Errors can be independent or occur in bursts (burst error).

The purpose of error-detecting codes is to check the validity of information. The basic principle relies on information redundancy. Indeed, it is necessary to add information that allows this detection.

Several solutions are possible. The earliest approaches used information redundancy, such as doubling or even tripling the information. Current classical approaches include detection of illegal codewords or adding so-called control data. These control data are the result of mathematical computations on the data.

This appendix begins with an example of illegal codeword detection using p out of n codes. Then, after the basic definitions, we examine simple detection codes based on logical parity. Finally, we address the concept of cyclic codes.

A1.1. A simple encoding: p out of n codes

The basic idea is to transform, in case of error(s), a codeword into an invalid word, i.e. one not belonging to the code. Thus, error detection becomes easy. The p out of n codes (other names: n choose p, p over n) allow checks since only codewords with p bits set to 1 are valid. If an error occurs, the "n choose p" rule is no longer satisfied and the resulting word does not belong to the code.

A1.1.1. *Example*

Let us take the 2 out of 5 code (Table A1.1). A word in this code always has 2 bits set to 1 among the 5 it contains.

	Weight				
Decimal	6	3	2	1	0
0	0	0	1	1	0
1	0	0	0	1	1
2	0	0	1	0	1
3	0	1	0	0	1
4	0	1	0	1	0
5	0	1	1	0	0
6	1	0	0	0	1
7	1	0	0	1	0
8	1	0	1	0	0
9	1	1	0	0	0

Table A1.1. *Two out of five codes*

A1.1.2. *Properties*

Each combination contains two 1-digits. A weight can be assigned to each position except for the value 0, which does not follow this rule. The main drawback is the representation of the zero value, which always contains p bits set to 1. This can cause issues with zero-testing in a machine.

There are therefore $C_n^p = \frac{n!}{p!\,(n-p)!} = M$ possible codewords. The efficiency, if all codewords are used, is equal to:

$$\eta = \frac{C_n^p}{2^n} \qquad [A1.1]$$

And there are $M!$ possible encodings.

Error detection simply consists of checking that the p out of n constraint is met.

A1.2. Control block concept

The previous technique is limited in its effectiveness. A more effective approach consists of adding control data (of size c bits) to the actual information (of size d bits) as shown in Figure A1.3. The part containing the information is called "systematic", and the part on the left added by the encoder is called redundant.

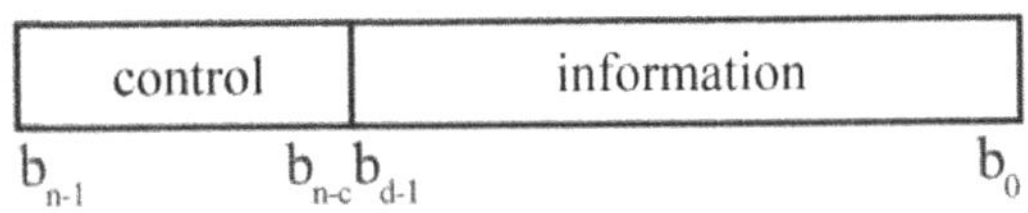

Figure A1.3. *Structure of the word*

In networking, the control block is called the FCS (frame check sequence) in the case of a cyclic code, used in the HDLC (high-level data link control – IBM) procedure. It is also called the BCC (block checking character) when a parity check is used.

Implementation occurs in the following order: generation or computation of the control data, then storing it with the original data. Verification is done by recalculating the control data on the data, then comparing it with the stored control data.

The efficiency η of this approach is given by the formula [A1.2]. An efficiency of 1 means that errors can be detected without adding extra bits. The lower the efficiency, the less effective the code is:

$$\eta = \frac{d}{c+d} = \frac{d}{n} \quad [A1.2]$$

Another measure is redundancy R, which expresses the code's efficiency (Hamming 1950). It is given by the formula [A1.3]. It is actually the inverse of efficiency. The higher its value compared to the minimum (= 1), the less effective the code is:

$$R = \frac{n}{d} = \eta^{-1} \quad [A1.3]$$

There is algebraic coding, also called block coding, and convolutional coding, also called recurrent or continuous coding. In the first case, the control applies directly to a block of fixed-size data. In the other case, the encoding generates control data from both current and past data. We only study the first case, as recurrent codes fall outside the scope of this book.

The Hamming weight of a codeword of length n is defined as the number of 1s it contains. The Hamming distance D between two codewords is the number of binary digits in which they differ. Figure A1.4 shows an example of distances between four words of size n = 4. Unit distance codes (D = 1), such as the Gray code (Gray 1953), are useful when transitioning from one value to another must occur unambiguously.

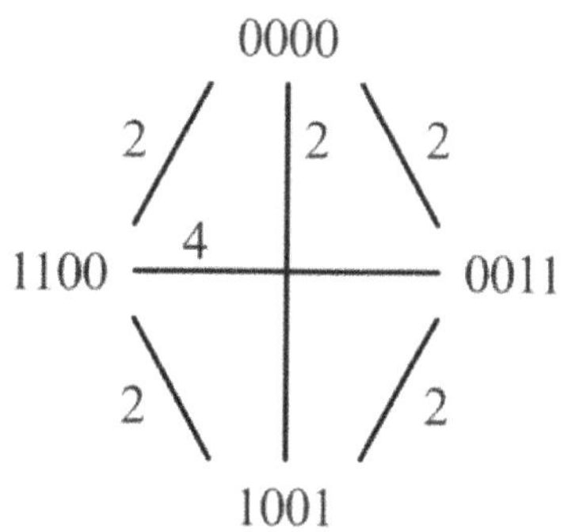

Figure A1.4. *Example of Hamming distance calculations (n = 4)*

The minimum Hamming distance D_{min} is defined as the smallest Hamming distance among a set of codewords. In the previous example, we have:

$$D_{min} = 2 \quad [A1.4]$$

These definitions are important because they allow us to define code performance in terms of error detection and correction (EDAC) (Cullmann 1967). A fundamental relation between the number of detectable errors e_d and the Hamming distance D is:

$$e_d \leq D - 1 \quad \text{[A1.5]}$$

$$\text{Hence, } D_{min} = e_d + 1 \quad \text{[A1.6]}$$

A fundamental relation also exists between the number of correctable errors e_c and the Hamming distance D, which is:

$$D_{min} = (2 \times e_c) + 1 \quad \text{[A1.7]}$$

To detect e_d errors and correct e_c with $e_c \leq e_d$, we must have:

$$e_c + e_d \leq D - 1 \quad \text{[A1.8]}$$

$$\text{Hence, } D_{min} = e_c + e_d + 1 \quad \text{[A1.9]}$$

When a dataset of size n is considered, two types of control must be distinguished: horizontal control or LRC (longitudinal redundancy check) and vertical control or VRC (vertical redundancy check). So, one control is done horizontally and another vertically. For each case, several techniques exist, such as the checksum (see section A1.2.3) and parity check (see section A1.3). Table A1.2 presents a few techniques that we will now detail.

VRC techniques	LRC techniques
AN code	
Modulo n remainder	
Crosswise parity	Longitudinal parity
Linear codes	Arithmetic sum (checksum)

Table A1.2. *Summary of redundancy-based control techniques*

A1.2.1. *AN code*

Its principle lies in multiplying the binary string N by a natural number A ($\in \mathbb{N}^*$), hence its name. The check consists of dividing the result by A. If the remainder is not zero, then there is an error.

An example is the 5N code. Let the binary value be 1001 0010. The codeword is calculated as: $(1001\ 0010)_2 = (146)_{10}$:

$$146 \times 5 = 730 = (10\ 1101\ 1010)_2$$

This type of code was mainly used for arithmetic operations (Chinal 1979). An extension corresponds to two-parameter codes AN + B. A theoretical study of both families can be found in Cullmann (1967) and Chinal (1979).

A1.2.2. *Modulo p remainder code*

The principle is to divide the binary string by p and attach the remainder to it. During transmission, the check involves recalculating this remainder and comparing it to the transmitted one.

Let us return to the example from section A1.2.1. First, 1001 0010 modulo 5 equals: 146 / 5 = 29.2, so 29 with a remainder of 1. Suppose an error occurs, for example, during data transmission, and we receive 1001 1010 (error in blue) and then 1001 1010 modulo 5 equals: 154 / 5 = 30.8, so 30 with a remainder of 4.

This type of code was mainly used for arithmetic operations (Chinal 1979).

A1.2.3. *Modulo checksum control*

Literally, the term checksum means "sum of control". It is one of the most basic controls. It consists of the arithmetic sum of all data without carrying and storing the result. The control is to recalculate this sum and compare it with the stored value (modulo checksum). It is used, for example, as protection against computer file copying. Any modification to a file is detected unless the change does not alter the checksum. The addition is generally done by bytes. If the final carry is not taken into account, it is a modulo $2^8 = 256$. Sometimes, the result can be complemented to the base, here 2's complement.

For example, consider the three following values: 0000 0000, 1111 1111 and 1000 0001, with decimal equivalents 0, 255 and 129. The checksum is equal to 384 modulo 256 = 128, which is appended to the data block.

The error is detected by recalculating the sum and comparing it to the transmitted value. If both values match, either there is no error (most likely), or the error introduced leaves the checksum unchanged. A solution is to increase the working format of the sum. In case of a difference, the data area and/or the checksum are incorrect. There is no issue anyway because the error is detected.

The simplest transmission protocols use this technique.

A1.3. Logical parity check

This is an extremely widespread technique.

A1.3.1. *Definition*

Logical parity characterizes the number of "1"s in the data. We speak of even and odd parity. It should not be confused with arithmetic parity, which determines whether a number is divisible by 2. Indeed, to check the validity of a binary word, it is more useful to consider each bit separately than to treat the word as a numerical value. Table A1.3 shows the calculation of the two possible parity functions for four examples.

	Logical parity functions	
Binary word	**Even**	**Odd**
0000 0000	1	0
0000 0001	0	1
0000 0011	1	0
0000 0111	0	1

Table A1.3. *Example of even and odd logical parity calculations*

We can observe that the odd parity calculation is equivalent to the modulo-2 sum of all bits, i.e. the exclusive OR (XOR) logical function.

The control data is the parity of the data. The check consists of calculating the parity and comparing it to the control bit. Some codes only detect one error; others detect multiple. In our example, this is a single-error-detecting code, where the total number of "1" bits including the control bit is even (odd parity function) or odd (even parity function).

We distinguish between longitudinal and crosswise logical parities.

NOTE.– On networks, the control covers both the data and the parity bit. This means that even parity control is equivalent to calculating the odd parity function and vice versa.

A1.3.2. *Crosswise parity*

Also called vertical parity or VRC. It consists of adding one parity bit. Even parity means the number of "1"s must be even; odd parity means it must be odd. Table A1.4 gives an example.

Parity	**Character**	**ASCII code**	**Parity bit**	**Resulting code word**
Even	"A"	41 h = $(0100\ 0001)_2$	0	82h
Odd	"A"	41 h = $(0100\ 0001)_2$	1	83h
Even	"B"	42 h = $(0100\ 0010)_2$	0	84h
Odd	"B"	42 h = $(0100\ 0010)_2$	1	85h

Table A1.4. *Examples of crosswise parity encoding*

Using formulas [A1.2] and [A1.3], the efficiency η and redundancy R for logical parity are:

$$\eta = \frac{d}{n} = \frac{n-1}{n} = 1 - \frac{1}{n} = \frac{8}{9} \qquad [A1.10]$$

$$R = \eta^{-1} = \frac{n}{d} = \frac{n}{n-1} = 1 + \frac{1}{n-1} \qquad [A1.11]$$

A1.3.3. *Longitudinal parity*

It is called horizontal parity and is designated as LRC. Each bit of the LRC character equals the parity of all corresponding bits in the block. Table A1.5 gives an example. We can see that even LRC is the modulo-2 sum column by column. Efficiency η and redundancy R are calculated the same way as for crosswise parity using equations [A1.10] and [A1.11].

A1.3.4. *Properties*

This method is simple and fast to detect a single error or an even/odd number of errors. It is likely one of the most common methods. Its drawback is that multiple-of-two errors cannot be detected.

	Characters
	01010101
	10101010
	00111000
	00011100
	01111100
	00000111
	11111111
	10000001
LRC (even parity)	11011110
LRC (odd parity)	00100001

Table A1.5. *Example of LRC parity calculation*

A1.3.5. *Field of use*

Parity check codes are mainly used in memory data verification. The memory word format is generally a multiple of the byte, and current dynamic random access memory or DRAM modules for servers use a format that is a multiple of 9, because one parity bit is added per memory byte.

A1.4. Cyclic codes

Cyclic codes are a subset of linear codes (see section A1.5.2). Cyclic codes are useful for their error detection capability, especially burst errors, and easy implementation. Some well-known cyclic codes include Bose–Chaudhuri–Hocquenghem (BCH), Reed–Solomon (RS) and Fire codes (Cullmann 1967). We focus on the most common type: polynomial codes, which are easy to implement and compute.

A1.4.1. *Definition*

A code is cyclic if rotating the bits of a code word still produces a valid code word. The main advantage is in hardware or software implementation, where bit rotation is easy. Let us now present one such code.

A1.4.2. *Polynomial codes*

Also called cyclic redundancy check (CRC) codes, these codes are characterized by a generator polynomial. After introducing the polynomial concept, we explain the principle and provide an example.

A1.4.2.1. *Modulo-2 polynomial arithmetic principle*

Consider binary data A of length n as a polynomial P(x), where each a_i is a coefficient of x^i. Thus, P(x) is written as:

$$P(x) = a_{n-1} \times x^{n-1} + a_{n-2} \times x^{n-2} + \cdots + a_1 \times x^1 + a_0 \times x^0 \\ = \sum_{i=0}^{n-1} a_i \times x^i \qquad [A1.12]$$

Figure A1.5 shows an example. The degree of a polynomial is the highest exponent of x. For our example, we write deg(P) = n – 1.

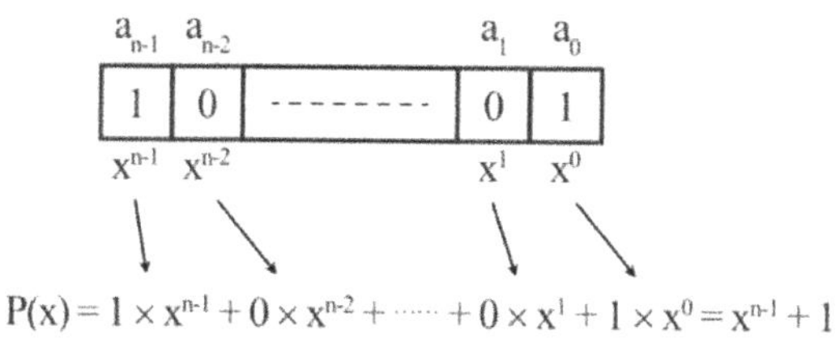

Figure A1.5. *Example of binary data conversion to a polynomial*

All arithmetic operations are done modulo 2. Addition and subtraction are therefore carryless. Figure A1.6 shows an example. These operations are equivalent.

	1	0	1	0	0	1	1	1
+	0	1	0	1	0	1	1	1
	1	1	1	1	0	0	0	0

	1	0	1	0	0	1	1	1
-	0	1	0	1	0	1	1	1
	1	1	1	1	0	0	0	0

Figure A1.6. *Examples of polynomial addition and subtraction*

Let us group the calculation rules in a table.

a_i	b_i	Addition or subtraction
0	0	0
0	1	1
1	0	1
1	1	0

Table A1.6. *Polynomial arithmetic rules*

If we see this table as a truth table, we can note that the logical operator for these arithmetic operations is the exclusive OR (EOR for exclusive OR, XOR for exclusive OR).

A1.4.2.2. *Encoding principle*

Let P(x) represent data A and G(x) be the generator polynomial. A logical left shift (see section 2.3.2.3 of Darche (2021d)) by n bits equals multiplying by x^n. The technique involves the Euclidean polynomial division. The polynomial $x^n \times$ P(x) is divided by G(x). So, we get the relation [A1.13] with deg(R) < deg(G). P(x) is the dividend, G(x) is the divisor, Q(x) is the quotient, and R(x) is the remainder:

$$x^n \times P(x) = \big(G(x) \times Q(x)\big) + R(x) \quad [A1.13]$$

The CRC is the remainder R(x) from dividing left-shifted binary data by G(x), where n is the degree of G(x). So, the remainder is n-1 bits long. Computing Q(x) is unnecessary, except perhaps to validate the result. Thus, CRC computation equals:

$$CRC = R(x) = \text{P(x) modulo G(x)} \quad [A1.14]$$

The CRC, such as a checksum, is the control field. The check is done with the same computation and consists of comparing the result with the stored CRC (control data).

The CRC's key characteristic is the degree and value of the generator polynomial. We do not detail how to choose G(x) here due to complexity. Interested readers can consult further sources (Cullmann 1967). Only the most common generator polynomials are presented in Table A1.7. In its second column, the number after "LRC-" or "CRC-" corresponds to the polynomial degree.

Generator polynomial G(x)	Use
$x + 1$	Even parity
$x^7 + x^3 + 1$	Minitel V-23
$x^8 + 1$	LRC-8
$x^{12} + x^{11} + x^3 + x^2 + x + 1$	CRC-12
$x^{16} + 1$	LRC-16
$x^{16} + x^{15} + x^2 + 1$	CRC-16
$x^{16} + x^{14} + x1 + 16$	Inverse CRC-16
$x^{16} + x^{12} + x^5 + 1$	CRC-16-CCITT/mass storage
$x^{16} + x^{11} + x^4 + 1$	CRC-16-CCITT inverse
$x^{32} + x^{28} + x^{26} + x^{19} + x^{17} + x^{10} + x^6 + x^2 + 1$ $x^{32} + x^{30} + x^{26} + x^{22} + x^{15} + x^{13} + x^6 + x^4 + 1$	Mass storage
$x^{32} + x^{26} + x^{23} + x^{22} + x^{16} + x^{12} + x^{11} + x^{10} + x^8$ $+ x^7 + x^5 + x^4 + x^2 + x + 1$	CRC-32 (IEEE 802.3)

Table A1.7. *Standard generator polynomials*

Famous file transfer protocols such as XMODEM/CRC and YMODEM/CRC use CRC-16. KERMIT uses CRC-CCITT; X-25 protocol uses it too. Ethernet and Token Ring use CRC-32. The term "inverse" means it operates on a reversed data stream.

CRC is computed either in software or hardware for speed. Software examples are in Boudreau and Steen (1971), Ramabadran and Gaitonde (1988) and Kientzle (1997); a hardware example is in Rallapalli (1978). Modern microprocessors often include specialized CRC instructions (see Chapter 2 of Darche (2021d)) such as CRC32 from SSE4.2 (streaming SIMD extensions) introduced by Intel's Nehalem or CRC32B/CB/H/CH/W/CW/X/CX from Arm A64 for CRC-32 and CRC-32C.

A1.4.2.3. *Example*

Take the binary data 1101. Its polynomial form is $P(x) = x^3 + x^2 + 1$. Let the generator polynomial $G(x) = x + 1$. We have:

$$P(x) \times x^1 = x^4 + x^3 + x$$

Figure A1.7 shows the division.

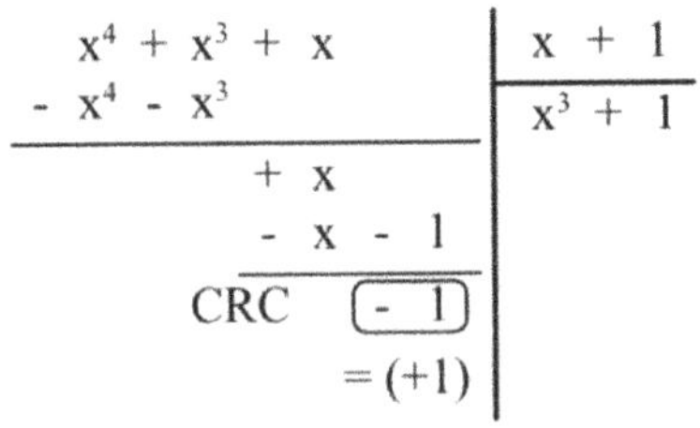

Figure A1.7. *Polynomial division example in decreasing powers (polynomial form)*

The stopping condition is deg(R) < deg(G). So, we have:

$$\deg(CRC) < \deg(G)$$

A more readable way to show polynomial division is binary notation. Take the binary data 1111. Its polynomial is: $P(x) = x^3 + x^2 + x^1 + 1$. Use the same generator polynomial as above. We have:

$$P(x) \times x^1 = x^4 + x^3 + x^2 + x^1$$

Figure A1.8 shows the division. We added one zero (n = 1) to the right; the remainder has length n. This generator polynomial computes even parity. In the above example, CRC = 0, which matches even parity. The CRC is then appended to the original data to create a packet ready for use. The set can, for example, be sent over in a network transmission or stored in a mass memory.

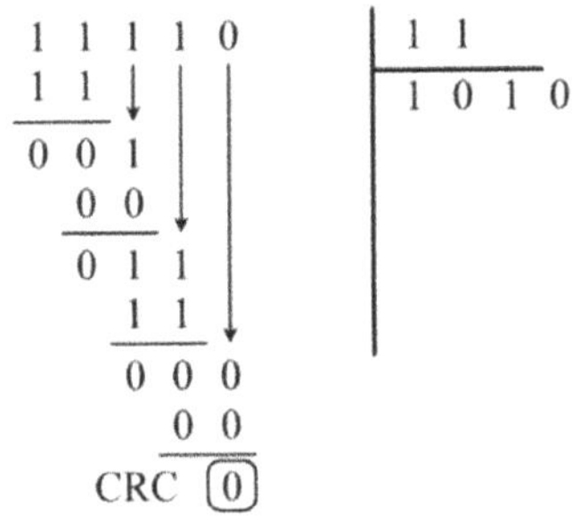

Figure A1.8. *Example of polynomial division in decreasing powers (binary form)*

A1.4.2.4. *Error detection*

To check if binary data match the original, for example, after transmission, the receiver must know G(x). There are two control methods: either recalculate the CRC and compare it with the original or compute the CRC on the entire set (data + CRC). In both cases, if the result is non-zero, there is an error. The second method is better, as encoding and decoding steps are identical. We use this method. Let T(x) be the transmitted polynomial. We have, with n the degree of the generator polynomial:

$$\mathrm{T(x)} = (\mathrm{P(x)} \times x^n) + CRC \qquad [A1.15]$$

Now, division of T(x) by G(x) gives zero remainder, meaning:

$$\mathrm{T(x)\ modulo\ G(x)} = 0 \qquad [A1.16]$$

with deg(CRC) < deg(G).

Let us model an error. It can also be seen as a polynomial. Let E(x) be this polynomial. If it equals 0, no error occurred. For a single-bit error, we have:

$$\mathrm{E(x)} = x^i \qquad [A1.17]$$

A burst error is a binary string with m incorrect bits. This means that, if we consider this burst as a polynomial, its first and last coefficients are equal to 1, and between the two 1s, there is any binary value. On reception, the data stream is R(x):

$$\mathrm{R(x)} = \mathrm{T(x)} + \mathrm{E(x)} \qquad [A1.18]$$

Since T(x) mod G(x) = 0, we have:

$$\mathrm{R(x)\ modulo\ G(x)} = \big(\mathrm{T(x)} + \mathrm{E(x)}\big)\ \mathrm{modulo\ G(x)} = \mathrm{E(x) modulo\ G(x)} \qquad [A1.19]$$

If this calculation of E(x) mod G(x) is not zero, an error occurred during transmission of the binary data. Several cases arise.

If G(x) has at least two “1” coefficients, the CRC can detect single-bit errors, since E(x) cannot be divisible by G(x). The non-zero remainder indicates the error location.

For double errors (two isolated bits), triple errors, odd numbers of errors or burst errors, choosing G(x) becomes more complex, and users must balance polynomial degree against error detection probability. An explanatory reference can be found in Tanenbaum (1989). Its degree especially defines the max data size for which detection is possible.

A1.4.2.5. *Application domains*

We saw that the same structure handles both generation and verification, and it is easy and cheap to implement in hardware and software. Also, this method supports variable-length binary data.

For all these reasons, this method is widely used. Its applications include mass storage devices (hard drives, floppy drives, magnetic tape drives), network protocols, backup/restore software and communication software (YMODEM, ZMODEM). A microelectronic implementation example is National Semiconductor's (NS) 74F401 chip, which acts as a CRC generator/verifier.

Theoretical supplements can be found in Macchi and Guilbert (1987), Nussbaumer (1987) and Tanenbaum (1989) and a practical study in Perez (1983).

A1.5. Error-correcting codes

Once an error is detected, it must be corrected. More or less complex error recovery strategies have been developed to solve this problem. We must distinguish between correction by retransmission (ARQ for automatic repeat request) and direct error correction (CED or FEC for forward error correction), or self-correction (see Figure A1.9), and hybrid approaches. The first approach generally belongs to communication protocol domains. It is often preferred because it is simple to implement. Deploying the second strategy requires adding more bits, which can be problematic for large amounts of data in terms of transmission time.

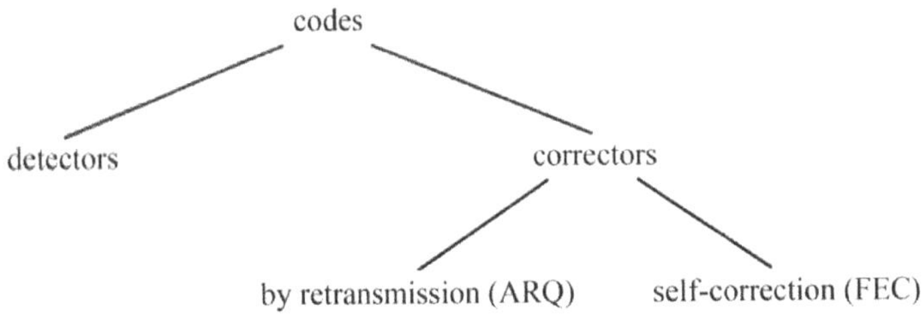

Figure A1.9. *Classification of error-detecting and error-correcting codes*

This second approach allows the receiver that detects the error to correct it. This latter case is what interests us here. It is necessary to know where the error is to correct it. These self-detecting/self-correcting codes therefore combine detection and especially correction of errors. We will study the Hamming code, which is the most well-known. We will use a practical approach, as the underlying mathematical theory goes beyond the scope of this book.

The generation and checking operations are done the same way as before. An additional step is added to correct any possible errors.

A1.5.1. *Technique of interleaved (logical) parities*

This technique allows error correction by extending parity control. It is a synthesis of the VRC and LRC techniques previously seen. It is sometimes incorrectly called the cross parity technique (see section A1.5.1.3).

A1.5.1.1. *Construction*

Let there be a block of k data items, each of n bits; this set can be seen as a matrix of k rows and n columns. For each row and column, we can compute the parity. We then distinguish between longitudinal and crosswise parities.

	Characters	**VRC (even logical parity)**	**VRC (odd logical parity)**
	01010101	0	1
	10101010	0	1
	00111000	1	0
	00011100	1	0
	01111100	1	0
	00000111	1	0
	11111111	0	1
	10000001	0	1
LRC (even logical parity)	11011110	0	
LRC (odd logical parity)	00100001		1

Table A1.8. *Example of VRC and LRC logical parity calculation*

If a single error occurs, that is, if only one bit value is flipped, then the recalculated VRC and LRC parities are incorrect compared to the transmitted ones (affected bits circled in Figure A1.10). An exercise (EA1.1) is given in the relevant section.

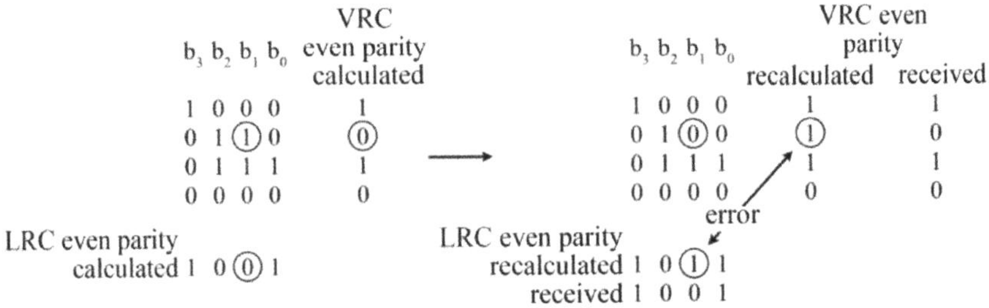

Figure A1.10. *Example of an error with cross parities*

A1.5.1.2. *Properties*

If an error occurs, both crosswise (vertical) and longitudinal (horizontal) parities are incorrect. It is then possible to correct it by flipping the faulty bit. A double error is also detected. This technique is mostly used in networking and data storage devices. The length of the binary string can vary.

A1.5.1.3. *Note*

There is an approach combining the VRC technique with the diagonal parity technique (cross parity check). It is called adaptive cross parity code (AXP) (Patel 1985). It is used for 18-track tape drives (Mee and Daniel 1996).

A1.5.2. *Linear codes*

Linear codes are an important class of error-detecting and correcting codes. A code is linear when the codeword is a linear combination of the data to be encoded. Another definition is that the sum of two codewords is still a codeword. Recall that addition and multiplication are done modulo 2.

The control part depends linearly on the data part. The need for matrix operations makes implementation complex. Some common codes include Hamming, Slepian, Golay or McDonald codes (Cullmann 1967). We deal with only one implementation example.

A1.5.2.1. *Hamming codes*

Hamming codes (Hamming 1950) rely on the concept of even parity. After the definition, we will study code generation, error detection and error correction in order.

A1.5.2.1.1. Principle

A set of c control bits is associated with data of length d. A control bit is a linear combination of certain data bits. These bits are chosen so that, when an error occurs, the control calculation indicates its position. This number indicating the error is called the checking number.

We call a Hamming code (n, d) a code that checks d data bits for a working format of n. There will thus be c (= n – d) control bits. These control bits form a number representing the position in error, if any. The value 0 is reserved to indicate no error. We then have the following relationship:

$$2^c \geq c + d + 1 \qquad [A1.20]$$

Since n = c + d, the previous inequality becomes:

$$2^d \leq \frac{2^n}{n+1} \qquad [A1.21]$$

Thus, it is possible, knowing the working format n, to calculate d_{max} and deduce c (Table A1.9).

n	**1**	**2**	**3**	**4**	**5**	**6**	**7**	**8**	**9**	**10**	**11**	**12**	**...**	**16**	**...**	**21**
d_{max}	0	0	1	1	2	3	4	4	5	6	7	8	...	11	...	16
$c = n - d_{max}$	1	2	2	3	3	3	3	4	4	4	4	4	...	5	...	5

Table A1.9. *Some d_{max} values for a given format*

We must choose codes with minimal redundancy to maximize the data area compared to the control area (Cullmann 1967), thus increasing the code's efficiency. We then obtain Table A1.10.

d	**c_{min}**	**n**		**C**	**d_{min}**	**n**
1	2	3		2	1	3
2	3	5		3	4	7
3	3	6		4	11	15
4	3	7		5	26	31
8	4	12		6	57	63
16	5	21		7	120	127

Table A1.10. *Some optimal Hamming codes*

A1.5.2.1.2. Reference example

We choose the Hamming code (7, 4) as the example for our explanation, which allows processing a quartet. The encoding is done in two phases: one for generating control data and one for checking.

Control data c_i must be generated from data bits d_i. The control positions correspond to columns whose number is a power of 22 (2^0, 2^1, 2^2), meaning it contains only one 1 in binary. By deduction, we get the positions of the data bits d_i. Table A1.11 shows the distribution of control bits (in bold) in a binary word of length n from 1 to 15 bits.

	Control bits					
	c_3	c_2	c_1	c_0		
	Weight					
Rank	2^3	2^2	2^1	2^0	**Assignment**	
1	0	0	0	**1**	c_0	a_0
2	0	0	**1**	0	c_1	a_1
3	0	0	**1**	**1**	d_0	a_2
4	0	**1**	0	0	c_2	a_3
5	0	**1**	0	**1**	d_1	a_4
6	0	**1**	**1**	0	d_2	a_5
7	0	**1**	**1**	**1**	d_3	a_6
8	**1**	0	0	0	c_3	a_7
9	**1**	0	0	**1**	d_4	a_8
10	**1**	0	**1**	0	d_5	a_9
11	**1**	0	**1**	**1**	d_6	a_{10}
12	**1**	**1**	0	0	d_7	a_{11}
13	**1**	**1**	0	**1**	d_8	a_{12}
14	**1**	**1**	**1**	0	d_9	a_{13}
15	**1**	**1**	**1**	**1**	d_{10}	a_{14}

Table A1.11. *Distribution of control and data bits in a binary word*

For our example, we have a_0, a_1 and a_3 as control positions and a_2, a_4, a_5 and a_6 as data positions (see Figure A1.11).

	a_6	a_5	a_4	a_3	a_2	a_1	a_0
	D	D	D	C	D	C	C
position	6	5	4	3	2	1	0
rank	7	6	5	4	3	2	1

Figure A1.11. *Binary word with its control data*

The result of the check must give the position of the bit in error. This means the result is weighted. We must treat the word to be checked as a number where each digit a_i has position i as defined in section 1.1.3 or rank i + 1. The value zero is reserved to indicate that there is no error.

Even parity is computed by successive additions of the selected digits modulo 2. We thus have the following system of linear equations:

$$a_3 = c_2 = a_6 + a_5 + a_4 = d_3 + d_2 + d_1$$

$$a_1 = c_1 = a_6 + a_5 + a_2 = d_3 + d_2 + d_0$$

$$a_0 = c_0 = a_6 + a_4 + a_2 = d_3 + d_1 + d_0$$

From these relations, we deduce that a_0 checks the parity of a_2, a_4 and a_6, that a_1 checks the parity of a_2, a_5 and a_6 and that a_3 checks the parity of a_4, a_5 and a_6. The control bits c_i self-check. The digits are chosen so that when there is an error at a rank, its number is calculated.

The check consists of recalculating the control data c_i and comparing it with the previously calculated ones. So, we have:

$$a'_3 - a'_6 - a'_5 - a'_4 = c_2$$

$$a'_1 - a'_6 - a'_5 - a'_2 = c_1$$

$$a'_0 - a'_6 - a'_4 - a'_2 = c_0$$

If the obtained values are zero, there is no error. Otherwise, they form, by their successive weights, a number that represents the rank of the error.

Using matrices helps simplify the calculations. We treat the data as row vectors. Generation consists of multiplying the data by a generation matrix called G (equation [A1.22]):

$$\text{data} \times \text{G} = \text{data} + \text{control data} \qquad \text{[A1.22]}$$

Checking consists of multiplying a control matrix called H by the data and control data (equation [A1.23]). The result is an error vector. It indicates the error position:

$$\text{H} \times (\text{data} + \text{control data}) = \text{error vector} \qquad \text{[A1.23]}$$

Figure A1.12 summarizes our proposition.

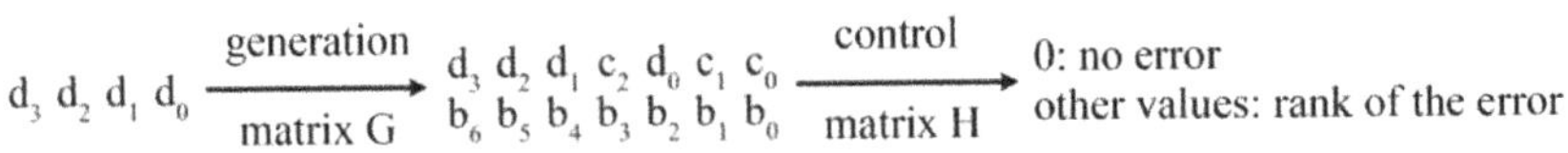

Figure A1.12. *Coding and error detection chain of Hamming code*

Let us now see how to build these two matrices.

A1.5.2.1.3. Generating control data

Generating control data consists of computing the generator matrix G. The data multiplied by it forms the complete codeword. So, we have:

$$(d_3\ d_2\ d_1\ d_0) \times G = (a_6\ a_5\ a_4\ a_3\ a_2\ a_1\ a_0)$$

We must obtain a codeword of format n, so a matrix of dimension (1, n). If there are d data bits and c control bits (n = c + d), matrix G is of size (d, n). We have the following system of linear equations:

$$a_6 = d_3$$

$$a_5 = d_2$$

$$a_4 = d_1$$

$$a_3 = d_3 + d_2 + d_1$$

$$a_2 = d_0$$

$$a_1 = d_3 + d_2 + d_0$$

$$a_0 = d_3 + d_1 + d_0$$

The corresponding generator matrix G is shown in Figure A1.13.

$$G = \begin{bmatrix} 1 & 0 & 0 & 1 & 0 & 1 & 1 \\ 0 & 1 & 0 & 1 & 0 & 1 & 0 \\ 0 & 0 & 1 & 1 & 0 & 0 & 1 \\ 0 & 0 & 0 & 0 & 1 & 1 & 1 \end{bmatrix} \begin{matrix} d_1 \\ d_0 \\ d_1 \\ d_0 \end{matrix}$$

$$\text{variables} \quad a_6 \; a_5 \; a_4 \; a_3 \; a_2 \; a_1 \; a_0$$

Figure A1.13. *Generator matrix G*

To generate a codeword, multiply the value by matrix G. Remember that all operations are done modulo 2. Let us take an example for illustration. Let the binary data $D_2 = 0101$; the codeword will be that shown in Figure A1.14.

$$\underset{d_3\, d_2\, d_1\, d_0}{[\,0 \;\; 1 \;\; 0 \;\; 1\,]} \times \begin{bmatrix} 1 & 0 & 0 & 1 & 0 & 1 & 1 \\ 0 & 1 & 0 & 1 & 0 & 1 & 0 \\ 0 & 0 & 1 & 1 & 0 & 0 & 1 \\ 0 & 0 & 0 & 0 & 1 & 1 & 1 \end{bmatrix} = \underset{b_6\, b_5\, b_4\, b_3\, b_2\, b_1\, b_0}{[\,0 \;\; 1 \;\; 0 \;\; 1 \;\; 1 \;\; 0 \;\; 1\,]}$$

Figure A1.14. *Codeword calculation*

Referring to Figure A1.15, we can locate the d_i in the expected data positions.

d_3	d_2	d_1	c_2	d_0	c_1	c_0
0	1	0	1	1	0	1
b_6	b_5	b_4	b_3	b_2	b_1	b_0

Figure A1.15. *Result of generating a codeword*

NOTE.– For easier reading of the error number, the bits c_i can be grouped at the start or end of the data. It is only necessary to move the corresponding columns in matrix G.

A1.5.2.1.4. Error detection

An error may occur on any bit. For detection, we must multiply the data to be checked by the parity-check matrix to get the error vector. If the result is zero, there is no error. This is expressed by equation [A1.24]. Otherwise, the binary value gives the rank of the error:

$$\text{codeword} \times H^t = 0 \qquad [A1.24]$$

So, we have:

$$H \times (a'_6\, a'_5\, a'_4\, a'_3\, a'_2\, a'_1\, a'_0) = \begin{pmatrix} b_2 \\ b_1 \\ b_0 \end{pmatrix} \qquad [A1.25]$$

We must obtain a result of format c, so a matrix of size (c, 1). If the multiplier is of size (1, n), matrix H is of size (c, n).

We have the following system of linear equations:

$$a'_3 - a'_6 - a'_5 - a'_4 = 0$$

$$a'_1 - a'_6 - a'_5 - a'_2 = 0$$

$$a'_0 - a'_6 - a'_4 - a'_2 = 0$$

Hence, the control matrix H is shown in Figure A1.16.

$2^3 - 1$ columns, weight

$$H = \begin{bmatrix} -1 & -1 & -1 & 1 & 0 & 0 & 0 \\ -1 & -1 & 0 & 0 & -1 & 1 & 0 \\ -1 & 0 & -1 & 0 & -1 & 0 & 1 \end{bmatrix} \quad \begin{matrix} 2^2 \\ 2^1 \\ 2^0 \end{matrix} \quad \text{3 rows}$$

rank 7 6 5 4 3 2 1

variables $a'_6\ a'_5\ a'_4\ a'_3\ a'_2\ a'_1\ a'_0$

Figure A1.16. *Control matrix H*

Recall that addition and subtraction are equivalent operations from the point of view of the result in the modulo 2 calculation. The equivalent control matrix H is that of Figure A1.17.

$$
\begin{array}{rccc}
 & 2^3 - 1 \text{ columns} & \text{weight} & \\
H = & \begin{bmatrix} 1 & 1 & 1 & 1 & 0 & 0 & 0 \\ 1 & 1 & 0 & 0 & 1 & 1 & 0 \\ 1 & 0 & 1 & 0 & 1 & 0 & 1 \end{bmatrix} & \begin{array}{c} 2^2 \\ 2^1 \\ 2^0 \end{array} & 3 \text{ rows} \\
\text{rank} & \begin{array}{ccccccc} 7 & 6 & 5 & 4 & 3 & 2 & 1 \end{array} & & \\
\text{variables} & \begin{array}{ccccccc} a'_6 & a'_5 & a'_4 & a'_3 & a'_2 & a'_1 & a'_0 \end{array} & &
\end{array}
$$

Figure A1.17. *Equivalent control matrix H*

We can see that each column of matrix H represents the binary value of the rank that could be in error. So, in the general case, it is of dimension $(c, 2^c-1)$ (see Figure A1.18).

$$
\begin{array}{rccc}
 & 2^c - 1 \text{ columns} & \text{weight} & \\
H = & \begin{bmatrix} 1 & 1 & \cdots & 0 & 0 & 0 \\ 1 & 1 & \cdots & 0 & 0 & 0 \\ & & & \vdots & & \\ 1 & 1 & \cdots & 0 & 0 & 0 \\ 1 & 1 & \cdots & 1 & 1 & 0 \\ 1 & 0 & \cdots & 1 & 0 & 1 \end{bmatrix} & \begin{array}{c} 2^{c-1} \\ 2^{c-2} \\ \vdots \\ 2^2 \\ 2^1 \\ 2^0 \end{array} & c \text{ rows} \\
\text{rank} & \begin{array}{cccccc} 2^c-1 & 2^c-2 & & 3 & 2 & 1 \end{array} & & \\
\text{variables} & \begin{array}{cccccc} b_{2^c-2} & b_{2^c-3} & & b_2 & b_1 & b_0 \end{array} & &
\end{array}
$$

Figure A1.18. *Generalized control matrix H*

To check a codeword, just multiply the value by matrix H. Using the previous result data, we now introduce an error at rank 2 (i.e. position 1), shown in bold. The data then becomes:

0 1 0 1 1 **1** 1

The control multiplication data × H gives Figure A1.19.

Value 2 points to the second bit from the left, i.e. bit number 1 as per the convention in Figure A1.11.

$$\begin{bmatrix} 1 & 1 & 1 & 1 & 0 & 0 & 0 \\ 1 & 1 & 0 & 0 & 1 & 1 & 0 \\ 1 & 0 & 1 & 0 & 1 & 0 & 1 \end{bmatrix} \times \begin{bmatrix} 0 \\ 1 \\ 0 \\ 1 \\ 1 \\ \mathbf{1} \\ 1 \end{bmatrix} = \begin{bmatrix} 0 \\ 1 \\ 0 \end{bmatrix} \begin{matrix} 2^2 \\ 2^1 \\ 2^0 \end{matrix}$$

Figure A1.19. *Error calculation*

A1.5.2.1.5. Error correction

In binary base, since there are only two possible states, if a bit is in error, it means it has been inverted. To correct it, once the error position is known, it is enough to complement the faulty bit.

A1.5.2.1.6. Correspondence between generation and control matrices

Until now, we have taken a pragmatic approach. We will show how to build matrix H from G and vice versa. From the generator matrix G in Figure A1.13, we permute the columns (in bold in Figure A1.20) to reveal the identity matrix I on the left in matrix G'. This latter is called the standard form.

$$G = \begin{bmatrix} 1 & 0 & 0 & 1 & 0 & 1 & 1 \\ 0 & 1 & 0 & 1 & 0 & 1 & 0 \\ 0 & 0 & 1 & 1 & 0 & 0 & 1 \\ 0 & 0 & 0 & 0 & 1 & 1 & 1 \end{bmatrix} \quad \text{hence} = (I, A) = \begin{bmatrix} 1 & 0 & 0 & \mathbf{0} & \mathbf{1} & 1 & 1 \\ 0 & 1 & 0 & \mathbf{0} & \mathbf{1} & 1 & 0 \\ 0 & 0 & 1 & \mathbf{0} & \mathbf{1} & 0 & 1 \\ 0 & 0 & 0 & \mathbf{1} & \mathbf{0} & 1 & 1 \end{bmatrix}$$
$$\begin{matrix} a_6 & a_5 & a_4 & a_3 & a_2 & a_1 & a_0 \end{matrix} \qquad\qquad \begin{matrix} a_6 & a_5 & a_4 & \mathbf{a_2} & \mathbf{a_3} & a_1 & a_0 \end{matrix}$$

Figure A1.20. *Generator matrix G' with identity matrix*

As H' = ($-A^t$, I), we compute $-A^t$ as shown in Figure A1.21.

$$A = \begin{bmatrix} 1 & 1 & 1 \\ 1 & 1 & 0 \\ 1 & 0 & 1 \\ 0 & 1 & 1 \end{bmatrix} \quad \text{hence } -A^t = \begin{bmatrix} -1 & -1 & -1 & 0 \\ -1 & -1 & 0 & -1 \\ -1 & 0 & -1 & -1 \end{bmatrix} = \begin{bmatrix} 1 & 1 & 1 & 0 \\ 1 & 1 & 0 & 1 \\ 1 & 0 & 1 & 1 \end{bmatrix}$$

Figure A1.21. *Transposed matrix*

Hence, the expression of the control matrix H is shown in Figure A1.22.

$$
H' = \begin{bmatrix} 1 & 1 & 1 & \mathbf{0} & \mathbf{1} & 0 & 0 \\ 1 & 1 & 0 & \mathbf{1} & \mathbf{0} & 1 & 0 \\ 1 & 0 & 1 & \mathbf{1} & \mathbf{0} & 0 & 1 \end{bmatrix} = (-A^t, I) \text{ hence } H = \begin{bmatrix} 1 & 1 & 1 & 1 & 0 & 0 & 0 \\ 1 & 1 & 0 & 0 & 1 & 1 & 0 \\ 1 & 0 & 1 & 0 & 1 & 0 & 1 \end{bmatrix}
$$

$$
\text{variables} \quad a'_6\, a'_5\, a'_4\, \mathbf{a'_2}\, \mathbf{a'_3}\, a'_1\, a'_0 \qquad\qquad a'_6\, a'_5\, a'_4\, a'_3\, a'_2\, a'_1\, a'_0
$$

Figure A1.22. *Calculation for the corresponding control matrix H*

To generate matrix G from H, all these operations must be done in reverse.

A1.5.2.1.7. Notes

In vector multiplications, order matters. Take the matrix equality:

$$Y = A \times X$$

where Y and X are the column matrices; this equality can also be written as in equation [A1.26] where Y and X are the row matrices. We prefer this form for presenting data as row vectors and the associated matrix. It is possible to represent data as a column vector; in that case, one must transpose the matrices and reverse the terms:

$$Y^t = X^t \times A^t \qquad \text{[A1.26]}$$

Matrices G and H are linked by the relationship (Cullmann 1967) as per equation [A1.27]:

$$G \times H^t = H \times G^t = 0 \qquad \text{[A1.27]}$$

A1.5.2.1.8. Summary

These codes thus allow detecting and correcting only one error among n. However, the binary string length must be fixed. It is therefore necessary to divide a large binary data into packets of n bits for this method to apply.

Hamming codes can be used to detect and correct multiple errors in RAM or ROM (read-only memory) (Gray 2000). They can be extended to any base B, for example, to detect and correct hardware errors in an adder or a subtractor (Robertson 1987).

Another example of a redundant polynomial code can be found in Reed and Solomon (1960).

A1.6. Summary

This appendix focused specifically on algebraic codes or block codes. In this first category, simple parity check codes are mainly used for memory data control. Linear codes are primarily used in networking due to their efficiency and implementation complexity.

For example, cyclic codes, especially CRC, are mainly used in mass storage and networks because they are easily implemented in hardware or software. Control data are generated from current and past data.

A second category includes convolutional codes (Elias 1955), also called recurrent codes. They are suited for protecting a continuous data stream, while algebraic codes protect data blocks independently.

The mixed version is the concatenation approach. A concatenated code has a multi-level (de)coding structure where the application can be serial (Forney 1965, 1966) or parallel (Berrou et al. 1993, 1996). Figure A1.23 shows a simplified classification.

The main drawback of most of these codes lies in the addition of control and/or error detection bits. Obviously, the number of control bits should be minimized to improve efficiency.

A complete theoretical study of these codes can be found in Cullmann (1967). Koopman (2024) is a reference work on checksums and CRC.

There is a metric to quantify the portion of erroneous data and that which cannot be corrected. This is the raw bit error rate or (R)BER and the post-correction uncorrectable bit error rate or UBER, found, for example, in industrial datasheets for mass memory devices based on flash EEPROM (electrically erasable programmable read-only memory) or SSDs (solid-state disks) (for more on this topic, refer to Mielke et al. (2008)).

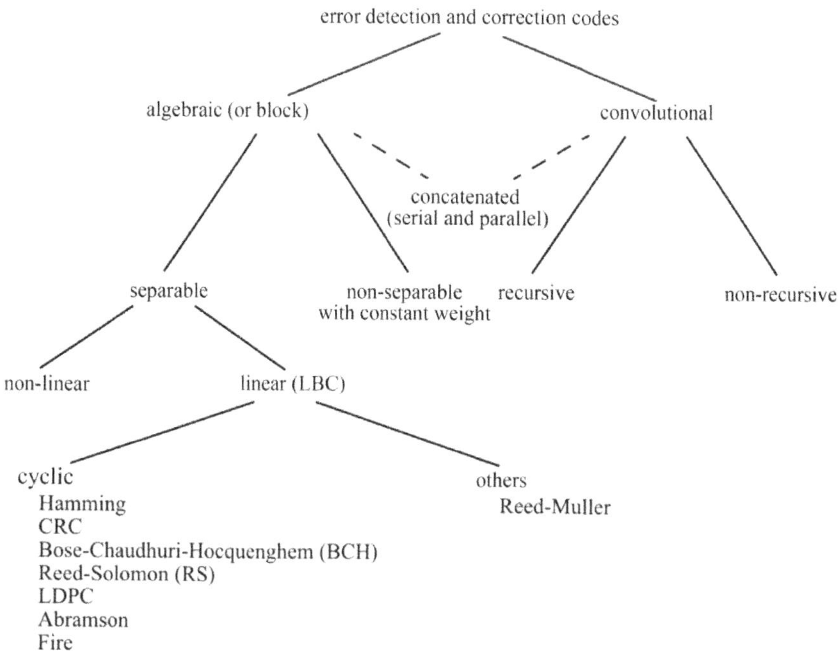

Figure A1.23. *Traditional non-exhaustive classification of error-detecting and error-correcting codes*

Appendix 2

Exercises

Here are some exercises that complement the concepts presented in this book. Their numbering refers to the chapter to which they are associated.

Chapter 1

E1.1 Justify the values of Table 1.3.

Answer. CD-quality sound is sampled at 44,100 Hz. A sample is digitized in format $n = 16$ bits. This gives for one left or right channel:

$$44{,}100 \text{ samples/s} \times 16 \text{ bits} = 705{,}600 \text{ b/s} = 705.6 \text{ kb/s} = 88.2 \text{ kB/s}$$

For stereo, the rate is doubled (left and right channels), i.e. 1,411.2 kb/s or 176.4 kB/s.

According to the Nyquist–Shannon sampling theorem (Nyquist 1928; Shannon 1948), the sampling rate must be greater than twice the maximum frequency.

For luminance, the standardized sampling frequency (International Radio Consultative Committee (CCIR) 601) is 13.5 MHz. The rate for sampling in format $n = 10$ bits is therefore:

$$13.5 \times 10^6 \times 10 = 135 \text{ Mb/s}$$

If chroma components Cr and Cb are added, sampled in format $n = 10$ bits with a standardized sampling rate (standard 4:2:2 CCIR 601) of 6.75 MHz, a total rate of 270 Mb/s is obtained.

The resolution of an image in XGA (extended graphics array) format is 1,024 × 768. If each pixel is digitized on 24 bits, then for a non-interlaced display (50 images/s), the bitrate equals:

$$1{,}024 \times 768 \times 24 \times 50 = 943{,}718{,}400 \text{ bit/s} = 973 \text{ Mb/s} \approx 118 \text{ Mb/s}$$

E1.2 Explain the principle of memory hierarchy.

Answer. Memory hierarchy is an abstraction organizing the various memory families along the data path. Memory hierarchy was invented for performance (latency, throughput, capacity, etc.) and cost reasons. It involves using memory technologies suited to processor use.

Chapter 2

E2.1 Justify the logic function of output enable (see Figure 2.7b) by studying it.

Answer. Studying the logic function means describing it graphically or textually (see section 1.2.4. of Darche (2002)). Since the function has two variables, the truth table (Table E2.1) has 2^2 rows. We saw that enabling a memory data output allows a bus connection. The output can only be enabled if the chip is selected (#CE = 0). The # symbol before the signal name indicates that the signal is active low.

#CE	#OE	#Command	Note
0	0	0	Output selected
0	1	1	High impedance output
1	0	1	High impedance output
1	1	1	High impedance output

Table E2.1. *Truth table of the control command for the output buffer*

The minterms of the algebraic equation are derived from the "1" values of the function. Thus, we obtain:

$$\#\text{Command} = \overline{\#\text{CE}} + \overline{\#\text{OE}} \qquad \text{[E.1]}$$

E2.2 Given the memory data path in Figure 2.8. Write the Boolean equations for the input buffer control (command_D) and data output (#command_Q).

Answer. Note that the output control works in negative logic (i.e. active low). To write the algebraic equations, simply read the logic symbols. Thus, we obtain:

$$\text{command\_D} = \overline{\#\text{CE}} \cdot \overline{\#\text{WE}} \qquad [\text{E.2}]$$

$$\#\text{command\_Q} = \#\text{CE} + \overline{\#\text{WE}} + \#\text{OE} = \overline{\overline{\#\text{CE}} \cdot \#\text{WE} \cdot \overline{\#\text{OE}}} \qquad [\text{E.3}]$$

E2.3 What is the difference between a block, a memory bank and a row?

Answer. A block is part of the memory area with its row and column address decoders and read amplifiers. A bank is an independent memory area made of one or more blocks with its I/O interface. Externally, several chips may form a row also called an "external bank". A row has its own buses.

E2.4 Draw the timing diagrams describing the operation of the logic diagram in Figure E2.1. What is the flaw in this approach?

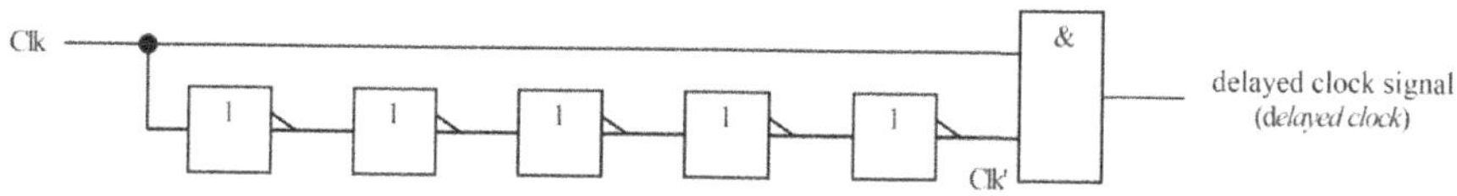

Figure E2.1. *Signal delay in an edge detector*

Answer. Figure E2.2 shows an example of a delayed signal generator. Due to variations in electrical and timing characteristics during manufacturing, the propagation delay time (t_{pd}) is imprecise. It varies from one component to another.

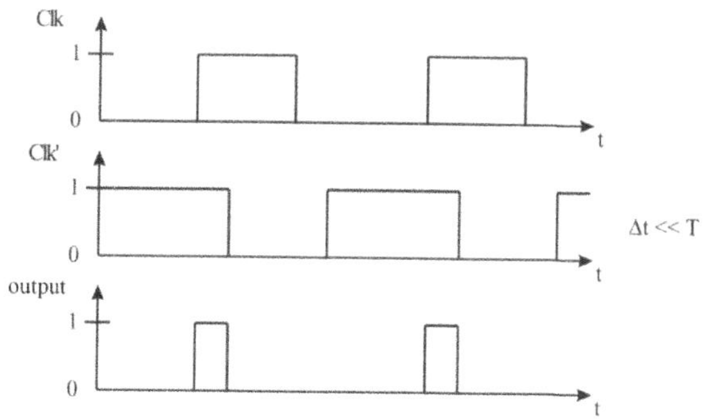

Figure E2.2. *Timing diagrams showing the behavior of a delayed signal generator*

E2.5 Draw the timing diagram of signal ATD from Figure E2.3 during the two address changes.

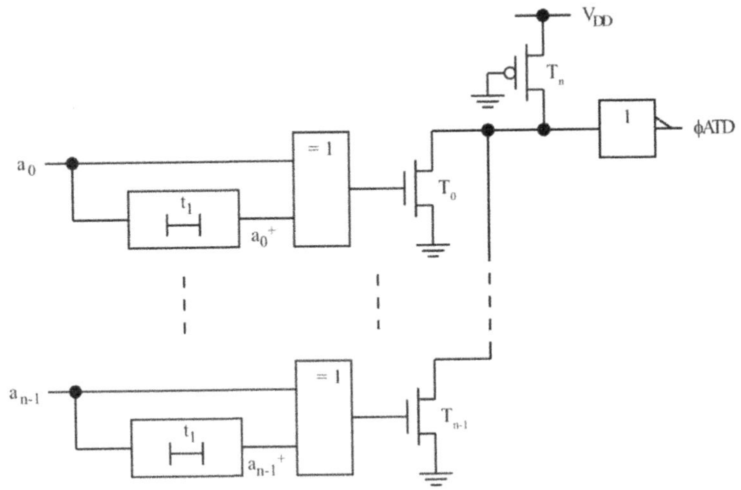

Figure E2.3. *Logic diagram of an address transition detector (ATD)*

Answer. We assume only one address wire varies, for example, a_0. The logic diagram is similar to the previous exercise. Figure E2.4 shows the example operation described there.

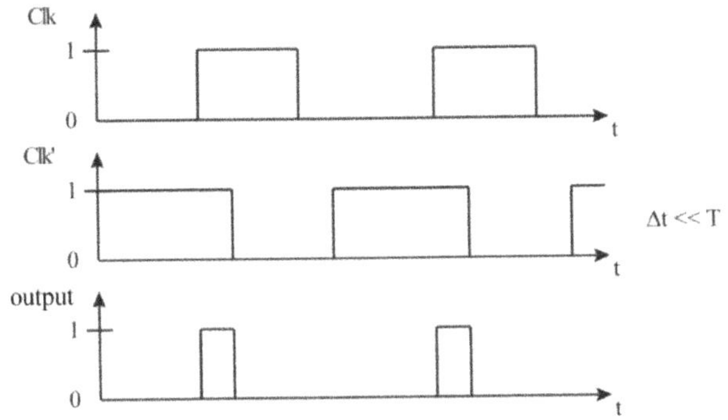

Figure E2.4. *Timing diagrams describing the behavior of an ATD*

If multiple address wires vary at once, the timing of signal ϕATD may be affected.

E2.6 How long would a microprocessor with a m = 32-bit address bus take to scan its full address space with a read cycle time t_{RC} of 20 ns?

Answer. $t_{tot} = 2^{32} \times t_c \approx 86$ s.

E2.7 Same question with m = 64 bits. What conclusion do you draw?

Answer. $t_{tot} = 2^{64} \times t_c \approx 368 \times 10^9$ s $\approx$ 11,699 years.

The number of years becomes too large compared to human life expectancy. Therefore, it is not feasible to exhaustively scan or test such a large address space.

E2.8 Write the logic equations of an m = three-bit wide one-hot address decoder in NOR (not OR), AND and NAND (not AND) versions. Then, draw the CMOS (complementary metal-oxide semiconductor) dynamic logic circuit.

Answer. For m = 3 bits, address A is written A = a_2 a_1 a_0. The decoder will have $2^m = 2^3$ outputs noted y_i, $i \in [0, 7]$, hence the 3:8 decoder name. "One-hot decoder" means only one output is active for a given address.

For the NOR form, we have:

$$y_0 = \overline{a_{m-1} + a_{m-1} + \cdots + a_0} = \overline{a_2 + a_1 + a_0}$$

$$y_{2^m-1} = \overline{\overline{a_{m-1}} + \overline{a_{m-1}} + \cdots + \overline{a_0}}$$

$$hence\ y_7 = \overline{\overline{a_2} + \overline{a_1} + \overline{a_0}}$$

For the AND form, we have:

$$y_0 = \overline{a_{m-1}} \cdot \overline{a_{m-2}} \cdot \cdots \cdot \overline{a_0} = \overline{a_2} \cdot \overline{a_1} \cdot \overline{a_0}$$

$$y_{2^m-1} = a_{m-1} \cdot a_{m-2} \cdot \cdots \cdot a_0$$

$$hence\ y_7 = a_2 \cdot a_1 \cdot a_0$$

The NAND form works in negative logic at the output level. "Negative logic" means the output active state is logic low. This means a logic 1 corresponds to the lowest voltage level (low-level voltage) (for more details, see section 2.1.4 of Darche (2004)). The NAND form is derived from the AND form by complementing the equations.

Thus, we have:

$$\#y_0 = \overline{\overline{a_{m-1}} \cdot \overline{a_{m-1}} \cdot \dots \cdot \overline{a_0}} = \overline{\overline{a_2} \cdot \overline{a_1} \cdot \overline{a_0}}$$

$$\#y_{2^m-1} = \overline{a_{m-1} \cdot a_{m-2} \cdot \dots \cdot a_0}$$

$$hence\ \#y_7 = \overline{a_2 \cdot a_1 \cdot a_0}$$

Figure E2.5 shows the NOR version circuit. A signal $\#\phi_P$ precharges the decoder output column.

Figure E2.6 shows the AND version circuit. The NAND version is obtained by removing the output inverter (shaded part). The drawback of both versions is that each extra variable adds a transistor to the stack, which increases the fan-in (see section 2.2.1 of Darche (2004)) and thus the decoder's response time. One solution is from Khanna and Partovi (2000), proposing an NAND decoder in a dynamic version.

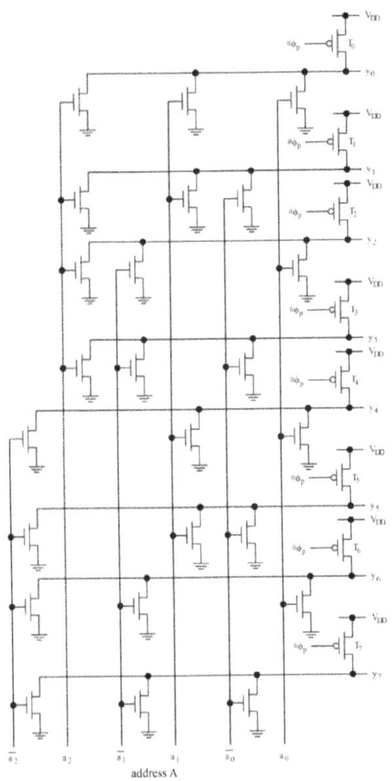

Figure E2.5. *Address decoder (m = 3) in NOR version*

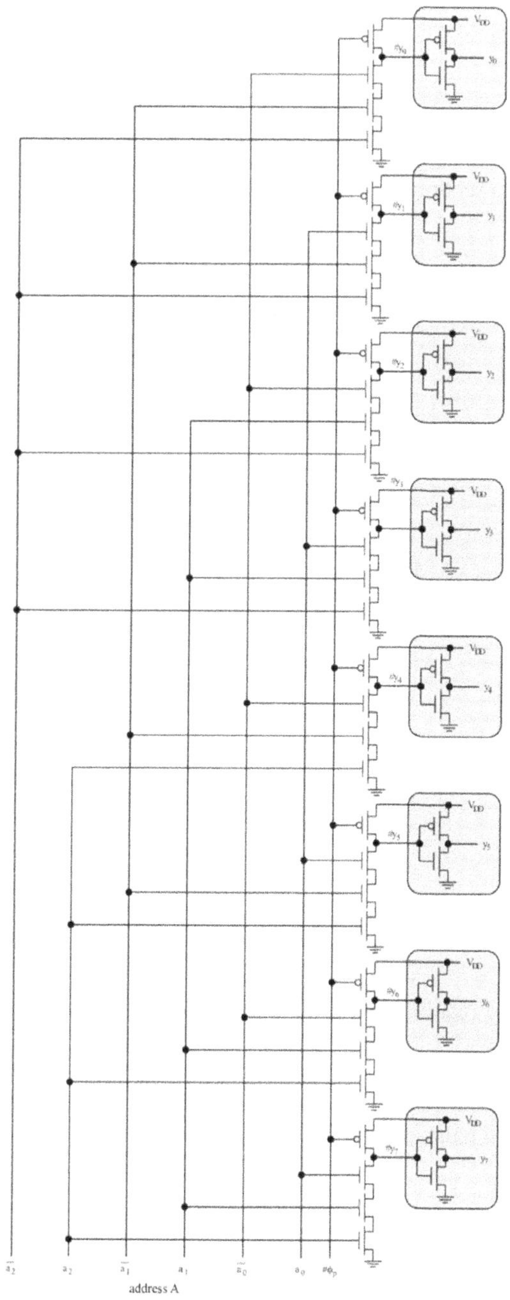

Figure E2.6. *Address decoder (m = 3) in (N)AND version*

E2.9 Draw the logic diagram of address decoding with predecoding in negative logic inspired by Figure 2.33.

Answer. "Negative logic" means the active state is logic low.

This means logic 1 corresponds to the lowest voltage level (low-level voltage) (for more details, see section 2.1.4 of Darche (2004)).

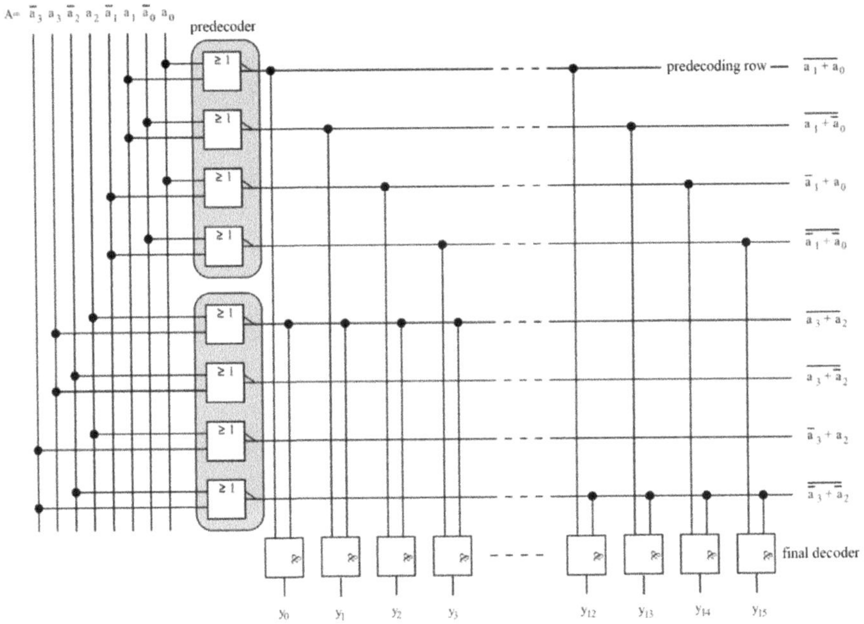

Figure E2.7. *Predecoding in negative logic*

E2.10 Draw the equivalent logic diagram of a sense amplifier (SA) with equalization.

Answer. Figure E2.8 shows the solution. It is a latch-type circuit with an enable signal and a potential balancing device.

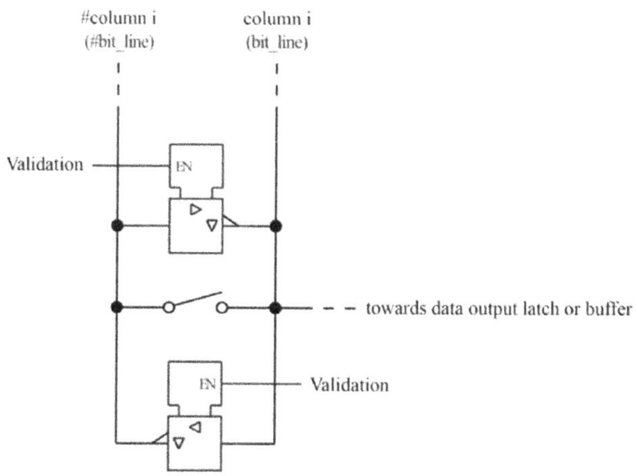

Figure E2.8. *Simplified logic diagram of an SA with equalization*

Chapter 5

E5.1 Spatial interleaving. Assume a memory space of 16 cells. Two memories are used to cover the full space. Draw the addressing logic diagram.

Answer. To address sixteen cells, a $m = 4$ wide address is needed. Since the space is covered by two memories, each has an address width m' = m – 1. The most significant bit a_3 is used as the chip select. Figure E5.1 shows the logic diagram.

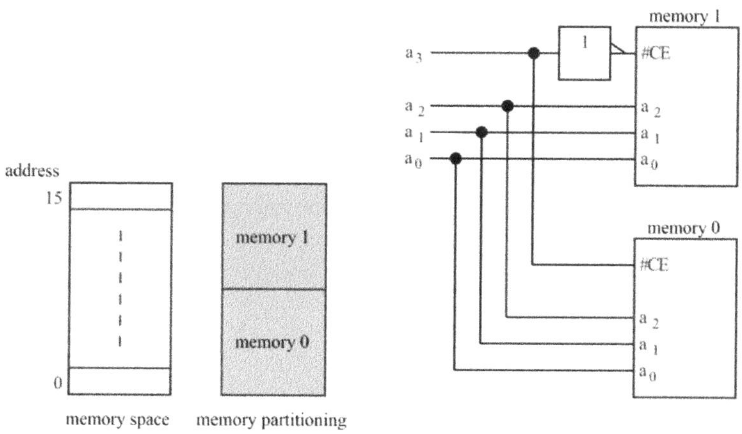

Figure E5.1. *Example of spatial memory interleaving (m = 4)*

E5.2 Temporal interleaving. Draw the memory space in the case of ROMs, using data from the previous exercise but now with temporal interleaving, and indicate which cell belongs to memory 0 or 1.

Answer. Note that the memories are permanently selected. The output enable signal activates the selected memory's output.

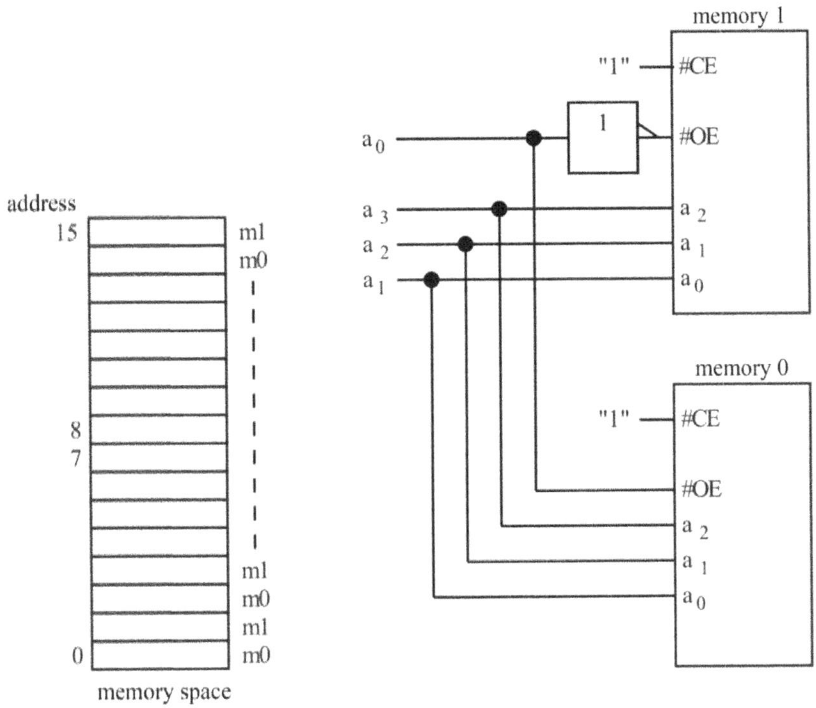

Figure E5.2. *Example of a temporal-type memory interleaving (m = 4)*

E5.3 Draw the memory space of a PMS (prime memory system) with three banks of unit size L = 8.

Answer. See Figure E5.3.

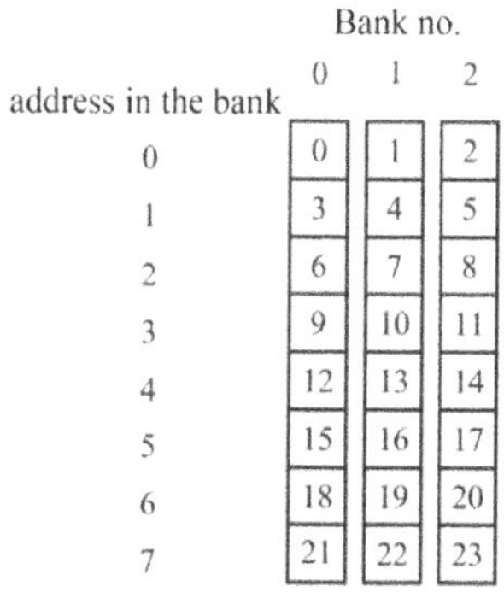

Figure E5.3. *Perfect PMS (PPMS) with B = 3 and L = 8*

Chapter 6

E6.1 EDAC introduces a cost in terms of extra bits. Fill in Table E6.1 to express this as a percentage of loss.

Original format n	**Extra bits**		**Loss percentage**	
	Parity	EDAC	Parity	EDAC
8	1	5		
16	2	6		
32	4	8		
64	8	8		

Table E6.1. *Comparison between error detection and correction*

Answer. The loss percentage is the ratio of bits added for correction (extra bits) to the original format n. It can be seen in the solution table (Table E6.2) that the percentage is constant for parity-based error detection, since one parity bit is added per data byte (next-to-last column). However, as the data format increases, fewer bits are needed for error detection and correction, and for a 64-bit format, EDAC becomes a better solution than parity. This is why parity has gradually been replaced by EDAC, as their efficiency was the same.

E6.2 Numerically justify that the loss, for format $n = 64$ bits and parity detection, is only 11% (last row of Table E6.2).

Answer. Out of 72 bits, one byte is used for error detection. The loss is 8/72 or about 11.2%.

Original format n	Extra bits		Loss percentage	
	Parity	EDAC	Parity	EDAC
8	1	5	11.2	38.5
16	2	6	11.2	27.3
32	4	7/8	11.2	18/20
64	8	8	11.2	11.2

Table E6.2. *Comparison between error detection and correction – solution*

E6.3 Checksum calculation. A RAM of 256 words in byte format is tested by filling each memory cell with an incremented value (initial value = 1). Calculate the checksum *s* or BCC (block-check character).

Answer. We have $U_{n+1} = U_n + 1$ with $U_0 = 1$. This is an arithmetic sequence (U_n) with first term U_0 and common difference 1. $U_{255} = 256$. The sum S_n of this sequence, i.e. the sum of the first *n* terms, is equal to:

$$S_n = \frac{n \times (n+1)}{2}$$

For $n = 256$, $S_{256} = 32{,}896$.

The checksum is calculated modulo 256. So, the sum *s* equals:

$$s = U_{256} \text{ modulo } 256 = 32{,}896 \text{ modulo } 256 = 128$$

Appendix 1

EA1.1 Crossed logical parities. Fill in Table EA1.1 using even logical parity. Note: in networks, logical parity is embedded in the transmitted data. What are the advantages and limitations of this approach? Justify your answer.

	b_7	b_6	b_5	b_4	b_3	b_2	b_1	b_0	**Horizontal parity (VRC)**
B_0	0	0	0	0	0	0	0	0	
B_1	0	1	0	1	0	1	0	1	
B_2	1	0	1	0	1	0	1	0	
B_3	1	1	1	0	0	0	0	0	
B_4	0	0	0	0	0	0	0	1	
B_5	0	0	1	1	0	1	0	1	
B_6	0	1	1	1	1	1	1	0	
B_7	1	1	1	1	1	1	1	1	
Vertical parity (LRC)									

Table EA1.1. *Even horizontal and vertical logical parities*

Answer. Table EA1.2 is filled to check even logical parity. This technique allows detection of two errors and correction of one.

	b_7	b_6	b_5	b_4	b_3	b_2	b_1	b_0	**Horizontal parity (VRC)**
B_0	0	0	0	0	0	0	0	0	0
B_1	0	1	0	1	0	1	0	1	0
B_2	1	0	1	0	1	0	1	0	0
B_3	1	1	1	0	0	0	0	0	1
B_4	0	0	0	0	0	0	0	1	1
B_5	0	0	1	1	0	1	0	1	0
B_6	0	1	1	1	1	1	1	0	0
B_7	1	1	1	1	1	1	1	1	0
Vertical parity (LRC)	1	0	1	0	1	0	1	0	

Table EA1.2. *Even horizontal and vertical logical parities – solution*

List of Acronyms

Memory systems make heavy use of acronyms. Here are their meanings.

General

A	address
AC	alternating current
A/D	address/data
AF	address fault
AGC	Apollo Guidance Computer
ARQ	automatic repeat request
ASCII	American Standard Code for Information Interchange
ASIC	application-specific integrated circuit
ASM	application-specific memory
ATD	address transition detection
ATM	asynchronous transfer mode
AU	memory-addressable unit
AXP	adaptive cross parity code
BCC	block-check(ing) character
BCH	Bose–Chaudhuri–Hocquenghem (code)
BE	big-endian
BER	bit error rate

BF	bridging fault
BHE	byte high enable
BiCMOS	bipolar and CMOS
BiE	bi-endian
BINAC	binary automatic computer
BIOS	basic input/output system
Bit	binary digit or binary digit
BL	bitline
BRAM	block RAM
BSB	back-side bus
BSP	burroughs scientific processor
C	cycle
C/A or CA	command/address
CAM	content-addressable memory, a form of associative memory
CAS	column address strobe
C/C/A or CCA	command/control/address
CCD	charge-coupled device
CD	compact disc
CDRAM	cache(d) DRAM
CD-ROM	CD ROM
CE	chip enable (see CS)
CF	coupling fault
CGA	color/graphics adapter
CIO	common (data) I/O
CISC	complex instruction set computer
CK	input and output clock
Clk	clock (see E)
CMOS	complementary MOS
CMP	chip multiprocessor

CPU	central processing unit
CRC	cyclic redundancy check
CRT	cathode ray tube
CS	chip select (see CE)
CTG	column transaction granularity
D	data (input)
D	device
DAC	digital-to-analog converter
DASD	direct access storage device
DBM	double-buffered memory
DC	direct current
DED	double-error detecting code
DDR	double data rate
DF	dynamic or delay fault
DIB	dual independent bus
DIMM	dual-in-line memory module
DLL	delay-locked loop
DMA	direct memory access
DP	datapath
DPM	dual-port memory
DPRAM	double port RAM
DQ	data input/output
DRAM	dynamic RAM
DRO	destructive read out
DSP	digital signal processor
DTD	data-transition detection
DVI	digital visual interface
DWL	divided word-line
E	clock signal (see Clk)

EAROM	electrically alterable ROM, one of the two EEPROM families
ECC	error checking and correcting (see ED(A)C/ error-correcting code)
ECL	emitter coupled logic
ED(A)C	error detection (and) correction (see ECC)
EDC	error-detecting circuit/code or error detection and correction
EEMS	enhanced EMS
EEPROM	electrically EPROM (see E^2PROM)
E^2PROM	electrically EPROM (see EEPROM)
EGA	enhanced graphics adapter
EMC	electromagnetic compatibility
EMS	expanded memory specification (LIM EMS)
ENIAC	electronic numerical integrator and computer
EOR	exclusive OR (see EXOR and XOR)
E2PROM	erasable PROM
ES	embedded system
ESD	electrostatic discharge
eSPI	enhanced serial peripheral interface
EXOR	exclusive OR (see EOR and XOR)
FCS	frame check sequence
FD	floppy disk
FDD	floppy disk drive
FEC	forward error correction
FEEPROM	flash EEPROM (definition JEDEC – JESD88C)
FF	fill frequency
FF	flip-flop
FIFO	first in, first out
FPGA	field-programmable gate array
FRAM	ferroelectric RAM

FSB	front-side bus
FW	firmware
G	output enable (see OE)
GaAs	gallium arsenide
GDDR	graphics DDR
GMCH	graphics and memory controller HUB
GPU	graphics Processing unit/graphics processor unit
GRAM	graphics RAM
GSI	gigascale integration
GUI	graphical user interface
HBM	high bandwidth memory
HD	hard disk
HDD	HD drive
HDL	hardware description language
HDLC	high-level data link control (IBM)
HDMI	high-definition multimedia interface
Hi-Fi	high fidelity
HMA	high memory area
HSB	high-speed buffer
HW	hardware
I	input
I^2C	inter-integrated circuit (Philips)
ICH	I/O controller HUB
INT	interrupt
I/O	input/output
IO	input/output (rarely used)
IOE	I/O element (see IOU)
IOU	I/O unit (see IOE)
IS	instruction set

ISBN	International Standard Book Number
JEP	JEDEC publications
JESD	JEDEC standards
LCM	loosely coupled memory
LE	little-endian
LIFO	last in, first out
LIW	long instruction word
LRC	longitudinal redundancy check
LSb	least significant bit
LSB	least significant byte
LSI	large scale integration
LSW	least significant word
LTO	linear tape open
M	memory
MCDIMM	multicore DIMM
MCH	memory controller HUB
MCU	microcontroller unit (preferred) or microcomputer unit (see μC)
MDA	monochrome display adapter
MDRAM	multibank DRAM®
ME	memory element (see MU)
MIPS	microprocessor without interlocked pipeline stages
MLC	multi(ple)-levels-per-cell
MMU	memory management unit
MoP	memory on package
MOS	metal-oxide semiconductor
MP3	MPEG-1 audio layer 3
MP	multiprocessor or multi-processor
MPDRAM	multiport DRAM
MPEG	Moving Picture Experts Group

MPM	multiport memory
MPRAM	multi-ported RAM
MPU	microprocessor unit (see μP)
MRAM	magnetoresistive RAM
MROM	mask ROM or mask-programmed ROM (JEDEC)
MS or M/S	master(s)/slave(s)
MSb	most significant bit
MSB	most significant byte
MSD	mass storage device
MSS	mass-storage system
MSW	most significant word
MT	micro-threaded
MU	memory unit (see ME)
NAND	not AND
NetRAM	network RAM
NMI	non maskable interrupt
NMOS	negative (channel) MOS
NOR	not OR
NUMA	non-uniform memory architecture
NVM	non volatile memory
O	output
OCD	off-chip driver
OE	output enable (see G)
ORTF	French national broadcasting office
OS	operating system
PAM	pointer-addresses memory
PATA	parallel advanced technology attachment
PC	personal computer
PC	phase comparator

PCB	printed circuit board
PCI	peripheral component interconnect
PD	phase detector
PDN	pull-down network
PDP	programmable data processor (DEC)
PE	processing element, processor element (see PU)
PLD	programmable logic device
PLL	phase-locked loop
PMOS	positive (channel) MOS
PMS	prime memory system
POST	power-on self-test
POWER	performance optimization with enhanced RISC
PowerPC	POWER performance computing
PPMS	perfect PMS
PRIM	pseudo-randomly interleaved memory
PROM	programmable ROM
PS/2	personal system/2
PSF	pattern-sensitive fault
PTL	pass-transistor logic
PU	processing unit (see PE)
PUN	pull-up network
Q	data output or data to write (data output)
QDR	quad-data-rate
R	read
R	register
RAID	redundant array of inexpensive disks
RAM	random access memory
RAMDAC/RAM-DAC	RAM DAC
RAS	row address strobe

RBER	raw BER
RC	read cycle
RC	resistor – capacitor
RDRAM	rambus DRAM
RISC	reduced instruction set computer
ROM	read-only memory
RQ	request
RS	Reed–Solomon (code)
RS	register select
RTG	row transaction granularity
RW or R/W	read/write
SA	sense amplifier
SAD	sum-addressed decoder
SAM	serial-access memory
SAM	sum-addressed memory
SATA	serial advanced technology attachment
SBM	single-buffered memory
SC	semiconductor
SCE	system control element
SDR	single data rate
SDRAM	synchronous DRAM
SEC	single-error correcting
SGRAM	synchronous GRAM
SIM	sequentially interleaved memory
SIO	separate(d) (data) I/O
SiP	system-in-a-package
SLDRAM	synchronous-link DRAM
S/N	signal/noise
SNR	S/N ratio

SoC	system on (a) chip, system-on-chip
SOI	silicon on insulator
SPA	sense preamplifier
SPARC	scalable processor architecture
SPI™	serial peripheral interface
SRAM	static RAM
SSD	solid-state disk
SSE	streaming SIMD extensions (Intel)
SSF	single-stuck fault
SSR	super self refresh (Elpida technology)
SSRAM	synchronous SRAM
ST	single-threaded
SW	software
TCM	tightly coupled memory
TF	transition fault
TTL	transistor transistor logic
UBER	uncorrectable BER
ULSI	ultra LSI
UMA	unified memory architecture
UNIVAC	universal automatic computer
USB	universal serial bus
UV	ultra-violet (old spelling)
VaWiRAM	variable width RAM
VAX	virtual addressed extended (DEC)
VGA	video graphics array
VHDL	VHSIC HDL
VHSIC	very high speed integrated circuit
VLIW	very LIW
VLSI	very LSI

VM	virtual memory
VMD	virtual memory device
VRAM	video RAM
VRC	vertical redundancy check
W	write
WC	write cycle
WE	write enable
WL	wordline
WOM	write-once memory (see WORM)
WORM	write-once-read-many times memory (see WOM)
WRAM	window RAM
XGA	extended graphics array
XOR	exclusive OR (see EOR and EXOR)

Miscellaneous

μC	microcontroller, or more rarely, microcomputer (see MCU)
μP	microprocessor (see MPU)
3D or 3-D	three-dimensional

Units of measurement or unit prefixes

b	bit
B	byte
b/s or bps	bit per second
bpspp	bps per pin
E	exa (= 10^{18})
exbi	exabinary, prefix Ei = 2^{60}
G	giga (= 10^{9})

Gb/GiB	gigabit/gigabyte
Gb/s or Gbps	gigabit per second
GB/s or GBps	gigabyte per second
Gib/GiB	gibibit/gibibyte
gibi	gigabinary, prefix Gi = 2^{30}
k	kilo (= 1,000)
K	kilobinary (= 1,024) – old prefix to avoid. only the uppercase or the context made it possible to distinguish the value of the prefix
kb/kB	kilobit/kilobyte (= 1,000 b/B)
Kb/KB	kilobit/Kilobyte (= 1,024 b/B) – old multiple to avoid
kb/s or kbps	kilobit per second
kB/s or kBps	kilobyte per second
Kib/KiB	kibibit/kibibyte
kibi	kilobinary, prefix ki = 2^{10}
M	mega (= 10^6)
Mb/MB	megabit/megabyte
Mb/s or Mbps	megabit per second
MB/s or MBps	megabyte per second
mebi	megabinary, prefix mi = 2^{20}
Mib/MiB	mebibit/mebibyte
P	peta (= 10^{15})
pebi	pebibinary, prefix pi = 2^{50}
T	tera (= 10^{12})
Tb/TB	terabit/terabyte
Tb/s or Tbps	terabit per second
TB/s or TBps	terabyte per second
tebi	tebibinary, prefix ti = 2^{40}
Tib/TiB	tebibit/tebibyte

Y	yotta (= 10^{24})
yobi	yobibinary, prefix yi = 2^{80}
Z	zetta (= 10^{21})
zebi	zebibinary, prefix zi = 2^{70}

Voltage characteristics

Gnd	ground
V_{BB}	bulk supply voltage
V_{DD}	drain drain (DC) supply voltage
V_{DH}	voltage drain high side
V_{DL}	data line voltage
$V_{GS(th)}$	gate (to) source threshold voltage
V_{PP}	programming power voltage
V_{SS}	source source (DC) voltage

Power characteristics

P_{max}	maximum power

Timing characteristics

t_a	access time
t_c	cycle time
t_{CC}	minimum time between two accesses to the same open page
t_{CCp}	partial t_{CC}
t_{pd}	propagation delay time

t_{PHL}	propagation delay time, high-to-low-level output
t_{PLH}	propagation delay time, low-to-high-level output
t_{RC}	read cycle time
t_{RR}	minimum time between two row activations in different banks
t_{RRp}	partial t_{RR}
t_{WC}	write cycle time

Companies or organizations

ACM	Association for Computing Machinery
AIEE	American Institute of Electrical Engineers
ANSI	American National Standards Institute
ARM	Acorn RISC Machine, then Advanced RISC Machines
CCIR	International Radio Consultative Committee (see IRCC)
CCITT	Consultative Committee for International Telegraph and Telephone
CEI	International Electrotechnical Commission (see IEC)
DEC	Digital Equipment Corporation
GSI	Giga Semiconductor, Inc.
HP	Hewlett-Packard
IBM	International Business Machines Corporation
IDT	Integrated Device Technology, Inc.
IEC	International Electrotechnical Commission (see CEI)
IEDM	International Electron Devices Meeting
IEEE	Institute of Electrical and Electronics Engineers
IRCC	International Radio Consultative Committee (see CCIR)
ISSCC	IEEE International Solid-State Circuits Conference

JEDEC	Joint Electron Device Engineering Council (Solid-State Technology Association)
LIM	Lotus Software, Intel, Microsoft
MIT	Massachusetts Institute of Technology
Mosys	Monolithic System Technology Incorporated
NS	National Semiconductor
NASA	National Aeronautics and Space Administration
RCA	Radio Corporation of America
SI	International System of Units

Trademarks (™)

Microwire	National Semiconductor
SPI	Motorola
VAX	Digital Equipment Corporation

Registered trademarks (®)

Ethernet	Xerox Corporation
HDMI	HDMI Licensing Administrator, Inc.
Intel	Intel
PS/2	International Business Machines Corporation

References

For reasons of domain consistency, the bibliographic references are organized into chapters.

Preface

Brewer, J.E. and Gill, M. (eds) (2008). *Nonvolatile Memory Technologies with Emphasis on Flash: A Comprehensive Guide to Understanding and Using NVM Devices.* John Wiley & Sons, New York.

Brown, W.D. and Brewer, J.E. (eds) (1997). *Nonvolatile Semiconductor Memory Technology: A Comprehensive Guide to Understanding and Using NVSM Devices.* John Wiley & Sons, New York.

Campardo, G., Micheloni, R., Novosel, D. (2005). *VLSI-Design of Non-Volatile Memories.* Springer, Berlin.

Chen, W.-K. (ed.) (2003). *Memory, Microprocessor, and ASIC.* CRC Press, New York.

Darche, P. (2000). *Architecture des ordinateurs. Représentation des nombres et codes. Cours avec exercices corrigés.* Gaëtan Morin, Quebec.

Darche, P. (2002). *Architecture des ordinateurs. Fonctions booléennes, logiques combinatoire et séquentielle. Cours avec exercices et exemples en VHDL.* Vuibert, Paris.

Darche, P. (2003). *Architecture des ordinateurs. Interfaces et périphériques. Cours avec exercices corrigés.* Vuibert, Paris.

Darche, P. (2004). *Architecture des ordinateurs. Logique booléenne : implémentations et technologies.* Vuibert, Paris.

Darche, P. (2021a). *Microprocessor 1: Prolegomenes – Calculation and Storage Functions – Models of Computation and Computer Architecture.* ISTE Ltd, London and John Wiley & Sons, New York.

Darche, P. (2021b). *Microprocessor 2: Core Concepts: Communication in a Digital System.* ISTE Ltd, London and John Wiley & Sons, New York.

Darche, P. (2021c). *Microprocessor 3: Core Concepts – Hardware Aspects.* ISTE Ltd, London and John Wiley & Sons, New York.

Darche, P. (2021d). *Microprocessor 4: Core Concepts – Software Aspects.* ISTE Ltd, London and John Wiley & Sons, New York.

Darche, P. (2021e). *Microprocessor 5: Software and Hardware Aspects of Development, Debugging and Testing – The Microcomputer.* ISTE Ltd, London and John Wiley & Sons, New York.

Itoh, K. (2001). *VLSI Memory Chip Design.* Springer, Berlin.

Redaelli, A. and Pellizzer, F. (eds) (2022). *Semiconductor Memories and Systems.* Elsevier, Amsterdam.

Yu, S. (2022). *Semiconductor Memory Devices and Circuits.* CRC Press, New York.

Introduction

Darche, P. (2003). *Architecture des ordinateurs. Interfaces et périphériques. Cours avec exercices corrigés.* Vuibert, Paris.

Darche, P. (2004). *Architecture des ordinateurs. Logique booléenne : implémentations et technologies.* Vuibert, Paris.

Darche, P. (2021a). *Microprocessor 1: Prolegomenes – Calculation and Storage Functions – Models of Computation and Computer Architecture.* ISTE Ltd, London and John Wiley & Sons, New York.

Darche, P. (2021b). *Microprocessor 2: Core Concepts: Communication in a Digital System.* ISTE Ltd, London and John Wiley & Sons, New York.

Darche, P. (2021c). *Microprocessor 3: Core Concepts – Hardware Aspects.* ISTE Ltd, London and John Wiley & Sons, New York.

Darche, P. (2021d). *Microprocessor 4: Core Concepts – Software Aspects.* ISTE Ltd, London and John Wiley & Sons, New York.

Darche, P. (2021e). *Microprocessor 5: Software and Hardware Aspects of Development, Debugging and Testing – The Microcomputer.* ISTE Ltd, London and John Wiley & Sons, New York.

Haraszti, T.P. (2002). *CMOS Memory Circuits.* Kluwer Academic Publishers, New York.

Keeth, B. and Baker, R.J. (2000). *DRAM Circuit Design: A Tutorial.* John Wiley & Sons, New York.

Prince, B. (1996). *Semiconductor Memories – A Handbook of Design, Manufacture, and Application.* John Wiley & Sons, New York.

Prince, B. (1999). *High Performance Memories-New Architecture DRAMs and SRAMs Evolution and Function*. John Wiley & Sons, New York.

Sharma, A.K. (2002a). *Semiconductor Memories: Technology, Testing, and Reliability*. John Wiley & Sons, New York.

Sharma, A.K. (2002b). *Advanced Semiconductor Memories: Architectures, Designs, and Applications*. John Wiley & Sons, New York.

Von Neumann, J. (1945). First draft of a report on the EDVAC. Report, University of Pennsylvania, Philadelphia.

Chapter 1

ANSI/IEEE (1991). IEEE standard for test procedures for magnetic cores. IEEE.

Bardeen, J. and Brattain, W.H. (1948). The transistor, a semiconductor triode. *Physical Review*, 74(2), 230–231.

Bashe, C.J., Johnson, L.R., Palmer, J.H., Pugh, E.W. (1986). *IBM's Early Computers*. MIT Press, Cambridge.

Beaulieu, N.C. (2002). Introduction to "Certain topics in telegraph transmission theory". *Proceedings of the IEEE*, 90(2), 276–279.

Belady, L.A., Parmelee, R.P., Scalzi, C.A. (1981). The IBM history of memory management technology. *IBM Journal of Research and Development*, 25(5), 491–504.

Bell, C.G., Mudge, J.C., McNamara, J.E. (eds) (1978). *Computer Engineering: A DEC View of Hardware Systems Design*. Digital Press, Waltham Cross.

Boland, K. and Dollas, A. (1994). Predicting and precluding problems with memory latency. *IEEE Micro*, 14(4), 59–67.

Bornhauser, H. (1964). Core storage matrix. Patent, 3154763.

Bromley, A.G. (1982). Charles Babbage's analytical engine, 1838. *IEEE Annals of the History of Computing*, 4(3), 196–217.

Burks, A.W. (1947). Electronic computing circuits of the ENIAC. *Proceedings of IRE*, 35(8), 756–767.

Burks, A.W. (1997). Electronic computing circuits of the ENIAC. *Proceedings of the IEEE*, 85(7), 1172–1182.

Burks, A.W., Goldstine, H.H., von Neumann, J. (1946). Preliminary discussion of the logical design of electronic computing instrument. Report, U.S. Army Ord. Dept., Washington, D.C.

Chen, P.M. and Patterson, D.A. (1993). Storage performance-metrics and benchmarks. *Proceedings of the IEEE*, 8(9), 1151–1165.

Chisvin, L. and Duckworth, R.J. (1989). Content-addressable and associative memory: Alternatives to the ubiquitous RAM. *IEEE Computer*, 22(7), 51–64.

Chu, J.C. and Klein, R.J. (1952). Williams tubes selection program. In *Proceedings of the 1952 ACM National Meeting*, 110–114.

Ciminiera, L. and Valenzano, A. (1987). *Advanced Microprocessor Architectures*. Addison-Wesley Publishing, Reading.

Cohen, E.I., King, G.M., Brady, J.T. (1989). Storage hierarchies. *IBM Systems Journal*, 28(1), 62–76.

Cragon, H.G. (1996). *Memory Systems and Pipelined Processors*. Jones and Bartlett Publishers, Burlington.

Darche, P. (2000). *Architecture des ordinateurs. Représentation des nombres et codes. Cours avec exercices corrigés*. Gaëtan Morin, Quebec.

Darche, P. (2002). *Architecture des ordinateurs. Fonctions booléennes, logiques combinatoire et séquentielle. Cours avec exercices et exemples en VHDL*. Vuibert, Paris.

Darche, P. (2003). *Architecture des ordinateurs. Interfaces et périphériques. Cours avec exercices corrigés*. Vuibert. Paris.

Darche, P. (2004). *Architecture des ordinateurs. Logique booléenne : implémentations et technologies*. Vuibert, Paris.

Darche, P. (2021a). *Microprocessor 1: Prolegomenes – Calculation and Storage Functions – Models of Computation and Computer Architecture*. ISTE Ltd, London and John Wiley & Sons, New York.

Darche, P. (2021b). *Microprocessor 2: Core Concepts: Communication in a Digital System*. ISTE Ltd, London and John Wiley & Sons, New York.

Darche, P. (2021c). *Microprocessor 3: Core Concepts – Hardware Aspects*. ISTE Ltd, London and John Wiley & Sons, New York.

Darche, P. (2021d). *Microprocessor 4: Core Concepts – Software Aspects*. ISTE Ltd, London and John Wiley & Sons, New York.

Darche, P. (2021e). *Microprocessor 5: Software and Hardware Aspects of Development, Debugging and Testing – The Microcomputer*. ISTE Ltd, London and John Wiley & Sons, New York.

Dewilde, P. and Vandewalle, J. (eds) (1992). *Computer Systems and Software Engineering: State-of-the-Art*. Kluwer Academic Publishers, New York.

Eccles, W.H. and Jordan, F.W. (1919). A trigger relay utilizing three-electrode thermionic vacuum tubes. *The Radio Review*, 1, 143–146.

Eckert, J.E. (1949). An electrostatic memory system. In *Proceedings of a Second Symposium on Large-Scale Digital Calculating Machinery*, 32–43.

Eckert, J.E. (1953). A survey of digital computer memory systems. *Proceedings of the IRE*, 41(10), 1393–1406.

Eveleth, J.H. (1965). A survey of ultrasonic delay lines operating below 100 Mc/s. *Proceedings of the IEEE*, 53(10), 1406–1428.

Forrester, J.W. (1951). Digital information storage in three dimensions using magnetic cores. *Journal of Applied Physics*, 22(1), 44–48.

Forrester, J.W. (1956). Multicoordinate digital information storage device. Patent, 2736880.

Godfrey, M.D. and Hendry, D.F. (1993). The computer as von Neumann planned it. *Annals of the History of Computing*, 15(1), 11–21.

Greifer, A.P. (1969). Ferrite memory materials. *IEEE Transactions on Magnetics*, 5(4), 774–811.

Grossman, C.P. (1985). Cache-DASD storage design for improving system performance. *IBM Systems Journal*, 24(3/4), 316–334.

Hake, J.-F. and Homberg, W. (1990). The impact of memory organization on the performance of matrix multiplication. In *Proceedings of Supercomputing '90*, 34–40.

Handy, J. (1998). *The Cache Memory Book*. Academic Press, New York.

Hartree, D.R. (1948). A historical survey of digital computing machines. *Proceedings of the Royal Society of London. Series A, Mathematical and Physical Sciences*, 195(104), 265–271.

Hartree, D.R., Newman, M.H.A., Wilkes, M.V., Williams, F.C., Wilkinson, J.H., Booth A.D. (1948). A discussion on computing machines. *Proceedings of the Royal Society of London. Series A, Mathematical and Physical Sciences*, 195(104), 265–287.

IEC (2000). Symboles littéraux à utiliser en électrotechnique. Télécommunications et électronique. International Electrotechnical Commission.

IEEE (1996). IEEE standard for high-bandwidth memory interface based on scalable coherent interface (SCI) signaling technology (RamLink). IEEE.

IEEE (2002a). Draft standard for prefixes for binary multiples. IEEE.

IEEE (2002b). IEEE 1541-2002: IEEE standard for prefixes for binary multiples. IEEE.

IEEE Spectrum (2000). A backward glance. Arriving at the punched-card system. *IEEE Spectrum*, 37(2), 58–61.

James, W. (1890). *The Principles of Psychology*. Henry Holt and Co, New York.

Julian, R.S. and Samuel, A.L. (1949). Coordinate tubes for use with electrostatic storage tubes. In *Proceedings of a Second Symposium on Large-Scale Digital Calculating Machinery*, 96–114.

Kaneko, T. (1974). Optimal task switching policy for a multilevel storage system. *IBM Journal of Research and Development*, 18(4), 310–315.

Katayama, Y. (1997). Trends in semiconductor memories. *IEEE Micro*, 17(6), 1017.

Kistermann, F.W. (1991). The invention and development of the Hollerith punched card: In commemoration of the 130th anniversary of the birth of Herman Hollerith and for the 100th anniversary of large scale data processing. *IEEE Annals of the History of Computing*, 13(3), 245–259.

Kistermann, F.W. (2005). Hollerith punched card system development (1905–1913). *IEEE Annals of the History of Computing*, 27(1), 56–66.

Knoll, M. and Kazan, B. (1952). *Storage Tubes and Their Basic Principles*. John Wiley & Sons, New York.

Marguin, J. (1994). *Histoire des instruments et machines à calculer. Trois siècles de mécanique pensante, 1642–1942*. Éditions Hermann, Paris.

Meinadier, J.-P. (1988). *Structure et fonctionnement des ordinateurs*. Larousse, Paris.

Nakagomi, T., Holzbach, M., Van Meter III, R., Ranade, S. (1993). Re-defining the storage hierarchy: An ultra-fast magneto-optical disk drive. In *Proceedings of the Twelfth IEEE Symposium on Mass Storage Systems: "Putting all that Data to Work"*, 29 April, 267–274.

Nyquist, H. (1928). Certain topics in telegraph transmission theory. *Transactions of the American Institute of Electrical Engineers (AIEE)*, 47(2), 617–644.

O'Brien, F. (2010). *The Apollo Guidance Computer: Architecture and Operation*. Springer, Berlin.

Patterson, D., Anderson, T., Cardwell, N., Fromm, R., Keeton, K., Kozyrakis, C., Thomas, R., Yelick, K. (1997). A case for intelligent RAM: IRAM. *IEEE Micro*, 17(2), 34–44.

Proebster, W.E. (1992). The evolution of data memory and storage: An overview. In *Computer Systems and Software Engineering: State-of-the-Art*, Dewilde, P. and Vandewalle, J. (eds). Kluwer Academic Publishers, New York, 1–23.

Przybylski, S.A. (1996). SDRAMs ready to enter PC mainstream. *Microprocessor Report*, 10(6), 17–23.

Pugh, E.W. (1971). Storage hierarchies: Gaps, cliffs, and trends. *IEEE Transactions on Magnetics*, 7(4), 810–814.

Pugh, E.W. (2000). *Memories that Shaped an Industry: Decisions Leading to IBM System/360*. MIT Press, New York.

Pugh, E.W., Critchlow, D.L., Henle, R.A., Russell, L.A. (1981). Solid state memory development in IBM. *IBM Journal of Research and Development*, 25(5), 585–602.

Puthuff, S.H. (1978). Technical innovations in information storage and retrieval. *IEEE Transactions on Magnetics*, 14(4), 143–148.

Rajan, S. (2009). Integrated memory core and memory interface circuit. Patent, 7515453.

Rajchman, J. (1948). The Selectron – A tube for selective electrostatic storage. In *Proceedings of a Symposium on Large-Scale Digital Calculating Machinery*, 133–135.

Rajchman, J. (1949). The Selectron. In *Proceedings of a Second Symposium on Large-Scale Digital Calculating Machinery*, 365–373.

Rajchman, J. (1951). The selective electrostatic storage tube. *RCA Review*, 12(1), 5397.

Rajchman, J. (1957). A survey of magnetic and other solid-state devices for the manipulation of information. *IRE Transactions on Circuit Theory*, 4(3), 210–225.

Rege, S.L. (1976). Cost, performance and size tradeoffs for different levels in memory hierachy. In *Proceedings of the Third Annual International Symposium on Computer Architecture (ISCA '76)*, 19–21 January, 64–67.

Schmitt, W.F. (1988). The UNIVAC short code. *Annals of the History of Computing*, 10(1), 7–18.

Schneck, P.B. (1997). Introduction to the classic paper: "A survey of digital computer memory systems". *Proceedings of the IEEE*, 85(1), 181–183.

Scrupski, S. (2001). Thin-film memory gives fast output. *Electronic Design*, 49, 50.

Self, K. (1999). Memory in megabytes and/or mebibytes. *IEEE Spectrum*, 36(8), 18.

Shannon, C.H. (1948). A mathematical theory of communication. *The Bell System Technical Journal*, 27, 379.

Shannon, C.H. (1993). *Claude Elwood Shannon: Collected Papers.* Wiley-IEEE Press, Piscataway.

Shriver, B. and Smith, B. (1998). *The Anatomy of a High-Performance Microprocessor: A Systems Perspective.* IEEE Computer Society Press, Los Alamitos, CA.

Slater, M., Farmwald, M., Hannah, M., James, D.V., Karp, J.A., Kumanoya, M., Szarek, J. (1993). Which DRAM will win the great DRAM sweepstakes? In *40th IEEE International Solid-State Circuits Conference (ISSCC 1993)*, 24–26 February, 76–77.

Von Neumann, J. (1945). First draft of a report on the EDVAC. Report, Universiy of Pennsylvania, Philadelphia.

Wang, A. (1955). Pulse transfer controlling device. Patent, 2708722.

Wang, A. and Woo, W.D. (1950). Digital information storage in three dimensions using magnetic cores. *Journal of Applied Physics*, 21(1), 49–54.

Williams, J.G. (1973). Asymmetric memory hierarchies. *Communications of the ACM (CACM)*, 16(4), 213–222.

Williams, M.R. (1997). *A History of Computing Technology*. IEEE Computer Society Press, Los Alamitos, CA.

Wulf, W.A. and McKee, S.A. (1995). Hitting the memory wall: Implications of the obvious. *ACM SIGARCH Computer Architecture News*, 23(1), 20–24.

Zilberstein, R.M. (1965). Variable ultrasonic delay line. Correspondence. *Proceedings of the IEEE*, 53(6), 637–637.

Chapter 2

Chan, Y.H., Srinivasan, U., Wadhwa, J.K. (2006). High performance CMOS NOR predecode circuit. Patent, 20060176757.

Darche, P. (2002). *Architecture des ordinateurs. Fonctions booléennes, logiques combinatoire et séquentielle. Cours avec exercices et exemples en VHDL*. Vuibert, Paris.

Darche, P. (2004). *Architecture des ordinateurs. Logique booléenne : implémentations et technologies*. Vuibert, Paris.

Davis, H.L. (1985). A 70ns word-wide 1-Mb ROM with on-chip error-correction circuits. *IEEE Journal of Solid-State Circuits (JSSC)*, 20(5), 958–963.

DiMarco, D.P., Nicholes, J.W., Smith, D.D. (1994). Sense amplifier and latching circuit for an SRAM. Patent, 5289415.

Dubujet, B. (1990). Circuit for the detection of address transitions. Patent, 4922122.

Foss, R.C. and Harland, R.H. (1975). Peripheral circuits for one transistor cell MOS RAMs. *IEEE Journal of Solid-State Circuits (JSSC)*, 10(5), 255–261.

Frederick, B.A. (1985). MOS depletion load circuit. Patent, 4516225.

Gerez, S.H. and Woutersen, E.G. (1996). Assignment of storage values to sequential read-write memories. In *Proceedings of the 1996 European Design Automation Conference (EURO-DAC '96) (with EURO-VHDL '96)*, 302–307.

Gubbels, W.C.H., Hartgring, C.D., Salters, R.H.W., Lammerts, J.A.M., Tooher, M.J., Hens, P.F.P.C., Bustiaens, J.J., van Dijk, J.M.F., Sprokel, M.A. (1987). A 40-ns/100-pF low-power full-CMOS 256K (32K × 8) SRAM. *IEEE Journal of Solid-State Circuits*, 22(5), 741–747.

Heald, R., Shin, K., Reddy, V., Kao, I., Khan, M., Lynch, W.L., Lauterbach, G., Petolino, J. (1998a). 64 KB sum-addressed-memory cache with 1.6 ns cycle and 2.6 ns latency. In *IEEE International Solid-State Circuits Conference (ISSC) Digest of Technical Papers*, 216–217.

Heald, R., Shin, K., Reddy, V., Kao, I., Khan, M., Lynch, W.L., Lauterbach, G., Petolino, J. (1998b). 64-KB sum-addressed-memory cache with 1.6 ns cycle and 2.6 ns latency. *IEEE Journal of Solid-State Circuits (JSSC)*, 33(11), 1682–1689.

Heller, L.G., Spampinato, D.P., Yao, Y.L. (1976). High sensitivity charge-transfer sense amplifier. *IEEE Journal of Solid-State Circuits (JSSC)*, 11(5), 596–601.

Hofmann, R.H. and Von Basse, P.W. (1978). Arrangement for addressing a MOS store. Patent, 4104735.

IEEE (1984). IEEE standard graphic symbols for logic functions. In *Electrical and Electronics Graphic & Letter Symbols and Reference Designations*. IEEE Standards Collection, New York.

IEEE (1991). Supplement to IEEE standard graphic symbols for logic functions. In *Electrical and Electronics Graphic & Letter Symbols and Reference Designations*. IEEE Standards Collection, New York.

IEEE (1996). *Electrical and Electronics Graphic & Letter Symbols and Reference Designations*. IEEE Standards Collection, New York.

Jordan, W.F. (1970). Read-only memory organization. Patent, 3653004.

Jordan, P.V., Palmieri, J.A., Wade, W.T. (1972). Read only memory and method of using same. Patent, 3678475.

Kimura, K., Itoh, K., Hori, R., Etoh, J., Kawajiri, Y., Kawamoto, H., Sato, K., Matsumoto, T. (1986). Power reduction techniques in megabit DRAM's. *IEEE Journal of Solid-State Circuits (JSSC)*, 21(3), 381–389.

Leak, D.A. (1995). Methods and apparatus for using address transition detection to reduce power consumption. Patent, 5423047.

Lynch, W.T. and Boll, H.J. (1974). Optimization of the latching pulse for dynamic flip-flop sensors. *IEEE Journal of Solid-State Circuits (JSSC)*, 9(2), 49–55.

Lynch, W.L., Lauterbach, G., Chamdani, J.I. (1998). Low load latency through sum-addressed memory (SAM). In *Proceedings of the 25th Annual International Symposium on Computer Architecture (ISCA '98)*, 369–379.

Matsui, Y. (1999). Semiconductor device having a latch circuit for latching data externally input. Patent, 5886553.

O'Connell, T.R. and Leach, G.S. (1980). Sense line termination circuit for semiconductor memory systems. Patent, 4195356.

Ochii, K., Yasuda, H., Kobayashi, K., Kondoh, T., Masuoka, F. (1985). A 17ns 64K CMOS RAM with a Schmitt trigger sense amplifier. In *1985 IEEE International Solid-State Circuits Conference (ISSCC 1985)*, 64–65.

Pascucci, L. (2001). Address transition detector in semiconductor memories. Patent, 6212128.

Proebsting, R. and Green, R.S. (1975). Dynamic data input latch and decoder. Patent, 3902082.

Regitz, W.M. (1973). Read-only memory organization. Patent, 3774171.

Simon, J.C. (1970). *Introduction au fonctionnement des ordinateurs*. Masson & Cie, Echandens.

Stewart, R.G. (1977a). High-density CMOS ROM arrays. In *1977 IEEE International Solid-State Circuits Conference (ISSCC 1977)*, 20–21.

Stewart, R.G. (1977b). High-density CMOS ROM arrays. *IEEE Journal of Solid-State Circuits (JSSC)*, 502–506.

Chapter 3

Boonstra, L., Lambrechtse, C.W., Salters, R.H.W. (1973). A 4096-b one-transistor per bit random-access memory with internal timing and low dissipation. *IEEE Journal of Solid-State Circuits (JSSC)*, 8(5), 305–310.

Brugler, J.S. and Jespers, P.G.A. (1969). Charge pumping in MOS devices. *IEEE Transactions on Electron Devices*, 16(3), 297–302.

Darche, P. (2004). *Architecture des ordinateurs. Logique booléenne : implémentations et technologies*. Vuibert, Paris.

Davis, H.L. (1985). A 70ns word-wide 1-Mb ROM with on-chip error-correction circuits. *IEEE Journal of Solid-State Circuits (JSSC)*, 20(5), 958–963.

Foss, R.C. and Harland, R. (1975). Peripheral circuits for one transistor cell MOS RAMs. *IEEE Journal of Solid-State Circuits (JSSC)*, 10(5), 255–261.

Fujii, S., Ogihara, M., Shimizu, M., Yoshida, M., Numata, K., Hara, T., Watanabe, S., Sawada, S., Mizuno, T., Kumagai, J. et al. (1989a). A 45ns 16Mb DRAM with triple-well structure. In *36th IEEE International Solid-State Circuits Conference (ISSCC 1989) Digest of Technical Papers*, 248–249.

Fujii, S., Ogihara, M., Shimizu, M., Yoshida, M., Numata, K., Hara, T., Watanabe, S., Sawada, S., Mizuno, T., Kumagai, J. et al. (1989b). A 45-ns 16-Mbit DRAM with triple-well structure. *IEEE Journal of Solid-State Circuits (JSSC)*, 24(5), 1170–1175.

Gillingham, P., Foss, R.C., Lines, V., Shimokura, G., Wojcicki, T. (1991). High-speed, high-reliability circuit design for megabit DRAM. *IEEE Journal of Solid-State Circuits (JSSC)*, 26(8), 1171–1175.

Igarashi, R., Kurosawa, T., Yaita, T. (1966). A 150-nanosecond associative memory using integrated MOS transistors. In *1966 IEEE International Solid-State Circuits Conference (ISSCC 1966)*, 104–105.

Itoh, K. (2001). *VLSI Memory Chip Design*. Springer, Berlin.

Joynson, R.E., Mundy, J.L., Burgess, J.F., Neugebauer, C.A. (1971). Eliminating threshold losses in MOS circuits by varactor bootstrapping. *Proceedings of the IEEE*, 59(9), 1365–1366.

Joynson, R.E., Mundy, J.L., Burgess, J.F., Neugebauer, C.A. (1972). Eliminating threshold losses in MOS circuits by bootstrapping using varactor coupling. *IEEE Journal of Solid-State Circuits (JSSC)*, 7(3), 217–224.

Kim, D., Park, M., Jang, S., Song, J.-Y., Chi, H., Choi, G., Choi, S., Kim, J., Kim, C., Kim, K. et al. (2019). A 1.1V 10-nm 6.4Gb/s/pin 16Gb DDR5 SDRAM with a phase-rotator-based DLL, high-speed SerDes and RX/TX equalization scheme. In *Proceedings of the 2019 IEEE International Solid-State Circuits Conference (ISSCC)*, 380–382.

Kim, D., Park, M., Jang, S., Song, J.-Y., Chi, H., Choi, G., Choi, S., Kim, C., Han, H., Koo, K. et al. (2020). A 1.1-V 10-nm class 6.4-Gb/s/pin 16-Gb DDR5 SDRAM with a phase rotator-ILO DLL, high-speed SerDes, and DFE/FFE equalization scheme for Rx/Tx. *IEEE Journal of Solid-State Circuits (JSCC)*, 55(1), 167–177.

Schnell, J. (2000). Delay lock loop. Patent, 6137327.

Smith, R.T., Chlipala, J.D., Bindels, J.F.M., Nelson, R.G., Fischer, F.H., Mantz, T.F. (1981). Laser programmable redundancy and yield improvement in a 64K DRAM. *IEEE Journal of Solid-State Circuits (JSSC)*, 16(5), 506–514.

Suzuki, M., Tachibana, S., Watanabe, A., Shukuri, S., Higuchi, H., Nagano, T., Shimohigashi, K. (1989). A 3.5-ns, 500-mW, 16-kbit BiCMOS ECL RAM. *IEEE Journal of Solid-State Circuits (JSSC)*, 24(5), 1233–1237.

Takano, S., Makino, H., Tanino, N., Noda, M., Nishitani, K., Kayano, S. (1987). A 16K GaAS SRAM. In *1987 IEEE International Solid-State Circuits Conference (ISSCC 1987)*, 30, 140–141.

Tan, S.C. and Sun, X.W. (2002). Low power CMOS level shifters by bootstrapping technique. *Electronics Letters*, 38(16), 876–878.

Taylor, R.T. and Johnson, M.G. (1985a). A 1Mb CMOS DRAM with a divided bitline matrix architecture. In *1985 IEEE International Solid-State Circuits Conference (ISSCC 1985)*, 28, 242–243.

Taylor, R.T. and Johnson, M.G. (1985b). A 1-Mbit CMOS dynamic RAM with a divided bitline matrix architecture. *IEEE Journal of Solid-State Circuits (JSSC)*, 20(5), 894–902.

Chapter 4

Ahn, J.H., Leverich, J., Schreiber, R.S., Jouppi, N.P. (2009a). Multicore DIMM: An energy efficient memory module with independently controlled DRAMs. *IEEE Computer Architecture*, 8(1), 5–8.

Ahn, J.H., Jouppi, N.P., Kozyrakis, C. (2009b). Future scaling of processor-memory interfaces. Report, HP Laboratories, Palo Alto.

Ayukawa, K., Watanabe, T., Narita, S. (1998). An access-sequence control scheme to enhance random-access performance of embedded DRAM's. *IEEE Journal of Solid-State Circuits (JSSC)*, 33(5), 800–806.

Darche, P. (2004). *Architecture des ordinateurs. Logique booléenne : implémentations et technologies*. Vuibert, Paris.

Darche, P. (2021a). *Microprocessor 1: Prolegomenes – Calculation and Storage Functions – Models of Computation and Computer Architecture*. ISTE Ltd, London and John Wiley & Sons, New York.

Darche, P. (2021b). *Microprocessor 2: Core Concepts: Communication in a Digital System.* ISTE Ltd, London and John Wiley & Sons, New York.

Giovannini, T., Best, S., Shaeffer, I., De Berti, K., Ching, M. (2009). Challenges and solutions for future main memory. Rambus White Paper, San Jose.

Hsu, F.C. (1998). Method and structure for improving display data bandwidth in a unified memory architecture system. Patent, 5790138.

John, L.K. (1996). VaWiRAM: A variable width random access memory module. In *Proceedings of 9th International Conference on VLSI Design*, 219–224.

Leung, W., Lee, W., Hsu, F.-C. (1997). Resynchronization circuit for a memory system and method of operating same. Patent, 5655113.

Ochii, K., Hashimoto, K., Yasuda, H., Masuda, M., Nozawa, H., Kohyama, S. (1982). A 15nW standby power 64Kb CMOS RAM. In *1982 IEEE International Solid-State Circuits Conference (ISSCC 1982)*, 260–261.

Ogawa, J. and Horowitz, M. (2001). A 64Mbit mesochronous hybrid wave pipelined multibank DRAM macro. In *Revised Papers from the Second International Workshop on Intelligent Memory Systems (IMS 2000)*.

Przybylski, S. (1995). MoSys reveals MDRAM architecture, radical alternative is not just another VRAM. *Microprocessor Report*, 9(17), 17–20.

Ware, F.A. and Hampel, C. (2005). Micro-threaded row and column operations in a DRAM core. Rambus White Paper, San Jose.

Ware, F.A., Hampel, C.E., Richardson, W.S., Bellows, C.A., Lai, L. (2006). Micro-threaded memory. Patent, US2006/0117155 A1.

Ware, F.A., Hampel, C.E., Richardson, W.S., Bellows, C.A., Lai, L. (2007). Multi-mode memory. Patent, US2007/0250677 A1.

Yoshimoto, M., Anami, K., Shinohara, H., Yoshihara, T., Takagi, H., Nagao, S., Kayano, S., Nakano, T. (1983). A divided word-line structure in the static RAM and its application to a 64K Full CMOS RAM. *IEEE Journal of Solid-State Circuits (JSSC)*, 18(5), 479–484.

Zheng, H., Lin, J., Zhang, Z., Zhu, Z. (2009). Decoupled DIMM: Building high-bandwidth memory system using low-speed DRAM devices. *ACM SIGARCH Computer Architecture News*, 37(3), 255–266.

Chapter 5

Asato, C., Montoye, R., Gmuender, J., Simmons, E.W, Ike, A., Zasio, J. (1995). A 14-port 3.8 ns 116-word 64b read-renaming register file. In *1995 IEEE International Solid-State Circuits Conference (ISSCC 1995)*, 345, 104–105.

Burnett, G.J. and Coffman, E.G. (1970). A study of interleaved memory systems. In *Proceedings of the 1970 Spring Joint Computer Conference, Session: Computer System Modeling and Analysis*, 467–474.

Darche, P. (2000). *Architecture des ordinateurs. Représentation des nombres et codes. Cours avec exercices corrigés*. Gaëtan Morin, Quebec.

Darche, P. (2002). *Architecture des ordinateurs. Fonctions booléennes, logiques combinatoire et séquentielle. Cours avec exercices et exemples en VHDL*. Vuibert, Paris.

Darche, P. (2003). *Architecture des ordinateurs. Interfaces et périphériques. Cours avec exercices corrigés*. Vuibert, Paris.

Dijkstra, E.W. (1965). Solution of a problem in concurrent programming control. *Communications of the ACM (CACM)*, 8(9), 569.

Gao, Q.S. (1993). The Chinese remainder theorem and the prime memory system. In *Proceedings of the 20th Annual International Symposium on Computer Architecture (ISCA '93)*, 337–340.

Harper III, D.T. and Jump, J.R. (1986). Performance evaluation of vector accesses in parallel memories using a skewed storage scheme. *ACM SIGARCH Computer Architecture News*, 14(2), 324–328.

Harper III, D.T. and Jump, J.R. (1987). Vector access performance in parallel memories using a skewed storage scheme. *IEEE Transactions on Computers*, 36(12), 1440–1449.

Hennessy, J.L. and Patterson, D.A. (1994). *Architecture des ordinateurs : une approche quantitative*. Morgan Kaufmann Publishers, Burlington.

JEDEC (2009). GDDR5 SGRAM. JEDEC Standard no. JESD212. JEDEC Solid State Technology Association.

JEDEC (2020). High bandwidth memory (HBM) DRAM. JEDEC Standard no. JESD235C (revision of no. JESD235B, November 2018). JEDEC Solid State Technology Association.

Kuck, D.J. (1968). ILLIAC IV software and application programming. *IEEE Transactions on Computers*, 17(8), 758–770.

Kuck, D.J. and Stokes, R.A. (1982). The Burroughs Scientific Processor (BSP). *IEEE Transactions on Computers*, 31(5), 363–376.

Lawrie, D.H. and Vora, C.R. (1982). The prime memory system for array access. *IEEE Transactions on Computers*, 31(5), 435–442.

Poppendieck, M. and Desautels, E.J. (1977). Special feature: Memory extension techniques for minicomputers. *IEEE Computer*, 10(5), 68–75.

Raghavan, R. and Hayes, J.P. (1990). On randomly interleaved memories. In *Proceedings of Supercomputing '90*, 49–58.

Rau, B.R. (1979). Program behavior and the performance of interleaved memories. *IEEE Transactions on Computers*, 28(3), 191–199.

Rau, B.R. (1991). Pseudo-randomly interleaved memory. *ACM SIGARCH Computer Architecture*, 19(3), 74–83.

Seznec, A. and Lenfant, J. (1994). Interleaved parallel schemes. *IEEE Transactions on Parallel and Distributed Systems*, 5(12), 1329–1334.

Teng, M.H. (1983). Comments on “The prime memory systems for array access”. *IEEE Transactions on Computers*, 32(11), 1072–1072.

Van Sas, J., Catthoor, F., De Man, H.J. (1993). Test algorithms for double-buffered random access and pointer-addressed memories. *IEEE Design & Test of Computers*, 10(2), 34–44.

Wyland, D.C. (1988). Dual-port RAMs simplify processor communications. *Microprocessors and Microsystems*, 12(10), 585–594.

Zhang, Z., Zhu, Z., Zhang, X. (2000). A permutation-based page interleaving scheme to reduce row-buffer conflicts and exploit data locality. In *Proceedings of the 33rdAnnual ACM/IEEE International Symposium on Microarchitecture (MICRO 33)*, 32–41.

Chapter 6

Amdahl, G.M., Blaauw, G.A., Brooks, F.P. (1964). Architecture of the IBM System/360. *IBM Journal of Research and Development*, 8(2), 87–101.

Becker, M.K., Allen, M.S., Moore, C.R., Muhich, J.S., Tuttle, D.P. (1993). The power PC 601 microprocessor. *IEEE Micro*, 13(5), 54–68.

Bell, C.G., Mudge, J.C., McNamara, J.E. (eds) (1978). *Computer Engineering: A DEC View of Hardware Systems Design*. Digital Press, Waltham Cross.

Berlekamp, E.R. (ed.) (1974). *Key Papers in the Development of Coding Theory*. IEEE Press, New York.

Blake, I.F. (ed.) (1973). *Algebraic Coding Theory: History and Development. Benchmark Papers in Electrical Engineering and Computer Science*. Dowden, Hutchinson & Ross, Stroudsburg, PA.

Chen, C.L. and Hsiao, M.Y. (1984). Error-correcting codes for semiconductor memory applications: A state-of-the-art review. *IBM Journal of Research and Development*, 28(2), 124–134.

Cohen, D. (1981). On holy wars and a plea for peace. *IEEE Computer*, 14(10), 48–54.

Collège d’experts (2003). Collège d’experts chargé du contrôle des systèmes de vote et de dépouillement automatisés. Report.

Darche, P. (2000). *Architecture des ordinateurs. Représentation des nombres et codes. Cours avec exercices corrigés*. Gaëtan Morin, Quebec.

Darche, P. (2002). *Architecture des ordinateurs. Fonctions booléennes, logiques combinatoire et séquentielle. Cours avec exercices et exemples en VHDL*. Vuibert, Paris.

Darche, P. (2003). *Architecture des ordinateurs. Interfaces et périphériques. Cours avec exercices corrigés*. Vuibert, Paris.

Darche, P. (2004). *Architecture des ordinateurs. Logique booléenne : implémentations et technologies*. Vuibert, Paris.

Darche, P. (2021a). *Microprocessor 1: Prolegomenes – Calculation and Storage Functions – Models of Computation and Computer Architecture*. ISTE Ltd, London and John Wiley & Sons, New York.

Darche, P. (2021c). *Microprocessor 3: Core Concepts – Hardware Aspects*. ISTE Ltd, London and John Wiley & Sons, New York.

Darche, P. (2021d). *Microprocessor 4: Core Concepts – Software Aspects*. ISTE Ltd, London and John Wiley & Sons, New York.

Darche, P. (2021e). *Microprocessor 5: Software and Hardware Aspects of Development, Debugging and Testing – The Microcomputer*. ISTE Ltd, London and John Wiley & Sons, New York.

Dell, T.J. (1997). *A white paper on the benefits of Chipkill correct ECC for PC server main memory*. White Paper, IBM Microelectronics Division.

Diefendorff, K. (1994). History of the power PC architecture. *Communications of the ACM (CACM)*, 37(6), 28–33.

Eto, A., Hidaka, M., Okuyama, Y., Kimura, K., Hosono, M. (1998). Impact of neutron flux on soft errors in MOS memories. In *1998 International Electron Devices Meeting (IEDM '98) Technical Digest*, 367–370.

George, J., Thompson, T.J., Conroy, D.G., Tudor, F.H. (1990). Method for canonical ordering of binary data for portable operating systems. Patent, 4956809.

Ghosh, S., Basu, S., Touba, N.A. (2004). Reducing power consumption in memory ECC checkers. In *Proceedings of the IEEE International Test Conference (ITC-2004)*, 1322–1331.

Gifford, D. and Spector, A. (1987). Case study: IBM's system/360-370 architecture. *Communications of the ACM (CACM)*, 30(4), 291–307.

GSI (2000). Using ByteSafe™ SRAMs in parity and non-parity applications [Online]. Available at: http://www.gsitechnology.com/an1001.pdf.

Hamming, R.W. (1950). Error detecting and error correcting codes. *The Bell System Technical Journal*, 29, 147–160.

Hennessy, J., Jouppi, N., Przybylski, S.A., Rowen, C., Gross, T., Baskett, F., Gill, J. (1982). MIPS: A microprocessor architecture. In *Proceedings of the Fifteenth Annual Workshop on Microprogramming*, Palo Alto, 17–22.

Hidaka, H., Matsuda, Y., Asakura, M., Fujishima, K. (1990). The cache DRAM architecture: A DRAM with an on-chip cache memory. *IEEE Micro*, 10(2), 14–25.

Horiguchi, M. (1997). Redundancy techniques for high-density DRAMs. In *Proceedings of the Second Annual IEEE International Conference on Innovative Systems in Silicon*, 22–29.

IBM (2000). PowerPC 405GP endianness and bit naming conventions. Application Note.

IEEE (1996). *Electrical and Electronics Graphic & Letter Symbols and Reference Designations*. IEEE Standards Collection, New York.

JEDEC (2003). Configurations for solid sate memories. JEDEC Standard no. 21-C (JESD21-C). JEDEC Solid State Technology Association.

Khanna, R. and Partovi, H. (2000). Dynamic NOR gates for NAND decode. Patent, 6081136.

May, T.C. and Woods, M.H. (1979). Alpha-particle-induced soft errors in dynamic memories. *IEEE Transactions on Electron Devices*, 26(1), 2–9.

Sharma, A.K. (2002). *Semiconductor Memories: Technology, Testing, and Reliability*. John Wiley & Sons, New York.

Swartzlander, E.E. (1990). *Computer Arithmetic*. IEEE Computer Society Press, Washington, D.C.

Swift, J. (1726). *Gulliver's Travels*. Oxford University Press, Oxford.

Yaney, D.S., Nelson, J.T., Vanskike, L.L. (1979). Alpha-particle tracks in silicon and their effect on dynamic MOS RAM reliability. *IEEE Transactions on Electron Devices*, 26(1), 10–16.

Ziegler, J.F. (1996). Terrestrial cosmic rays. *IBM Journal of Research and Development*, 40(1), 19–39.

Ziegler, J.F., Curtis, H.W., Muhlfeld, F.P., Montrose, C.J., Chin, B., Nicewicz, M., Russell, C.A., Wang, W.Y., Freeman, L.B., Hosier, P. et al. (1996). IBM experiments in soft fails in computer electronics (1978–1994). *IBM Journal of Research and Development*, 40(1), 3–16.

Appendix

Berlekamp, E.R. (ed.) (1974). *Key Papers in the Development of Coding Theory*. IEEE Press, New York.

Berrou, C. and Glavieux, A. (1996). Near optimum error correcting coding and decoding: Turbo-codes. *IEEE Transactions on Communications*, 44(10), 1261–1271.

Berrou, C., Glavieux, A., Thitimajshima, P. (1993). Near Shannon limit error-correcting coding and decoding: Turbo-codes (1). In *Proceedings of IEEE International Conference on Communications (ICC '93)*, 1064–1070.

Boudreau, P.E. and Steen, R.F. (1971). Cyclic redundancy checking by program. In *Proceedings of the Fall Joint Computer Conference (AFIPS '71 (Fall))*, 9–15.

Chinal, J. (1979). *Circuits logiques de traitement numérique de l'information*. Éditions Cépaduès, Toulouse.

Cullmann, G. (1967). *Codes détecteurs et correcteurs d'erreurs*. Dunod, Paris.

Darche, P. (2004). *Architecture des ordinateurs. Logique booléenne : implémentations et technologies*. Vuibert, Paris.

Darche, P. (2021a). *Microprocessor 1: Prolegomenes – Calculation and Storage Functions – Models of Computation and Computer Architecture*. ISTE Ltd, London and John Wiley & Sons, New York.

Darche, P. (2021d). *Microprocessor 4 : Core Concepts – Software Aspects*. ISTE Ltd, London and John Wiley & Sons, New York.

Elias, P. (1955). Coding for noisy channels. *IRE International Convention Record*, 3(4), 37–44.

Forney, G.D. (1965). Concatenated codes. Report.

Forney, G.D. (1966). *Concatenated Codes*. MIT Press, New York.

Gray, F. (1953). Pulse code communication. Patent, 2 632 058.

Gray, K. (2000). Adding error-correcting circuitry to ASIC memory. *IEEE Spectrum*, 37(4), 55–60.

Hamming, R.W. (1950). Error detecting and error correcting codes. *The Bell System Technical Journal*, 29, 147–160.

Kientzle, T. (1997). Understanding CRCs. *Dr. Dobb's Journal*, 22(4), 103–107.

Koopman, P. (2024). *Understanding Checksums and Cyclic Redundancy Checks*. Self-published.

Macchi, C. and Guilbert, J.-F. (1987). *Téléinformatique*. Dunod, Paris.

Mee, C.D. and Daniel, E.D. (eds) (1996). *Magnetic Storage Handbook*. McGraw-Hill, New York.

Mielke, N., Marquart, T., Wu, N., Kessenich, J., Belgal, H., Schares, E., Trivedi, F., Goodness, E., Nevill, L.R. (2008). Bit error rate in NAND flash memories. In *Proceedings of the 46th Annual IEEE International Reliability Physics Symposium (IEEE CFP08RPS-CDR)*, 9–19.

Nussbaumer, H. (1987). *Téléinformatique I : Circuits de données - Les erreurs et leur traitement. Liaisons de données*. Presses Polytechniques Universitaires Romandes, Lausanne.

Patel, A.M. (1985). Adaptive cross-parity (AXP) code for high-density magnetic tape subsystem. *IBM Journal of Research and Development*, 29(6), 546–562.

Perez, P. (1983). Byte-wise CRC calculations. *IEEE Micro*, 3(3), 40–50.

Rallapalli, K. (1978). CRC error-detection schemes ensure data accuracy. *EDN*, 23(16), 119–123.

Ramabadran, T.V. and Gaitonde, S.S. (1988). A tutorial on CRC computations. *IEEE Micro*, 8(4), 62–75.

Reed, I.S. and Solomon, G. (1960). Polynomial codes over certain finite fields. *Journal of the Society for Industrial and Applied Mathematics (SIAM)*, 8(2), 300–304.

Robertson, J.E. (1987). Error detection and correction for addition and subtraction, through use of higher radix extensions of hamming codes. In *Proceedings of the Eighth Symposium on Computer Arithmetic*. 87–94.

Swartzlander, E.E. (1990). *Computer Arithmetic.* IEEE Computer Society Press, Washington, D.C.

Tanenbaum, A. (1989). *Computer Networks*. Prentice Hall, London.

Index

E, F

O, P

Q, R

S, T

U, V, W

Other titles from

iSTE

in

Computer Engineering

2025

CHIKH Azeddine
Systemic Approach to Categorizing and Modeling Requirements

TANEJA Ashu, KUMAR Abhishek, LIMKAR Suresh Vishnudas, OUAISSA Mariya, OUAISSA Mariyam
Driving Innovation through AI and Digital Twin for 6G Powered Sustainable Ultra Smart Cities

TANEJA Ashu, KUMAR Abhishek, LIMKAR Suresh Vishnudas, OUAISSA Mariya, OUAISSA Mariyam
6G Urban Innovation: AI and Digital Twin for Next-Gen Sustainable Cities

2024

CHAKRABORTY Rajdeep, GHOSH Anupam, KUMAR MANDAL Jyotsna, CHOUDHURY Tanupriya, CHATTERJEE Prasenjit
Smart Edge Computing: An Operation Research Perspective (International Perspectives in Decision Analytics and Operations Research Set – Volume 2)

HOMÈS Bernard
Fundamentals of Software Testing (2nd edition, revised and updated)

JERBI Abdessalem
Discrete-Event Simulation: Concepts and Production in Arena

PRADHAN Devasis, KUMAR SAHU Prasanna, MYO TUN Hla, CHATTERJEE Prasenjit
Artificial and Cognitive Computing for Sustainable Healthcare Systems in Smart Cities
(International Perspectives in Decision Analytics and Operations Research Set – Volume 3)

2023

CHOUDHURY Tanupriya, KHANNA Abhirup, CHATTERJEE Prasenjit, UM Jung-Sup, BHATTACHARYA Abhishek
Blockchain Applications in Healthcare: Innovations and Practices
(International Perspectives in Decision Analytics and Operations Research Set – Volume 1)

PAI G A Vijayalakshmi
A Textbook of Data Structures and Algorithms 1: Mastering Linear Data Structures
A Textbook of Data Structures and Algorithms 2: Mastering Nonlinear Data Structures
A Textbook of Data Structures and Algorithms 3: Mastering Advanced Data Structures and Algorithm Design Strategies

2022

HOMÈS Bernard
Advanced Testing of Systems-of-Systems 1: Theoretical Aspects
Advanced Testing of Systems-of-Systems 2: Practical Aspects

MEHTA Shikha, TIWARI Sanju, SIARRY Patrick, JABBAR M.A.
Tools, Languages, Methodologies for Representing Semantics on the Web of Things

SIDHOM Sahbi, KADDOUR Amira
Systems and Uses of Digital Sciences for Knowledge Organization
(Digital Tools and Uses Set – Volume 9)

ZAIDOUN Ameur Salem
Computer Science Security: Concepts and Tools

2021

DELHAYE Jean-Loïc
Inside the World of Computing: Technologies, Uses, Challenges

HARDIN Thérèse, JAUME Mathieu, PESSAUX François,
VIGUIÉ DONZEAU-GOUGE Véronique
Concepts and Semantics of Programming Languages 1: A Semantical Approach with OCaml and Python
Concepts and Semantics of Programming Languages 2: Modular and Object-oriented Constructs with OCaml, Python, C++, Ada and Java

MKADMI Abderrazak
Archives in The Digital Age: Preservation and the Right to be Forgotten (Digital Tools and Uses Set – Volume 8)

TOKLU Yusuf Cengiz, BEKDAŞ Gebrail, NIGDELI Sinan Melih
Metaheuristics for Structural Design and Analysis
(Optimization Heuristics Set – Volume 3)

2020

DARCHE Philippe
Microprocessor 1: Prolegomenes – Calculation and Storage Functions – Models of Computation and Computer Architecture
Microprocessor 2: Core Concepts – Communication in a Digital System
Microprocessor 3: Core Concepts – Hardware Aspects
Microprocessor 4: Core Concepts – Software Aspects
Microprocessor 5: Software and Hardware Aspects of Development, Debugging and Testing – The Microcomputer

DUVAUT Patrick, DALLOZ Xavier, MENGA David, KOEHL François,
CHRIQUI Vidal, BRILL Joerg
Internet of Augmented Me, I.AM: Empowering Innovation for a New Sustainable Future

LAFFLY Dominique
TORUS 1 – Toward an Open Resource Using Services: Cloud Computing for Environmental Data
TORUS 2 – Toward an Open Resource Using Services: Cloud Computing for Environmental Data
TORUS 3 – Toward an Open Resource Using Services: Cloud Computing for Environmental Data

LAURENT Anne, LAURENT Dominique, MADERA Cédrine
Data Lakes
(Databases and Big Data Set – Volume 2)

OULHADJ Hamouche, DAACHI Boubaker, MENASRI Riad
Metaheuristics for Robotics
(Optimization Heuristics Set – Volume 2)

SADIQUI Ali
Computer Network Security

VENTRE Daniel
Artificial Intelligence, Cybersecurity and Cyber Defense

2019

BESBES Walid, DHOUIB Diala, WASSAN Niaz, MARREKCHI Emna
Solving Transport Problems: Towards Green Logistics

CLERC Maurice
Iterative Optimizers: Difficulty Measures and Benchmarks

GHLALA Riadh
Analytic SQL in SQL Server 2014/2016

TOUNSI Wiem
Cyber-Vigilance and Digital Trust: Cyber Security in the Era of Cloud Computing and IoT

2018

ANDRO Mathieu
Digital Libraries and Crowdsourcing
(Digital Tools and Uses Set – Volume 5)

ARNALDI Bruno, GUITTON Pascal, MOREAU Guillaume
Virtual Reality and Augmented Reality: Myths and Realities

CARDON Alain
Beyond Artificial Intelligence: From Human Consciousness to Artificial Consciousness

HOMAYOUNI S. Mahdi, FONTES Dalila B.M.M.
Metaheuristics for Maritime Operations
(Optimization Heuristics Set – Volume 1)

JEANSOULIN Robert
JavaScript and Open Data

PIVERT Olivier
NoSQL Data Models: Trends and Challenges
(Databases and Big Data Set – Volume 1)

SEDKAOUI Soraya
Data Analytics and Big Data

SALEH Imad, AMMI Mehdi, SZONIECKY Samuel
Challenges of the Internet of Things: Technology, Use, Ethics
(Digital Tools and Uses Set – Volume 7)

SZONIECKY Samuel
Ecosystems Knowledge: Modeling and Analysis Method for Information and Communication
(Digital Tools and Uses Set – Volume 6)

2017

BENMAMMAR Badr
Concurrent, Real-Time and Distributed Programming in Java: Threads, RTSJ and RMI

BOUHAÏ Nasreddine, SALEH Imad
Internet of Things: Evolutions and Innovations
(Digital Tools and Uses Set – Volume 4)

HÉLIODORE Frédéric, NAKIB Amir, ISMAIL Boussaad, OUCHRAA Salma, SCHMITT Laurent
Metaheuristics for Intelligent Electrical Networks
(Metaheuristics Set – Volume 10)

MA Haiping, SIMON Dan
Evolutionary Computation with Biogeography-based Optimization
(Metaheuristics Set – Volume 8)

PÉTROWSKI Alain, BEN-HAMIDA Sana
Evolutionary Algorithms
(Metaheuristics Set – Volume 9)

PAI G A Vijayalakshmi
Metaheuristics for Portfolio Optimization: An Introduction using MATLAB®
(Metaheuristics Set – Volume 11)

REYES-GARCIA Everardo
The Image-Interface: Graphical Supports for Visual Information
(Digital Tools and Uses Set – Volume 3)

REYES-GARCIA Everardo, BOUHAÏ Nasreddine
Designing Interactive Hypermedia Systems
(Digital Tools and Uses Set – Volume 2)

SZONIECKY Samuel, BOUHAÏ Nasreddine
Collective Intelligence and Digital Archives: Towards Knowledge Ecosystems
(Digital Tools and Uses Set – Volume 1)

2016

BLUM Christian, FESTA Paola
Metaheuristics for String Problems in Bio-informatics
(Metaheuristics Set – Volume 6)

DEROUSSI Laurent
Metaheuristics for Logistics
(Metaheuristics Set – Volume 4)

DHAENENS Clarisse, JOURDAN Laetitia
Metaheuristics for Big Data
(Metaheuristics Set – Volume 5)

LABADIE Nacima, PRINS Christian, PRODHON Caroline
Metaheuristics for Vehicle Routing Problems
(Metaheuristics Set – Volume 3)

LEROY Laure
Eyestrain Reduction in Stereoscopy

LUTTON Evelyne, PERROT Nathalie, TONDA Alberto
Evolutionary Algorithms for Food Science and Technology
(Metaheuristics Set – Volume 7)

MAGOULÈS Frédéric, ZHAO Hai-Xiang
Data Mining and Machine Learning in Building Energy Analysis

RIGO Michel
Advanced Graph Theory and Combinatorics

ZELM Martin, DOUMEINGTS Guy, MENDONÇA Joao Pedro
Enterprise Interoperability: in the Digitized and Networked Factory of the Future

2015

BARBIER Franck, RECOUSSINE Jean-Luc
COBOL Software Modernization: From Principles to Implementation with the BLU AGE® Method

CHEN Ken
Performance Evaluation by Simulation and Analysis with Applications to Computer Networks

CLERC Maurice
Guided Randomness in Optimization
(Metaheuristics Set – Volume 1)

DURAND Nicolas, GIANAZZA David, GOTTELAND Jean-Baptiste, ALLIOT Jean-Marc
Metaheuristics for Air Traffic Management
(Metaheuristics Set – Volume 2)

MAGOULÈS Frédéric, ROUX François-Xavier, HOUZEAUX Guillaume
Parallel Scientific Computing

MUNEESAWANG Paisarn, YAMMEN Suchart
Visual Inspection Technology in the Hard Disk Drive Industry

2014

BOULANGER Jean-Louis
Formal Methods Applied to Industrial Complex Systems
Formal Methods Applied to Complex Systems: Implementation of the B Method

EXPOSITO Ernesto, DIOP Codé
Smart SOA Platforms in Cloud Computing Architectures

GARDI Frédéric, BENOIST Thierry, DARLAY Julien, ESTELLON Bertrand, MEGEL Romain
Mathematical Programming Solver based on Local Search

KRICHEN Saoussen, CHAOUACHI Jouhaina
Graph-related Optimization and Decision Support Systems

LARRIEU Nicolas, VARET Antoine
Rapid Prototyping of Software for Avionics Systems: Model-oriented Approaches for Complex Systems Certification

LAURAS Matthieu, ZELM Martin, ARCHIMÈDE Bernard, BÉNABEN Frédérick, DOUMEINGTS Guy
Enterprise Interoperability: Interoperability for Agility, Resilience and Plasticity of Collaborations

OUSSALAH Mourad Chabane
Software Architecture 1
Software Architecture 2

QUESNEL Flavien
Scheduling of Large-scale Virtualized Infrastructures: Toward Cooperative Management

RIGO Michel
Formal Languages, Automata and Numeration Systems 1: Introduction to Combinatorics on Words
Formal Languages, Automata and Numeration Systems 2: Applications to Recognizability and Decidability

SAINT-DIZIER Patrick
Musical Rhetoric: Foundations and Annotation Schemes

TOUATI Sid, DUPONT DE DINECHIN Benoit
Advanced Backend Code Optimization

2013

ANDRÉ Etienne, SOULAT Romain
The Inverse Method: Parametric Verification of Real-time Embedded Systems

BOULANGER Jean-Louis
Safety Management for Software-based Equipment

DELAHAYE Daniel, PUECHMOREL Stéphane
Modeling and Optimization of Air Traffic

FRANCOPOULO Gil
LMF — Lexical Markup Framework

GHEDIRA Khaled
Constraint Satisfaction Problems: CSP Formalisms and Techniques

GOVAERT Gérard, NADIF Mohamed
Co-Clustering: Models, Algorithms and Applications

LANDRAGIN Frédérick
Man–Machine Dialogue: Design and Challenges

LUCAS Laurent, LOSCOS Céline, REMION Yannick
3D Video: Models, From Capture to Diffusion

ROCHANGE Christine, UHRIG Sascha, SAINRAT Pascal
Time-Predictable Architectures

WAHBI Mohamed
Algorithms and Ordering Heuristics for Distributed Constraint Satisfaction Problems

ZELM Martin, VAN SINDEREN Marten, FERRAIRA PIRES Luis, DOUMEINGTS Guy
Enterprise Interoperability: Research and Applications in the Service-oriented Ecosystem

2012

ARBOLEDA Hugo, ROYER Jean-Claude
Model-Driven and Software Product Line Engineering

BLANCHET Gérard, DUPOUY Bertrand
Computer Architecture

BOULANGER Jean-Louis
Industrial Use of Formal Methods: Formal Verification
Formal Methods: Industrial Use from Model to the Code

CALVARY Gaëlle, DELOT Thierry, SÈDES Florence, TIGLI Jean-Yves
Computer Science and Ambient Intelligence

MAHOUT Vincent
Assembly Language Programming: ARM Cortex-M3 2.0: Organization, Innovation and Territory

MARLET Renaud
Program Specialization

SOTO Maria, SEVAUX Marc, ROSSI André, LAURENT Johann
Memory Allocation Problems in Embedded Systems: Optimization Methods

2011

BICHOT Charles-Edmond, SIARRY Patrick
Graph Partitioning

BOULANGER Jean-Louis
Static Analysis of Software: The Abstract Interpretation

CAFERRA Ricardo
Logic for Computer Science and Artificial Intelligence

KORDON Fabrice, HADDAD Serge, PAUTET Laurent, PETRUCCI Laure
Distributed Systems: Design and Algorithms
Models and Analysis in Distributed Systems

LORCA Xavier
Tree-based Graph Partitioning Constraint

RIDHA MAHJOUB A.
Progress in Combinatorial Optimization: ISCO2010

TRUCHET Charlotte, ASSAYAG Gerard
Constraint Programming in Music

VICAT-BLANC Pascale, GOGLIN Brice, GUILLIER Romaric,
SOUDAN Sébastien
Computing Networks: From Cluster to Cloud Computing

2010

AUBRUN Christophe, SIMON Daniel, SONG Ye-Qiong
Co-design Approaches for Dependable Networked Control Systems

AUDIBERT Pierre
Mathematics for Informatics and Computer Science

BABAU Jean-Philippe, BLAY-FORNARINO Mireille, CHAMPEAU Joël,
ROBERT Sylvain, SABETTA Antonino
Model Driven Engineering for Distributed Real-Time Systems: MARTE Modeling, Model Transformations and their Usages

BOULANGER Jean-Louis
Safety of Computer Architectures

SIGAUD Olivier, BUFFET Olivier
Markov Decision Processes in Artificial Intelligence

MONMARCHÉ Nicolas, GUINAND Frédérick, SIARRY Patrick
Artificial Ants

SOLNON Christine
Ant Colony Optimization and Constraint Programming

2009

FOURNIER Jean-Claude
Graph Theory and Applications: with exercises and problems

GUÉDON Jeanpierre
The Mojette Transform: theory and applications

JARD Claude, ROUX Olivier H.
Communicating Embedded Systems: Software and Design

LECOUTRE Christophe
Constraint Networks: Techniques and Algorithms

2008

BANÂTRE Michel, MARRON Pedro Jose, OLLERO Anibal, WOLITZ Adam
Cooperating Embedded Systems and Wireless Sensor Networks

MERZ Stephan, NAVET Nicolas
Modeling and Verification of Real-time Systems: Formalisms and Software Tools

PASCHOS Vangelis Th.
Combinatorial Optimization and Theoretical Computer Science: Interfaces and Perspectives

WALDNER Jean-Baptiste
Nanocomputers and Swarm Intelligence

2007

BENHAMOU Frédéric, JUSSIEN Narendra, O'SULLIVAN Barry
Trends in Constraint Programming

JUSSIEN Narendra
A to Z of Sudoku

2006

BABAU Jean-Philippe, CHAMPEAU Joël, GÉRARD Sébastien
From MDD Concepts to Experiments and Illustrations – DRES 2006

HABRIAS Henri, FRAPPIER Marc
Software Specification Methods: An Overview Using a Case Study

MURAT Cécile, PASCHOS Vangelis Th.
Probabilistic Combinatorial Optimization on Graphs

PANETTO Hervé, BOUDJLIDA Nacer
Interoperability for Enterprise Software and Applications: Proceedings of the Workshops and the Doctorial Symposium of the Second IFAC/IFIP I-ESA International Conference: EI2N, WSI, IS-TSPQ 2006

2005

GÉRARD Sébastien, BABAU Jean-Philippe, CHAMPEAU Joël
Model Driven Engineering for Distributed Real Time Embedded Systems

PANETTO Hervé
Interoperability of Enterprise Software and Applications: Workshops of the INTEROP-ESA 2005 International Conference (EI2N, WSI, ISIDI and IEHENA 2005)

Printed and bound by CPI Group (UK) Ltd, Croydon, CR0 4YY

13/09/2026

14961012-0004